Praise for
A Walk through the Forest of Souls

"A beautiful book of connections and correspondences or, perhaps, a book of beautiful connections and correspondences that is like being taken by the hand by the wisest person you know and taught about the Tarot: what it is, ways to think about it, and ways we can use it in our lives or our stories. For forty years, Rachel Pollack has been one of the finest writers and thinkers about Tarot, and *A Walk through the Forest of Souls* feels like a distillation of everything she has been trying to get us to see. A must for people who want the Tarot in their lives or just for people like me who want it in our stories."

—**Neil Gaiman**, bestselling author of *American Gods, Sandman,*
and numerous other works

"*A Walk through the Forest of Souls* is a master work by one of the great thinkers of our time. I've taught Tarot with Rachel Pollack for over thirty years and deeply admire the wisdom and knowledge she brings to the cards. Of all her books, I love this one the most. She is a fascinating storyteller and a master in the art of asking questions and exploring analogies that surprise and enlighten us. Rachel shows how Tarot weaves a wide-ranging fabric that integrates myth, science, music, literature, history, spirituality, psychology, human anatomy, and soul. Additionally, she tells us we can ask Tarot questions about all these things and get meaningful answers. If we approach Tarot as a gamble, with a spirit of play and wonder, it will awaken and inspire us to do more with it than we've ever imagined. This is being an adept at using Tarot as an instrument of wisdom."

—**Mary K. Greer**, author of *Archetypal Tarot* and *Tarot for Your Self*

"Perhaps Rachel Pollack's best work yet, *A Walk through the Forest of Souls* will be heralded as a landmark moment in the philosophical explorations of the Tarot. This book inspires your personal journey to answer life's biggest and hardest questions. Each chapter's thought-explorations will expand your mind. Integrating Kabbalist thought, myth, and folklore, *A Walk through the Forest of Souls* is meditation, nourishment, and written for the reader who is ready to receive truths about human existence. A must-read for both the inquisitive newcomer and the seasoned practitioner."

—**Benebell Wen,** author of *Holistic Tarot*

"This is one of my favourite books on Tarot. Rachel Pollack leads us into the deep truth of the mythic forest where Kabbalah and Tarot hold the patterns still. When we stand before these living powers, our soul's questions find profound answers for life's rich mysteries."

—**Caitlín Matthews,** author of *Untold Tarot* and
The Celtic Book of the Dead

"Rachel Pollack's scholarship is both deep and broad. Yet more impressive is her original thought, as well as her fearlessness in following the breadcrumbs through the winding woods of our souls. *A Walk through the Forest of Souls* is the most interesting and transformative Tarot book I've ever read."

—**Ellen Lorenzi-Prince,** creator of *Dark Goddess Tarot,*
Greek Goddess Tarot, and *Tarot of the Crone*

"Only Rachel Pollack could have written this. Her wit and wisdom, heart and soul, and above all, her vast knowledge are all in this extraordinary book. Here are thoughts about the origins of Tarot, the best ways to read the cards—and how not to, and some immensely exciting readings concerning huge subjects far and away from the personal issues we tend to bring to the cards. No one with even the smallest interest in Tarot should be without it."

—**John Matthews,** cocreator of *The Wildwood Tarot*
and author of *The Goblin Market Tarot*

In *A Walk through the Forest of Souls*, readers experience Rachel Pollack's skillful interweaving of diverse wisdom, established teachings, and her application of Tarot. This highly readable book is brilliant in its perspective and aims to enable any student of Tarot to deepen their relationship with the cards and find themselves on the Tarot journey."

—**Gina G. Thies**, creator of *Tarot of the Moors*
and author of *Tarot Coupling*

"Many years ago, I was gifted a copy of Rachel Pollack's *The Forest of Souls*. It was unlike any Tarot book I had encountered—instead of the standard 'how to,' this one took a different approach, one that weaves a magical journey through story and inquiry as only the legendary Pollack can do. How lucky we are that this book is back in print and updated! *A Walk through the Forest of Souls* will pull you in from the start, turn you around, challenge your assumptions, and have you looking at the cards with new eyes. It's one of those books you'll want to read again and again because each time you do, you'll walk away with another Tarot epiphany. A must-have for every serious Tarot reader."

—**Theresa Reed,** author of *Tarot: No Questions Asked*

"This is a must-have book for any serious (and seriously playful) student of tarot. While there are lots of great books that teach tarot card meanings—and Rachel Pollack has written some of the best of them—Pollack's *A Walk through the Forest of Souls: A Tarot Journey to Spiritual Awakening* will take you deep into the meaning of tarot itself. And while the book draws on the wisdom of many spiritual traditions, it is Pollack's ability to make seemingly complex Kabbalistic concepts simple and relatable that will enable the reader to connect with the deepest wisdom of their soul, the tarot, and the universe itself."

—**Mark Horn,** author of *Tarot and the Gates of Light*

"Rachel Pollack's *A Walk through the Forest of Souls* is a love letter to all those who feel drawn to the mystery of tarot. Pollack's mastery of her craft is evident in the way she seamlessly weaves together art, history, religion, science, psychology, and magic to create a tapestry that prompts readers to question their assumptions about themselves, tarot, the nature of God, and time itself. The essential premise of this book is that tarot reveals more than we can possibly imagine, if we let it, and Pollack encourages readers to release themselves from a formulaic relationship with tarot in order to fall deeply in love with all that it has to offer. A thought-provoking masterpiece that asks readers to play with the impossible and gamble with their most preciously held beliefs to find tarot right at the heart of it all, Pollack's guidance and curiosity-prompting questions make this book a must-read for anyone looking to deepen their understanding and appreciation of tarot. Whether you're a seasoned tarot reader or just getting started, this book is sure to provide a rich and rewarding tarot awakening."

—**Jenna Matlin,** author of *Will You Give Me a Reading?*

"Rachel Pollack's *A Walk through the Forest of Souls* will be essential reading for anyone interested in the spiritual dimensions of Tarot. Pollack brings to the subject her extraordinary depth of knowledge and a lifetime of experience, not only of Tarot, but also of magic and the occult, mythologies, archaeology, spiritualities and religions and their histories. She proposes a creative approach to Tarot and a multiplicity of meanings that will enable the reader, whatever their cultural or spiritual background, to use the cards as a means of exploring their magical inner world and gaining self-knowledge and wisdom. In a book packed with stories and imagery, she writes with erudition, wit, and a beguiling sense of humor. This is a book that will stand alongside Pollack's *Seventy-Eight Degrees of Wisdom* as a Tarot classic."

—**Levannah Morgan,** author of *A Sea Witch's Companion*
and *A Witch's Mirror*

"Although I am a Tarot author myself, I find that I don't read most Tarot books. Rachel Pollack's *A Walk through the Forest of Souls* is an exception. Her approach to the Tarot is refreshing and unique. She merges mythology and philosophy with Tarot imagery in a way that is empowering."

—**Robert M. Place,** creator of *The Alchemical Tarot*
and author of *The Tarot: History, Symbolism, and Divination*

"Among the glories of picking up any book by Rachel Pollack is that you will put it down a different person. You will be challenged, beguiled, and given a fresh set of tools for your Tarot work. Rachel's mind is elastic, curious, wry, and wise—her way of conveying wisdom is frequently entertaining and never less than fascinating. Her authorial voice is clear, engaging, and reassuring through the bumps and bends of the Royal Road. *A Walk through the Forest of Souls* may be Rachel's best book yet—full of fascinating insights and valuable knowledge, presented with clarity, humor, and stunning new directions to guide us through our journey. Every aspect of this book yields rich treasure. Rachel is generous and engaging; sharing the discoveries of her lifetime of study and practice in this 'forest' is a priceless, gorgeous gift to Tarot enthusiasts from eager beginners to well-seasoned travelers."

—**Thalassa**, founder of the San Francisco Bay Area
Tarot Symposium (SF BATS)

"*A Walk through the Forest of Souls* by Rachel Pollack takes us, as Tarot readers, whether new or decades experienced, well past the boundaries of what we think the Tarot is and provides us with keys in the form of poems, tales, and myths that unlock the doorways to the universal mysteries held within each one of us and captured in the images of the seventy-eight cards. Rachel hands us our own painter's palate and invites us to draw deep from within, create our own colors, and paint the story of the universe anew each time we shuffle and draw the cards. This is a book of discovery. Be open to the unexpected when you cross the threshold and turn to page one."

—**Rhonda Alin**, founder of the Northern New Jersey Tarot Meetup

"The beauty of *A Walk through the Forest of Souls* is that it addresses the possibility of asking the impossible questions. No one can trump Rachel Pollack when she demonstrates just how we can have an infinite conversation with the cards. In her hands, the cards move from the intangible symbol to the concrete manifestation of a solution that is always anchored in astonishment. We go, 'aha,' and that's where the magic is."

—**Camelia Elias, PhD,** director of studies at Aradia Academy
and editor-in-chief at EyeCorner Press

"Rachel Pollack's *A Walk through the Forest of Souls* is a must-read for tarot enthusiasts of all levels. Pollack's expertise in Tarot has made her an authority on the subject for decades, and this book clearly showcases why. A comprehensive guide, Pollack's beautiful book contains unparalleled wisdom and observations of the potency of the Tarot in our spiritual lives, utilizing the cards as tools of mysticism to gain access to profound insight and reflection into the deeper secrets of the soul, life, and the universe."

—Mat Auryn, author of *Psychic Witch* and *Mastering Magick*

A WALK
through the
FOREST
OF SOULS

A TAROT JOURNEY TO
SPIRITUAL AWAKENING

RACHEL POLLACK

WEISER BOOKS

For all her insights and knowledge,
for her wit and commitment to truth, and for her kind soul,
this book is dedicated to Zoe Matoff.

This edition first published in 2023 by Weiser Books, an imprint of
Red Wheel/Weiser, LLC
With offices at:
65 Parker Street, Suite 7
Newburyport, MA 01950
www.redwheelweiser.com

ISBN: 978-1-57863-770-6
Library of Congress Cataloging-in-Publication Data available upon request.

Cover and text design by Sky Peck Design
Interior images are used by permission and credits may be found on page 263
Typeset in Adobe Text Pro

Printed in the United States of America
IBI
10 9 8 7 6 5 4 3 2 1

Contents

Acknowledgments

So many people, knowing and unknowing, go into the making of a book. I have found inspiration in many places, from many sources. Though I have never met David Rosenberg, my debt to his book *Dreams of Being Eaten Alive* will be very clear to anyone who reads this book. I have indeed met Stephen Karcher, whose work on divination holds up a light to all would-be seers. For insights and knowledge of Kabbalah, as well as for her warmth and generosity, I owe a special thanks to Judith Laura. My friend and some-time teaching partner, Mary K. Greer, continues to inspire and amaze me with her scholarship, her teaching skills, and her love of Tarot. Cynthia Giles and Camelia Elias have each, in their different ways, shown what is possible in Tarot. Reb Avigayil Landsman has taught me of letters, the joy of Torah and laughter, and doorways into the heart. I thank all these, and all others cited in this book, for their wisdom and knowledge. I apologize deeply for any mistakes or misuse I may have made of their ideas.

And finally, my special gratitude to Red Wheel/Weiser, and especially the marvelous Judika Illes, brilliant writer and superb editor, for her love and support of this book.

A Gallery of Quotations

Many people assume that the inspiration for a book about Tarot must be other books about Tarot—its history, the meanings of the cards, occult correspondences, spreads. For me, the books and teachings and stories—always stories—that helped give life to this book often don't mention Tarot at all. They may be about other forms of divination—the *I Ching,* for example—but not techniques or lists of meanings. Rather, they concern the ways divination allows us to experience the world, its mysteries, its magic. "The first thing that happens is that the world comes alive," writes Stephen Karcher.

During the research for this book certain phrases and statements have come to me from many sources. Some address Tarot directly, others divination, or spiritual development, or the ways we know things. There are statements about Kabbalah, but again, not lists of doctrines or facts. ("The most important thing to say about Kabbalah is that it is always the wrong idea to clarify it."—Poet and translator David Rosenberg.) Every one of these quotes, however, in some way concerns the experience of working with Tarot. Rather than sprinkle them through the book at the heads of chapters, I have decided to offer them all together, as a kind of portrait of this work. The author, and the source, follows each statement. Where it says "from the notebooks," the words come from my notes or previous publications. Where only "self" and a title appears after the statement, the source is a work of my own. Some are what I call "Directives," ways to open up that landscape. The thing that binds together all these statements and fragments is that they open the way. They lead us into the world of Tarot, a world often stranger and more wondrous than we expected, and help us find our own pathways through the Forest of Souls.

"Tarot is a dream that stands still."
—JOANNA YOUNG, IN CONVERSATION

"I work as a midwife of the soul."
—MARY K. GREER, IN CLASS

"Symbols are the very stuff of time."
—STEPHEN KARCHER, *TA CHUAN, THE GREAT TREATISE*

*"Erect the gates
Then the transformation can take place between them."*
—TA CHUAN, TRANSLATED BY STEPHEN KARCHER

*"If you got a good plan, follow it.
If you don't got a good plan, don't follow it."*
—CONVERSATION WITH JAMES WELLS

"I don't believe there is an outcome until you are dead."
—MARY K. GREER, IN CLASS

"Nothing is learned except through joy."
—IOANNA SALAJAN

*"We can try to disarm the other side with knowledge and more
knowledge. But there will never be enough knowledge."*
—DAVID ROSENBERG, *DREAMS OF BEING EATEN ALIVE: THE LITERARY CORE
OF THE KABBALAH*

"*The most important thing to say about Kabbalah is that it is always the wrong idea to clarify it.*"

—DAVID ROSENBERG, *DREAMS OF BEING EATEN ALIVE:*
THE LITERARY CORE OF THE KABBALAH

"*What is the sacred? The divine breath that animates dead bones.*"

—SELF, FROM THE NOTEBOOKS

"*Where were you when I laid the foundations of the world?*"

—GOD, IN THE BOOK OF JOB

"*All measurement is a lie.*"

—SELF, FROM *THE TRANSSEXUAL BOOK OF THE DEAD*

"*Look closely.*"

—MOSES DE LEON, *THE ZOHAR*, TRANSLATED BY DAVID ROSENBERG

"*There is something you should know.*
And the right way to know it
Is by a cherrying of the mind."

—ANNE CARSON, "FIRST CHALDAIC ORACLE,"
IN *MEN IN THE OFF HOURS*

"*The Common Language—bone, fabric, song, dream.*"

—AVIGAYIL LANDSMAN, PRIVATE CORRESPONDENCE

"*Ancient To The Future.*"

—MOTTO OF MUSIC GROUP, THE ART ENSEMBLE OF CHICAGO

*"There are no rules except discovery.
There is no tradition except invention."*

—SELF, FROM *UNQUENCHABLE FIRE*

"To stand in the middle and know who you are."

—LYNDEL ROBINSON, PRIVATE CORRESPONDENCE

"God lives in the spaces between the cards."

—MARI GEASAIR

*"It is not in heaven or across the sea but in your heart and in your
mouth, that you may know it."*

—GOD, THROUGH HIS SPOKESPERSON, MOSES, THE BOOK OF
DEUTERONOMY

"The first thing that happens is that the world comes to life."

—STEPHEN KARCHER, *THE ILLUSTRATED GUIDE TO DIVINATION*

"Give me not words of consolation. Give me magic."

—NORMANDI ELLIS, *AWAKENING OSIRIS*

*"And as for me, my prayer is for You, Gentle One, that it be for You
a time of desire."*

—FROM THE RECONSTRUCTIONIST JEWISH PRAYERBOOK

"Blessed are You, the Imageless, who has made me in Your image."

—MORNING BLESSING, FROM THE RECONSTRUCTIONIST JEWISH PRAYERBOOK

"*Whom does the Grail serve?*"

—QUESTION NOT ASKED BY PERCIVAL, IN THE MEDIEVAL GRAIL LEGENDS

"*Why is there a plague in Thebes?*"

—QUESTION OEDIPUS SENT TO THE ORACLE AT DELPHI

"*Time present and time past
Are perhaps present in time future
And time future contained in time past.*"

—T. S. ELIOT, "BURNT NORTON," FROM *THE FOUR QUARTETS*

"*Turn it, and turn it, for everything is in it.*"

—RABBI BEN BAG BAG, IN *PERKEI AVOT* (SAYINGS OF THE FATHERS)

"*Shuffle it and shuffle it, for everything is in it.*"

—SELF

"*I suppose we were given two decks of cards at Mount Sinai. One,
the Torah, would allow us to love our neighbors, to learn from
teachers, to cross the mighty river. . . . The cards of this deck are
shuffled to us and dealt to us. . . . However, the mysteries of the other
deck, the Tarot, are the deeds about which the Torah can only be
silent: the shuffling, the drawing, and the dealing of cards.*"

—JOEL NEWBERGER

"*An outlawed way of knowing and speaking with a living world.*"

—STEPHEN KARCHER, *THE ILLUSTRATED GUIDE TO DIVINATION*

"The Tarot is a structure of possibilities that can be used by almost anyone for almost any reason in almost any manner."

—Cynthia Giles, Tarot: History, Mystery, and Lore

"The only thing I can say for certain is that you will never come to the end of it."

—Self, in The New Tarot Handbook

Directives

See what there is to see	*The eye can't hit what the hand can't see*
Hear what there is to hear	*Dream like a butterfly*
Touch whatever you touch	*Go home like a bee*
Speak the thing you must speak	*Shuffle, Tarot girl, shuffle*

  —Self,   —Self,

    from *Unquenchable Fire*   after Muhammad Ali

Pay Attention!

At Play in the Fields of Tarot

The subtitle of this book may surprise some people. What does it mean to *journey* in the Tarot? For some, the phrase suggests predictions of soulmates or career changes or family struggles or legal matters (all deeply important to those who seek answers).

Others, who know the Tarot's esoteric traditions, may think they know exactly what I mean by journeys. For them, the Tarot contains the keys to a vast system of correspondences. These include the laws of nature, both known and unknown, magic, Jewish mysticism, astrology, Pagan Gods and Goddesses, Christian revelations, secret knowledge, Egyptian initiations, angels, demons, but most especially journeys along the twenty-two pathways on the Kabbalah Tree of Life.

This book takes neither of these approaches. While it does not give any instructions on how to tell fortunes or any card-by-card list of meanings, it does in fact include quite a few readings. But instead of asking whom someone will marry or where to look for a job, the readings in this book ask questions like "How do I open my heart?" or "What nourishes the soul?" and even "What reading did you give God to create the universe?"

Readings in this book become a means to explore unknown territory—in ourselves, but also in the world outside us, and in the sacred mysteries and riddles of existence. They take advantage of the Tarot's most distinctive feature. Unlike books of spiritual ideas and the lessons of famous teachers, the pages of the Tarot are not bound in any real order. The cards appear to contain a linear message, for they come to us numbered and labeled, with such titles as "The High Priestess," or "Judgement." Many books describe the step-by-step development of this great message, but unlike sacred books or the works of psychologist sages, the Tarot can change and become new every time we pick it up. This is because we can shuffle it. We can take the cards, with all their intense symbols, mix them, and lay them out as a new work.

In *The Silence of the Lambs*, the genius psychopath Dr. Hannibal Lecter tells FBI agent Clarice Starling that to catch the killer she must go back to what Marcus Aurelius called "first principles." What is something—in this case the unidentified killer's—essence? What is it "in and of itself"?

To me, this speaks to the fact that unlike a book the "pages" of the Tarot are not fixed. They may be numbered and arranged according to groups (the named and numbered Major Arcana and the four suits of the Minor Arcana), but at any moment we can shuffle them and get a whole new deck.

Divinatory systems that are not fixed are called "aleatory," that is, a set of symbols or bits of information that we can randomize and thus create a new order every time we use them. The *I Ching* and the Tarot are both aleatory. So is Ifa, an African system that uses scattered sand or cowrie shells to create images that then lead the diviner to instructions to guide the querent.

Interestingly, I do not know of any generic term for what I think of as "fixed" systems of divination. The great example is astrology. No matter how many times you cast your birth chart, it will always be the same. The skill of the diviner lies in understanding what it says. You can "progress" your chart to the present day and get a whole new life structure, but still, each time you progress it to a specific moment the result will be the same. Much the same goes for palmistry or phrenology.

I confess that I sometimes joke that I belong to "Team Aleatory." To me, the Tarot opens up the world and is new at every moment. In this book readings do not reveal a fixed future. Just the opposite. They become a means to gain new perspectives and explore possibilities outside our normal ways of thought.

Those who know the Tarot's esoteric tradition, with its symbols and lists, also may find some surprises here. Just as we will not give recipes for fortune-telling, we will not give charts of correspondences or lists of strict ideas the reader should memorize for spiritual advancement. We will draw on these systems and their long history, but will not simply lay them out, for our purpose here is a *search* for meaning. We will look into the mysteries that can unfold before us when we allow symbols and stories and the beauty of images to entice us into new ways of understanding.

An old rabbinical story tells of a farmer whose goat wanders off one day and returns with a sweet-smelling branch in its mouth. The next day the same thing happens, and the farmer becomes intrigued. The day after that he follows the goat as it wanders into a cave. The cave opens into a tunnel, and as they walk along, the farmer becomes inexplicably joyous; all his life's weariness begins to lift off him. Finally he sees a light and smells sweet air. He emerges from the tunnel to fragrant trees and flowers and a glorious soft light, and he realizes that the animal has led him to Eden, the lost garden of our imagined first ancestors (and presumably an unguarded back door, as legend suggests that the front gate is guarded by an angel with a flaming sword, placed there after the expulsion of Adam and Eve).

The Star from the Rider Tarot

I think of the Tarot as a little like that goat. If we let go of the desire to define the pictures or explain them once and for all or determine their exact meanings and purposes, if we simply follow the images, who knows where they may take us? This does not mean that we abandon scholarship or the great work of esoteric interpreters. These have become part of the pictures, and we can use them to find the tunnel, maybe even open the door.

In the card of the Star from the Rider pack of Arthur Edward Waite and Pamela Colman Smith, the world's most famous Tarot, a small bird appears on a tree in the back of the picture.

A quick glance at the image might not even register the bird's presence. Or it might just seem a decoration. Someone who ponders the picture might think about birds and what they inspire in us. But if we know that the bird is actually an ibis and that an ibis represented the Egyptian God Thoth, then the bird suddenly gives us access to a whole range of stories and ideas. Thoth is the god of knowledge, magic, science, and writing, as well as the legendary creator of the Tarot itself.

Through the ibis—and our knowledge of its esoteric symbolism—we gain access to Egyptian myths, with all their history and wisdom. We will come back to Thoth, and his stories, many times in this book.

And what of the woman in the picture? We notice first of all her nakedness, her ease, and we recognize hope and confidence in life. But notice the two gourds of water poured out so freely. At the end of the Greater Mysteries of Eleusis, a mass initiation held for over two thousand years in ancient Greece, the Goddess Persephone returned from the Underworld of Death. At the visionary moment of her return, her celebrants poured water from two vessels into two cracks in the Earth. Persephone is the Queen of the Dead, a Goddess who died and come back to life, and who promised life after death to her initiates.

In this she resembles not only Jesus, but also Osiris, an Egyptian God murdered by his brother and restored to life by his wife Isis, with the help of—Thoth.

Do we need to know all these stories to appreciate the Star? Certainly not, and in fact, if we allow our knowledge of such things to distract us, we might forget to follow the goat through the tunnel. But the stories are there, hidden in the pictures, along with so much more. Why not make use of them? Maybe we can think of the various myths and doctrines coded into the Tarot as the branch in the goat's mouth. They entice us and lead us to follow. Or maybe we can switch metaphors (what are metaphors for, if not to switch and play with them—the way we shuffle cards?) and describe symbolism as the tunnel itself. We need the symbolism because it will lead us to the garden, but we should not confuse it with the goal. We do not want to get stuck in the tunnel.

This book is for anyone interested in spiritual discovery. It is also for anyone interested in Tarot. I have tried to write it in such a way that people who know nothing beforehand about Tarot can follow it (a tunnel is no good if you can't find your way through it), while people who have spent their lives in Tarot study can still find new things in it. This may seem an impossible task, but it is not so difficult as it seems. It only requires a willingness to look at the Tarot in a fresh way.

We will not go through each card in systematic fashion, though the course of our explorations will lead us to a great many traditional meanings. Other books have illuminated the wonders and meanings of the cards in their numerical order. Our purpose here is to use the Tarot images as openings to spiritual wonder.

For the newcomer to the subject, a brief description: The Tarot consists of seventy-eight cards. There are four suits of fourteen cards each, plus twenty-two "trump" cards numbered 0–21. *Trump* means "triumph," for in the card game Tarot or *tarocchi*—related to bridge and whist—these cards will triumph over the fifty-six suit cards. The trumps contain odd names, like the Magician or the Hanged Man, and bright vivid scenes. In the esoteric tradition the twenty-two trumps became known collectively as the Major Arcana (*arcana* means "secrets"), while the suit cards receive the collective title of Minor Arcana.

Structurally, the four suits resemble ordinary playing cards, with Ace through Ten, plus Page, Knight, Queen, and King. The Page is equivalent to the jack in regular decks, with the Knight as an extra card. At one time most playing cards had the same suit emblems as the Tarot. These are Wands (or Staves), Cups, Swords, and Coins (Pentacles in many modern Tarot decks). Over time the suits in regular playing cards changed, at least in northern European countries and the United States. Wands became clubs, Cups became hearts, Swords spades, and Coins diamonds. In some countries, such as Spain, playing cards still carry the same emblems as Tarot cards.

We will look at the question of the Tarot's origin in chapter one, but for now we can say that as far as scholarship can tell us, it began as a game. This may startle many people, especially those who have heard exaggerated stories of the Tarot's mythic origin. The more I think about it, however, the more it appeals to me that these are *playing* cards. When we play, we can do so much more—we can *allow* so much more—than when we make everything solemn and literal.

This book contains some outrageous ideas and questions. We will play with the idea that the Tarot images existed before the creation of the universe, that God somehow consulted the cards to make the world, and even that we can use the cards to find the very reading that God received. Now, I would never expect—or want—anyone to take this idea as literally true. If we had to limit all our Tarot investigations to ideas we consider literally true, how would we ever discover new things? If we remember that the Tarot is a game, cards that we shuffle and make new every time, the images on the cards can take us to wondrous gardens.

Does this make the Tarot frivolous? Absolutely not. To learn to play seriously is one of the great secrets of spiritual exploration. This is why so many traditions convey wisdom in the form of comical stories or riddles. If this book conveys nothing more than how to play seriously with Tarot cards, I will be more than pleased.

We will look at various different decks in our play. This too may surprise people. Part of the myth of Tarot is the idea that one true deck exists, with correct symbolism, from which all others deviate. Again, as far as scholarship can tell us, there simply is no original, official, pure Tarot. The earliest known decks look very different from the pictures that later became taken for standard or classic. Today there are literally thousands of decks available, and these are only a portion of all the decks that have existed.

Virtually all of the new decks in recent years have abandoned any claims of "restoring" an "original" and long-lost Tarot. We still see such claims, but most prefer to see themselves as *opening up* the Tarot to new consciousness and possibilities.

There is no single true Tarot. The Tarot has become an art form, or maybe an archetype. All the different decks together, with all their variations, make up the Tarot. We will return to this idea in the course of this book.

Of the various decks used, the most commonly cited will be the *Shining Tribe Tarot*. Partly, this is simply because I myself designed and drew this deck. It is also because I did my best to make the *Shining Tribe* cards a tool for people to open up and explore sacred pathways. The pictures for this deck derive partly from tribal and prehistoric art from all over the world. Please note—I have not actually *copied* any of these cultural images, and certainly do not claim to be a worshipper in their traditions. I have let them inspire me, just as the stories and symbolic ideas of many traditions (including Einstein's special theory of relativity) have inspired parts of this book.

Other decks used include the Rider Tarot for its comprehensive symbolism, the Thoth deck of Aleister Crowley and Lady Frieda Harris for its deep esoteric meanings, the classic Tarot de Marseille, and a range of contemporary decks.

The word *God* appears with some regularity in this book. So does *Goddess,* and the names of various mythological figures, as well as ideas of Paganism, Judaism, Christianity, and other established religions. None of these references are meant to endorse any of these traditions, let alone the churches or organizations that claim to speak for them. *God* in these pages becomes a way to express our universal desire to know and comprehend the sacred.

I offer this book to all playful seekers, all those who would travel through the tunnel to the garden of delight.

One

Myths of Origin

Where does Tarot come from? No matter how we treat the subject, whether we dive deep into the symbolic mysteries, recite formulas for fortune-telling, or play with the pictures, we cannot escape the question. There are certainly enough answers. Enter the world of Tarot and stories of its origin move around you like excited birds. Here is a sample:

❖ The Tarot depicts the sacred myths of the Romani, disguised in cards for the centuries of exile from the Rom homeland in India— or Egypt—or outer space (the last is favored by many Romani themselves).

❖ The Tarot is a Renaissance card game inspired by annual carnival processions called Triumphs.

❖ The Tarot is a card game derived from annual processions called thriambs, in honor of the God Dionysos, the creator of wine.

❖ The Tarot conceals/reveals the secret number teachings of Pythagoras, a Greek mystic who lived at the time of Moses, and who influenced Plato.

❖ The Tarot depicts the secret oral teachings of Moses, who received them directly from God.

❖ The Tarot contains the lost knowledge of Atlantis, a drowned continent first described by Plato.

❖ The Tarot is a card game imported from Palestine and Egypt during the Crusades.

❖ The Tarot is a vast memory system for the Tree of Life, a diagram of the laws of creation.

❖ The Tarot hides in plain sight the wisdom of the Egyptian God Thoth, master of all knowledge.

❖ The Tarot shows Egyptian temple initiations.

❖ The Tarot shows Tantric temple initiations.

❖ The Tarot preserves the wisdom of Goddess-initiated witches during the long dark centuries of patriarchal religion.

❖ The Tarot maps the patterns of the moon in Chaldean astrology.

❖ The Tarot was created by papermaker guilds who were the last remnants of the Cathars, Christians considered heretics by the Church of Rome and brutally suppressed.

Tarot writers have proclaimed all of the above and more as the one true authentic origin of the Tarot.

The great mythographer Joseph Campbell once commented that the world is full of creation stories and all of them are wrong. The Tarot is like that—full of origin stories, and probably all of them wrong. They are wrong because they take a compelling idea as literal truth. Wrong because they need that literal belief to take the idea seriously, and if someone should disprove once and for all these origin tales, they will have lost their hold on Tarot's meaning and value. But if we can learn to take these origin tales as myths, as divine play, then not only can we let go of this need to prove the superiority of one to all others, we also can appreciate the poetic truth of each one. We can marvel at this amazing work, this pack of seventy-eight pictures that somehow adapts itself to so many spiritual and historical traditions.

The secret origin of the Tarot is part of its myth. One of the most remarkable things about the cards is the way people snapped at this idea the moment it appeared and have clung to it tenaciously ever since. Here is a personal story. Years ago, I was in Denmark shortly after the publication of the Danish edition of my book *Seventy-Eight Degrees of Wisdom*. Two radio stations wanted to interview me. The first, on national radio, went very well. The second was for a New Age program and I looked forward to it as a chance to discuss the Tarot in some more depth. The day before, the host called me to go over some topics. When I told him that I did not believe the Tarot came from Atlantis or that secret occult masters crafted it and disguised it as a game, he canceled my appearance.

Ironically, though we cannot determine the exact origin of the cards, we can, in fact, pinpoint the origin of the myth. In the 1770s and '80s, a man named Antoine Court de Gébelin published a nine-volume study of eso-teric ideas called *Le Monde Primitif* (The Primitive World). The very idea of a primitive human state is itself a myth. In our time, the term *primitive* suggests people unformed, ignorant, savage. In earlier times it meant the opposite—a supposed Golden Age in which people knew spiritual truth and lived in perfect peace. The Garden of Eden is a variation on this myth.

In the course of his work, Court de Gébelin visited a friend, Madame la C. d'H., who showed him the latest fad: an Italian card game popular in the southern countries, called in Italy *tarocchi*, and in France *les tarots*. Court de Gébelin looked through the bright pictures and had an epiphany: the ordinary card game was, in fact, a disguised great work of occult mystery! He called it the Book of Thoth, the very sum of all knowledge.

Thoth is an Egyptian God, the quintessential master of wisdom. Thoth guided the boat of the Sun God Ra across the sky, invented mummifi-cation to resurrect the slain God Osiris, helped judge dead souls for the afterlife, and even gambled with the Moon to create extra days for the year (more about *that* story in a while). The Greeks linked Thoth with their own Hermes, God of magic, healing, wisdom, science, commerce, and not inci-dentally, patron of swindlers and thieves. (You have to love a religion with a God of swindlers.)

Much of the esoteric tradition originates with a shadowy figure known as Hermes Trismegistus, or Thrice-great Hermes, author of *The Emerald Tablet*, a work composed in Alexandrian Egypt in the early Christian era. The myth of the Emerald Tablet considers Hermes Trismegistus to be another name for Thoth. Now Antoine Court de Gébelin had described the Tarot as an even more fundamental divine work than the Emerald Tablet itself. Thoth, he said, had given the symbolic pictures to his human disciples and disguised them as a game so that it could move through the centuries undetected.

What a wonderful idea! How amazing that this moment's inspiration took such a powerful hold on people's imaginations that it reverberates to this day. Court de Gébelin and his nine volumes would be long forgotten were it not for this one short essay in volume eight. The compelling part of the myth was not really the claim of Egyptian origins. That was just the particulars. The core idea, the one that took hold so powerfully it dominates subsequent origin stories (at least the occult ones), is that the Tarot forms the basis of all knowledge, the key of keys, or *clavicle*, as occultists sometimes call it. In other words, the Tarot lies behind all other knowledge systems. The Tarot summarizes all the mysteries and discoveries of ancient masters. Know the Tarot, understand it correctly, and you will know everything. When Tarot interpreters say it is not Egyptian but Hebrew, or not Hebrew but Tantric, or Chaldean, or heretical Christian, or Wiccan, they begin with the same assumption: that whatever the origin, the Tarot *must* contain ultimate secrets. They may argue over just which secrets it contains, but they never doubt its esoteric significance.

If we let go of literal belief in all these stories, if we accept the strong likelihood that the Tarot began in the fifteenth century as a popular card game with well-known allegorical images, do we lose the value of the myth? Can we play with myth rather than believe in it? It seems to me, and to many modern Tarotists, that we actually gain when we see the Tarot's multiple origins as stories rather than history. For one thing, we can stop arguing, stop trying to prove our version of the origin is correct. Instead, we can look at the subtle beauty and inner truths of the varied esoteric systems entwined with the Tarot.

One of the major traditions looks at the Tarot as a representation of Kabbalah, a vast system of Jewish mystical ideas and practices. We will look at how this idea originated in a moment, but for now there is a Kabbalist myth that illuminates the question of literal belief. The Kabbalists teach that the universe exists in ten levels of divine energy, called *sephiroth* (the word is connected to "sapphire"). They picture these sephiroth in various ways, sometimes as concentric circles with God in the center and the physical world at the outermost circle, or more commonly with the sephiroth arranged as small circles on a "Tree of Life," with the ultimate energy at the top sephirah, called *Kether* (Hebrew for "crown"), and the material universe, called *Malkuth* (Hebrew for "kingdom"), at the bottom. God created Adam, the first human, with the ability to see and understand all the levels. However, Adam looked at the beauty of Malkuth and allowed himself to mistake it for all creation. And so Adam "sinned" and lost the closeness to God, and he took us all with him. Or maybe we ourselves repeat Adam's error of our own free will and continuously confuse the material world with the whole of existence.

A literal belief in any particular origin for the Tarot seems to me a little like Adam's great mistake. We become entranced by the claim and lose sight of the poetic levels and what they actually can teach us. Similarly, if we debunk the specific assertions—if we say no, the Tarot did not come from Egypt, or Atlantis, or ancient rabbis—we would make a great error to think such beliefs no longer mean anything.

The link of Tarot and Kabbalah also goes back to *Le Monde Primitif*, and a certain Comte (Count) de Mellet, who wrote a backup essay to Court de Gébelin's comments on the Tarot. Court de Gébelin wrote "the set of XXI or XXII trumps, the XXII letters of the Egyptian alphabet common to the Hebrews and the Orientals, which also served as numerals, are necessary in order to keep count of so many countries." [1]

Contrary to popular belief about the Egyptian hieroglyphs, they are indeed an alphabet, and not picture writing. However, there are not twenty-two of them. Nor can we determine just who "the Orientals" might be. The Hebrew alphabet, on the other hand, does indeed have twenty-two letters, and Jewish mystical thought considers them the very

---

1   Quoted in *A Wicked Pack of Cards,* Decker, Depaulis, and Dummett, Bristol Classical Press, 1996.

The Fool and Lovers from the Tarot of Ceremonial Magick

basis of existence. They link up the sephiroth emanations on the Tree of Life via twenty-two pathways, each with the special quality of one of the letters. Just as Court de Gébelin said, they have numerical value, so that each word adds up to a number, and we can discover secret connections in pairs of words that have the same numbers (this practice is called *gematria*). We also can move through mystical worlds with the letters and perform acts of magic using the divine names and other letter combinations. It was the Comte de Mellet's idea to link each Tarot trump to a particular Hebrew letter, so that the individual cards would take on the magical powers of the letters.

Tarot scholar and teacher Mary K. Greer has suggested an interesting revisionist history of the articles in *Le Monde Primitif*. Court de Gébelin and de Mellet were both Freemasons. Greer considers it likely that the Masons had developed the esoteric theory of Tarot over some time and gave permission to the two writers to make it public (she also thinks it likely that de Mellet's essay came first). Madame la C. d'H. may have been a cover story. If Greer is correct in her speculations, it still does not diminish the remarkable impact the announcement had on the history of Tarot.

Christian mystics and magicians became interested in Kabbalah around the same time as the first appearance of the Italian card game tarocchi, so it is not impossible that the Tarot indeed derived from Kabbalistic ideas (though modern scholarship suggests that the cards existed a few decades before the first Christian use of Kabbalah). And the structural comparisons are indeed impressive. Twenty-two is not as common a mystical number as say, twenty-one. (Numerologists describe twenty-two as a "master" number, but this is probably a Kabbalistic influence). Kabbalah describes four distinct worlds of creation, each with ten sephiroth. In Tarot we find four suits with cards Ace–Ten. Kabbalah also makes much of the mystical meaning of the four letters in God's most holy name: יהוי. (In English, this is sometimes called a Tetragrammaton.) Meanwhile the Tarot has four Court cards: Page, Knight, Queen, and King in each suit. No wonder the idea took hold so powerfully.

In the nineteenth century an occultist and magician named Éliphas Lévi (originally Alphonse Louis Constant) developed the Kabbalistic symbolism of the Tarot in great detail, especially for the trump cards and their Hebrew letters. At the end of that century, a Rosicrucian group with the wonderful name of The Hermetic Order of the Golden Dawn took Lévi's work and expanded and revised it to construct a magical universe of Kabbalah, ritual, Pagan Gods, Hindu philosophy, Freemasonry and other occult traditions, astrology, alchemy, and secret names. The key to all this, the Key of Keys that would enable the highest adepts (*adept* was a favorite word and there were many levels) to move through all these different worlds of consciousness and magical power, was—of course—the Tarot. Antoine Court de Gébelin had claimed it as the Book of Thoth. Éliphas Lévi had made it the embodiment of the Hebrew letters. Now the Golden Dawn had made these beliefs a reality, or at least a fully developed system.

Does it matter that there was no historical evidence for a Kabbalist, or for that matter an Egyptian, origin for the Tarot? It does if you need to believe in the literal truth of your magical system. The Golden Dawn included poets, artists, scholars, even a scientist or two. For such an intellectual group, they seem to have been remarkably gullible. One of the founders, Samuel Liddell "MacGregor" Mathers, produced the group's official Tarot deck, which differed in some interesting ways from the traditional cards.

Apparently, one evening Mathers took a set of blank cards, went into a room for a short time, and emerged with a complete deck of painted cards. This was enough to convince the group of the deck's divine inspiration. It does not seem to have occurred to them that Mathers (or possibly his artist wife Moina) might have painted seventy-eight pictures in the usual manner and concealed them somewhere in the room. But then, the Order's founders—Mathers, Dr. Wynn Westcott, and Rev. W. R. Woodman—based the whole thing on a fraud. They claimed to have received a "cypher manuscript" that included a page with information about a Frau Sprengel in Germany, who could authorize them to start an English branch of a secret mystical order. After decades of debate, scholars such as Israel Regardie (himself a former member of the Golden Dawn) demonstrated that Frau Sprengel never existed. Westcott himself seems to have written the vital page. Does such proof discredit the Golden Dawn and all its productions? The word *Hermetic* in the title comes from Hermes Trismegistus, but ultimately from that Greek God of swindlers. Hermes might have delighted in such a daring enterprise. Perhaps the Order's great success owes much to Hermes's blessing.

***

Note—the personal story below comes from the earlier edition of this book. Since then, my dog, Wonder, has died. We miss her. She was a special soul, and her memory is a blessing.

A personal story: While I was writing the above paragraphs, my dog, whose name is Wonder, decided to chew up one of my decks of cards, something she never has done before (or since). To do this, she had to pull the cards off a table, then bite off the silk scarf that enwrapped them, and scatter the cards about the floor. She actually chewed up only one card before she returned to the room where I sat at my desk. When I discovered what she had done (and had gotten over the shock), I checked to see which card she had destroyed. The deck is not Tarot, but an Egyptian-based oracle called *The Book of Doors*, and the card that Wonder chewed up was called Kerhet, after an Egyptian Goddess of secret initiation. Secret initiations were the Golden Dawn's whole manner of operation.

The deck's writers, Athon Veggi and Alison Davidson, write of this card, "the quality of secrecy is recognized in the oath to Keep Silent, to keep the creative operation in perfect secrecy." The Golden Dawn took this concept so seriously that members took an oath, with a sword on their shoulders, that they invited the spirits to strike them down dead if they ever revealed anything to the outside world.

Was Hermes, or to use his Egyptian name, Thoth, showing his displeasure at my lack of respect for his followers' beliefs? Was he warning me? Personally, I prefer to believe he was playing a joke. Or maybe Thoth was even endorsing openness, for after all, now that *Wonder* has removed the card of *secrecy*, any shuffle of the deck can no longer bring forth a card that means "the oath to Keep Silent."

***

The greatest of all Kabbalah texts, the source of so much that came after it, a work called the Zohar, describes itself as the product of a rabbi two thousand years ago, named Simeon bar Yohai. Bar Yohai dictated the Zohar to his son while they hid from the Romans in a cave for thirteen years, or so the story goes. The Zohar appeared about the year 1100, brought forth by a writer in Spain named Moses de Leon. More than eight hundred years later, in the 1930s, a scholar named Gershom Scholem demonstrated that de Leon himself created the Zohar.

Did de Leon commit fraud? Did Kabbalists need to believe the Zohar's claim of ancient authority to take it seriously? David Rosenberg, a contemporary poet whose book *Dreams of Being Eaten Alive: The Literary Core of the Kabbalah* greatly influenced this work, writes that Moses de Leon was not the sole author of the Zohar but rather the leader of a group that worked together on it. De Leon's own wife later claimed that he had written it. That is, according to an account I read, after his death someone asked her, "Did Moses write the Zohar?" to which she answered, "Yes, of course." This suggests that people at the time knew very well who actually had produced the Zohar, and it was only later generations that somehow needed to take the text at face value.

I suggest that we approach the Tarot in the spirit of Moses de Leon's writers' group—that we take it seriously by not taking it literally, that we play, with all our hearts, with the most daring of ideas.

Here is a myth of the Tarot's origin. In contrast to all those stories of a mysterious past, this one is a myth of the future. In further contrast, I do not expect people to take it with utmost seriousness. It is a strategy to open up the usual way we view reality. And isn't that why many people come to Tarot in the first place?

How do we know that time works the way we think it does? Time appears to move in a line, from past to future. Events in the past, it seems, cause the future to come into existence. I exist because my parents met and fell in love and had sex. Their past caused my present. This is simply common sense. But sometimes sense is *common* only because it's commonly agreed upon. For many centuries people assumed the Earth lay at the center of a series of concentric spheres, largely because it looked that way, and because it was just common sense. Of course the sun revolves around the Earth: you can see it every day. It rises in the east, moves overhead in an arc, and sets in the west, only to do it again the next day. The sun moves, and we stay where we are. It took a long time for people to get the idea that maybe the sun is stationary and the Earth spins around.

Notice that our language makes it very difficult to describe events in any way other than past to future. We say that people *used* to believe the sun moved, *then* they realized the Earth itself moved. Our common sense about time lies partly in our language. The past is primary because it causes the present. But suppose it were the other way around? Suppose we make existence now a primary fact, and the past secondary? Then we can say, for instance, that my presence now reached back in time and brought my parents together so that they would produce me. And perhaps the people in the future who are reading this book caused me to write it.

Dizzy yet? Think how people felt in the Renaissance when naturalists told them that the sun does not actually move, the Earth spins.

Physicists long ago noticed an odd quality about equations that involve a process over time. Nothing in the equations implies a direction. They always work as efficiently from the future to the past as they do from the past to the future. Quantum theory (the branch of physics that deals with the behavior of infinitesimal particles) produces an even more interesting view of time. Events occur through a process called "transactional interpretation." A wave ripples out from the present moment, the now. This wave must meet a resonating wave from the future. The interaction between these two waves produces a probability field in which events occur. At any moment the future is as real as the present.

The future can "cause" the past as much as the past causes the future. In fact, neither one causes the other, they exist in a relationship that goes in many directions at once. Imagine a web with a vast number of points, all connected to each other, with no single point as the origin or primary cause of the others. Our consciousness places us in one point, convincing us that a single line from the past has caused our current situation to come into being. But this may be an illusion. The physicist Louis de Broglie wrote that elementary particles sometimes seem to come out of nowhere because they can move freely through space-time, and our awareness reaches a point where they happen to exist.

If you find it difficult to follow these ideas, try to experience them as a kind of meditation. Stand outside on a pleasant day (so no rain or cold wind will distract you). Close your eyes and try to sense *this* moment, right now. Then see if you can feel the past rippling backward from where you are.

Think of your parents, and their parents, and the people who have influenced you, the events that shaped and even created you, such as the first time your parents met, and more subtly, the moment a friend showed you the Tarot, or the first time you saw that book or movie that changed your life. Now see if you can sense a wave equal in size that ripples out to the future, as real as the one to the past. Think of the friends you will influence, the lovers who will move through your life, the children you have or will have, and their children, and their children's children. The *now* shifts constantly and is different for each person, but it always contains the past and the future, and both perhaps as real as the present.

Here is how the poet T. S. Eliot (whose great poem, "The Wasteland" first introduced me to the Tarot) put it in "Burnt Norton," from *The Four Quartets*:

> *Time present and time past*
> *Are both present in time future*
> *And time future contained in time past.*

The image of a web does not imply that all time is fixed and rigid. It would if the "web" were a solid structure. But if we think of its many paths as probabilities or simply energy, we actually come to a greater sense of freedom than the usual view of time as a fixed past determining a likely future. All time, all events, exist and influence each other, but none of it controls us.

This view of time is a myth, just like that of three Goddesses called Fates who weave the pattern of our lives and cut the thread at the determined moment of our death or the medieval idea that a disembodied soul passes through successive planetary spheres on its way to lodge itself in a body. Can we acknowledge that our ordinary view of time is also a myth, and not an absolute truth?

All myths have their uses. One use of a myth of time as a web is a way to imagine the origin of Tarot. Suppose our collective beliefs about the Tarot as the key of keys—Antoine Court de Gébelin's "discovery," the Golden Dawn, the modern psychological approach to the cards, whatever "future" developments we do not know about—suppose all these beliefs and uses somehow reached back in time to draw the Tarot into existence in Renaissance Italy? When Court de Gébelin proclaimed the Tarot the Book of

Thoth, the idea took hold so powerfully because it "already" existed in the future.

We, all of us, caused the Tarot to come into the minds of cardmakers in such a perfect form and structure that in our own time we can adapt it to an almost endless series of esoteric, mythological, and cultural ideas. My friend and fellow Tarotist Zoe Matoff points out that our own view of the Tarot may come from future generations who need us to believe what we believe for them to develop their own ideas. We know (or think we know) the ways in which past concepts, such as the Golden Dawn, have influenced our current views (we may follow the past or rebel against it, but we still react to it). But maybe the future influences us in ways we have not learned how to recognize, and maybe neither the future nor the past *causes* the other, but all time is a web.

To see all time as existent and connected in a web opens up ways to understand divination. Maybe a Tarot reading helps us glimpse a slightly larger part of the web than we would otherwise recognize. At any moment the shifting energy of past-present-future creates a vast pattern, one that ultimately contains all existence. Or maybe a vast *potential* pattern, what physicists call a wave of probabilities. When we shuffle the cards (and therefore give up conscious control of how they fall), we allow them to form a very small pattern that mimics the very large one. They do not control or show an unchangeable fate. Instead, they reveal possibilities.

Stephen Karcher, an expert on the *I Ching* and world divination, has written that divination helps us to act with free will because it frees us from slavery to our conditioning. Is this just because it increases our awareness and shows us our choices? Or does divination liberate us in some basic way? Can our play with the cards actually open up our destiny and not just reveal it? Can a reading change reality?

An Egyptian myth about the calendar suggests a whole new way to look at what we do when we mix Tarot cards and lay them out for a reading. It features our good friend Thoth, the God of All Things Worth Knowing, and legendary inventor of the Tarot. I call this story Gambling with the Moon, and like any myth it resonates far beyond its literal subject. We will look at it in the next chapter.

Two

Gambling with the Moon: Divination and Freedom

Egyptian tales often come in many variant forms, that is, different versions of the same basic story (like the Tarot itself, with all the different decks). For example, in the myth that follows, Thoth aids in the birth of Seth and Horus. But Horus is also the name of Seth's nephew, and in another story Seth somehow "impregnates" his nephew so that a golden disk grows on the young Horus's head, and eventually Horus "gives birth"—to none other than Thoth himself.

The following myth also comes in variant forms. In this version, Thoth gambles with the Moon. In other versions, Thoth himself is the Moon God and gambles with the other Gods as a group. I've used the version below partly because it's the first one I read and partly just because I like it and find it useful. This, too, is like Tarot. Many Tarotists who become collectors, and may own hundreds of decks, still read or do other work (meditation, for instance) with the first deck they saw, the deck that made them fall in love with Tarot.

Here, then, is Thoth and the Moon, with some details of my own invention.

Nut (rhymes with root), Goddess of the Night Sky, was married to Ra, the all-powerful God of the Sun. Like many wives, she strayed, and took up with Geb, the God of the Earth. Readers alert to esoteric symbolism will recognize this situation as the universal tale of spirit "descending" into matter—in other words, taking on a physical form. Many people see this theme in the Tarot card of the Fool, who steps off a cliff and will fall to Earth.

The Sun God represents pure light, which may be a metaphor for divine spirit, or may in fact be the very essence of spirit itself, the true nature of reality (we will return to this concept in later chapters). For creation to take place, spirit must enter matter. (We will see, in chapter thirteen, that we might describe matter, physical bodies, as light slowed down.) The dark sky, married to light, must become the lover of Earth and become pregnant. For this is how new things emerge, whether a new generation of Gods or new ideas and discoveries, when we break the rules and allow ourselves to become pregnant.

When Ra discovers his wife pregnant from an affair, he issues a command. Nut will not bear her children on any day of any month of the year. Obviously, this means she must stay pregnant forever. We are dealing with the calendar and the zodiac here. The Egyptians imagined that before the birth of the new generation of Gods, those who would deal directly with human culture, the year consisted of twelve months of exactly thirty days each. Perfect regularity, the same clockwork existence over and over. This is the world of the sky, and not of Earth, where life is dynamic and ever-changing.

Clearly in a dilemma, Nut does the only sensible thing and turns to the expert of experts, Thoth. Now, we might expect that Thoth will persuade Ra or find some ingenious solution (for those of you who remember Uncle Scrooge McDuck comic books, Thoth reminds me of the great inventor Gyro Gearloose). Instead, Thoth gambles. If you want to step outside a closed system, you cannot do so through plans within that system, you have to break it open. Gambling does this because it removes control. Thoth gambles with the Moon, who after all determines the months with its cycle of twenty-nine and a half days.

Again, I should comment that in most versions Thoth is himself the Moon God and gambles with a group of the other Gods—I have stayed with the version as I first learned it.

As good at gambling as he is at everything else, Thoth wins 1/72nd of each day to produce five extra days that stand independently and are not in any month of the year (360 divided by 72 equals 5). Nut gives birth to a baby each day: Seth, Osiris, Isis, Nephthys, and Horus. Isis appears in many Tarot decks as the High Priestess card, while Seth sometimes shows up in his Greek form of Typhon, as the serpent of destruction on the Wheel of Fortune card.

The High Priestess and Wheel of Fortune from the Rider deck

The five days at the end of the year, not in any month, became a time of celebration in Egypt, when the rigid rules of society relaxed and perhaps people experimented with their lives and identities.

Let's stop for a moment and look at that number seventy-two. It appears later in the mythology as well, when Seth has decided to destroy Osiris. To help him, he brings together a group of seventy-two henchmen.

If we happen to know that the Kabbalists claimed there were seventy-two names for God or that a famous name contains seventy-two letters or even that the first translation of the Hebrew Bible into Greek was called the Septuagint because a commission of seventy-two scholars did the work, we will understand that seventy-two does not appear in the story as a random number. Nor does it appear only to produce five days out of 360, for the relationship between seventy-two and 360 also is not a chance occurrence.

The zodiac consists of twelve star clusters, or constellations, that lie more or less in a flat plane (called the *ecliptic*) created by the apparent paths of all the principal planets. (One reason Pluto was "demoted" from planetary status was because its orbit does not lie along the ecliptic.) Because humans live such a short time the stars appear stationary in their seasonal positions year after year. In fact, due to a wobble in the Earth's orbit caused by the gravitational pull of the sun and moon, the constellations actually shift very, very slowly. Over the course of 2,160 years, the constellations—the signs of the zodiac—shift an entire month in relation to the Earth. In other words, astrological calendars will say that the sun enters Aries on the spring equinox, but this is really an agreed-upon fiction. The sun has not actually entered Aries on the equinox for about four thousand years. Those who follow astrology should be aware that modern astrology is not in fact related to the actual positions of stars and planets. Some already know this, and there is a branch of astrology, called sidereal, that *is* based on the current sky. But if you are an Aries worrying that you've secretly been a Pisces all along, don't panic! Regardless of these astronomical facts, your astrological sign remains intact and valid.

About two thousand years ago, around the time of Jesus, the sun began to enter Pisces, the sign of the fish, at the beginning of spring. This is one reason why Christ often is compared to a fish and why bishops wear fish-shaped hats, called miters. Since that time, the signs have shifted again, so that the sun enters Aquarius around the time of the equinox, and we get the expressions New Age and Age of Aquarius.

My astrologer friends have pointed out to me that Western astrology actually follows the *signs*, not the constellations. That is, the sun is said to enter Aries in spring because the sign of Aries bears qualities of spring. Astrology, therefore, is more a *divinatory* system than an astronomical one.

What does all this have to do with Thoth and the number seventy-two? The amount of time for the full zodiac to turn around the Earth, the Great Year as Plato called it, is 25,920 (12 times 2,160). The zodiac is a circle, and long ago, astrologers organized circles into 360 degrees (based upon the constellations, with an arbitrary designation of thirty degrees for each of the twelve signs). One degree of the Great Year, 1/360th of 25,920 is seventy-two.

When Thoth gambles with the Moon—or the other Gods—to win 1/72nd of the year, he is opening up one degree of a fixed circle. Fate, closed destiny, opens, and new possibilities emerge into existence to change the course of humanity.

Seth uses seventy-two in exactly the opposite way—negatively. Here is what he does to destroy Osiris: he measures him. While Osiris sleeps, Seth and his gang of seventy-two carefully measure every turn of the God's body. Then they construct a magnificent jeweled box that will exactly fit and enclose him. At a party they pretend to discover the box and Seth says, "Hey, I know. Let's play a game. Whoever can fit inside this box gets to keep it." With fake enthusiasm, the seventy-two all lie down, and like Cinderella's sisters none of them fit.

Finally, Osiris tries it, and of course it fits him so tightly he cannot get up. Seth and his henchmen slam on the top, nail it down, seal it with lead, and float it off down the Nile. Osiris suffocates to death. (Don't worry, his wife Isis retrieves him and with the aid of—who else, Thoth—brings him back to life.)

When the seventy-two measure Osiris, they limit him to one degree of the infinite circle of his possibilities. Such measurement suffocates, becomes a coffin. It is the same for us. Virtually from the moment of our birth, society measures us. Doctors measure our physical (and more and more our psychological) abilities; schools measure our intelligence and "aptitude" for future careers; bosses measure our worth; family and friends all measure our character. We measure and weigh our bodies to judge our attractiveness. Potential partners place us on a scale of one to ten. Polls measure our beliefs and convictions; corporations measure our tastes. With every measurement, the box becomes tighter and more elaborate. Just like Osiris, we suffocate in a cramped space that limits us to one degree of who we can become.

Why should a Tarot reading play this game? Any reading that defines you, that says you are such and such a person, or that describes your destiny in fixed terms becomes part of Seth's gang of suffocators. Can we learn to read Tarot like Thoth—that is, to gamble with our supposed fate and open it up to new possibilities? Like the new Gods, born outside any day of the year, can we use divination to bring new things into our reality?

What game did Thoth play to create extra days? Some ancient versions of the old myth say dice, but ever since 1781 and *Le Monde Primitif*, we have known better. Thoth did not invent Tarot to describe a fixed universe. He invented it so he could go to the Moon and say, "Want to play some cards?" The God of magic invented Tarot to liberate us from measurements.

A Reading to Gamble with the Moon

If we want to read cards to liberate our destiny rather than define our fate, what kind of questions would we ask? Such a reading style requires a shift in thinking that makes it hard for us to formulate what we need to ask. That is, we know the kind of questions to tease out a determinist future. *When and where will I meet my soulmate? Will my restaurant succeed? When and how will I die?*

Luckily, we have a way to get beyond such limitations. We have the Tarot.

We use the cards to answer questions, why not use them to ask questions as well? I first began this kind of approach to the Tarot when people would ask me to teach at a center and no great subject came into my head. As a result, I decided to ask the cards something like, "What do you want to teach next April in New York?" The cards that came up invariably suggested dynamic topics that people found useful for their own work with the Tarot.

More recently, I have found it valuable to use the cards to set up the questions for a reading. It works like this: Someone will say that she wants to do a reading about how to integrate her spiritual work into her career. (This is an actual example.) Now, the traditional approach would be to choose an existent spread with set questions that seems best for what she wants to discover. However, some years ago I began to follow a suggestion that Gail Fairfield makes in her wonderful book, *Choice Centered Tarot*, and that is to make up a spread just for that person. And so we will discuss her issues and maybe frame some questions to put into a spread. This is what Fairfield describes, and she gives some excellent examples of questions people might want to ask for various situations. Sometimes, however, I will ask the person to mix the cards and choose, say, three or five cards. These cards will help us come up with valuable further questions. So in the example above, when the Magician came up, it inspired the woman to ask the question, "What will my life look like if I really live out my dreams?" Once we have formulated the questions, we return the cards to the deck, and the woman mixes them once more in the usual way to discover what answers the cards can show her.

After I had written the passage about using Tarot to gamble for our lives, I wondered what such a reading would look like. I knew it would not resemble the usual "past-present-future" style of reading, but just because it was not common, I had trouble thinking of what questions we might want to ask. Then I realized I could use the cards. The layout on pages 30–31 shows the cards that came up, from the *Shining Tribe Tarot*, exactly in the order they revealed themselves. For reasons of space, I will not give detailed explanations of their meaning (though a few, especially the Spiral of Fortune, appear in greater detail later in the book). Instead, I will briefly state the qualities of each card and the question it inspires.

❖ The Spiral of Fortune: This card (a variation on the traditional Wheel of Fortune) shows a spiral that breaks through a closed circle to become the neck of a bird. It gives us the question, "How can I break through my limited view of what is possible for me?"

❖ The Five of Birds: We see a shamanic sacrifice, in which magical multicolored vultures will take away the shaman's outer flesh to release his inner being of pure light. "What must I release or offer of myself to find the will to touch my power?"

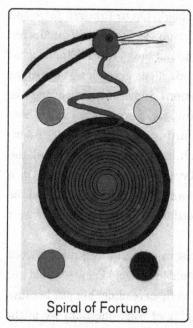

Spiral of Fortune

How can I break through my limited view of what is possible for me?

Five of Birds

What must I release or offer of myself to find the will to touch my power?

Chariot

How do I use my power beyond my limitations?

The Empress

What deep passion moves me?

Hermit

What doorway into the unknown opens for me?

Knower of Rivers

What power will I find if I go through that doorway?

Speaker of Trees

How can I speak my passion and bring it into the world?

❖ The Chariot: Traditionally a card of will, this Chariot figure also reaches into a river of divine energy that flows through the world. "How do I use my power beyond my limitations?" (Will is necessary because freedom does not just happen, we must choose it.)

❖ The Empress: A card of great passion, especially primal physical passions, such as sexuality and motherhood. "What deep passion moves me?"

❖ The Hermit: Unlike some older decks that show a wise old man, the *Shining Tribe* version of this card portrays a semiabstract figure joyously approaching a doorway to the astral world. "What doorway into the unknown opens for me?"

❖ The Knower of Rivers: Based on the Knight of Cups, this shaman, much more fully realized than the Hermit, emerges from a dark cave with fierce intensity. "What power will I find if I go through that doorway?" And perhaps, "What new version of myself will emerge?"

❖ Speaker of Trees: A variant on the King of Wands, this card shows how we share with other people the Fire energy of our lives. "How can I speak my passion and bring it into the world?"

Interlude—Writing and the Snake

During a break from my work on the "real" reason Thoth invented the Tarot, I did a short reading with a storytelling deck called *Life in the Garden*. Now that the Tarot has become popular, the concept of card decks for various subjects has really taken hold. There are Goddess cards, *I Ching* cards, Rune cards, Kabbalah cards, animal wisdom cards, and so on. Among the more interesting are decks that take story elements and place them on cards so that you can mix them together and create your own tales.

One of my favorites is *Life in the Garden*, by Eric Zimmerman and Nancy Nowacek. Each of the fifty-four cards contains a short dreamlike description about one or more of four characters: Adam, Eve, the serpent, and God. You mix the cards and choose however many you want to make a story. If you like, you can see them as a kind of divination. Here are the two I picked at random. I should add that the cards have no numbers, the numbers below are simply the order in which I drew them.

Card One:

> *The serpent*
> *invented writing*
> *as it worked the earth*
> *sliding through*
> *the fertile dirt*
> *of the garden.*

Card Two:

> *And Adam spent all night counting stars.*

Though Tarot cards show images, a Tarot reading is also about language. We get a set of pictures and must translate them into words. We might say, "The Lovers reversed means you turn away from love," or, "The Chariot indicates you can succeed if you focus your actions and take a strong stand." This is one reason we call them *readings*, because we translate the pictures into a story that the person who knows the Tarot can read and explain to the questioner.

But what about writing? When we write something down as an absolute statement, when we condemn—or praise—someone as if they had hired us to pass judgement on them, when we categorize ("You are a King of Wands, you are optimistic, energetic, etc."), when we *measure* people, we seek control. Not wisdom or discovery, but control. This is like Adam counting the stars, one by one by one. You can't really see the stars when you count them, you can't stop or you might lose track. "The King of Swords says that you are highly intelligent but judgemental."

There is another kind of language—a language of instinct and wonder connected to movements of energy and delight in the body and in nature. This language is like the flash of a snake as it marks the dirt with its passage.

A reading in such a language often contains questions as much as answers. "Who do you see in the King of Swords? Do you see yourself? What would it be like to sit on that throne and hold that sword, with all its weight and sharpness? How do you deal with people who bow down to you and ask for wisdom? Or is it someone else, someone who sits in judgement over you? What does it take to go to that person and ask for help or wisdom?"

When we *read* Tarot cards, let us try to see them as writing invented by the snake and not one more night spent counting the stars.

Three

The Instrument of Our Wisdom

I n the years spent on this work, various images and definitions for the
Tarot have come to mind, both for me and for my friends and students.
Some of these we will look at through the course of this book, especially in the section "The Tarot While Standing on One Foot." There is one,
however, that will help us enter into the worlds the Tarot reveals to us, and
that is that the Tarot is *the instrument of our wisdom*. Tarot is the tool that
teaches us, but also the means to find our own wisdom and then to express
it, to ourselves and to others. Like so many things with Tarot, the expression conveys many meanings, more and more as we consider what it means
to describe an instrument.

The Tarot encodes wisdom, and this makes it an instrument for discovering and expressing what lies inside the code. What does this mean? We
do not have to accept the literal claim of the occult tradition that the Tarot
is the key of keys to recognize that the potency of this claim, and the occultists' belief in it, brought about its own reality. In other words, because they
believed the Tarot expressed an entire universal system, the occultists
designed decks to do exactly that, in as thorough a way as possible. For
example, Aleister Crowley and Frieda Harris's *Book of Thoth* deck encodes

---

35

Kabbalistic doctrine, the Hebrew letter system, Crowley's own concepts, and astrological designations for each of the seventy-eight cards. The ideas and connections largely follow the Hermetic Order of the Golden Dawn, but they also go beyond it, not just through various changes but even more with Harris's striking paintings.

When someone reads with the Thoth deck, they will receive a great amount of information with every card. This makes the Tarot a little bit like a thumb drive. You code a vast amount of information into the small detachable device, so that later you can retrieve what you need. To the extent that you consider the information coded into any Tarot deck *wise*, you are getting a lot of wisdom in a small package. At the same time, the cards are not lists of properties or schematic designs. They are works of art and they stir us beyond the coded information.

Many modern decks have built on this esoteric tradition of the key of all knowledge. Some, such as the *Tarot of the Holy Light*, by Christine Payne-Towler and Michael Dowers, have used different elemental systems than the standard Golden Dawn arrangement, which runs Wands-Fire, Cups-Water, Swords-Air, and Pentacles-Earth.

The *Tarot of the Holy Light Tarot* follows a European tradition in which Cups are Air and Swords are Water. *The Alchemical Tarot* of Robert Place follows the traditional system but also encodes complex doctrines of Renaissance alchemy.

The *Haindl Tarot* includes the Kabbalistic Hebrew letters and post-Golden Dawn astrology (the Golden Dawn did not include Neptune, Uranus, and Pluto—the last of which had not been discovered yet—when they formulated their system), but also includes runes (ancient Germanic magical letters) on the Major cards, and on the Minor cards hexagrams from the *I Ching*, the three-thousand-year-old Chinese oracle. (A *hexagram* consists of six broken or unbroken lines arranged in a vertical pattern.)

The quality of encoded wisdom can take on a life of its own. Not long before the original edition of this deck, Hermann Haindl told me that he planned a new edition of his Tarot in which he would take out the hexagrams. The *I Ching* seemed unnecessary and perhaps extraneous to the Tarot, which after all, was quintessentially European. Just a few days later, he told me he had changed his mind. When he looked over the cards, he discovered that the hexagrams had entwined their meanings with the pictures. They were more than a detail printed in the corner of the cards; instead they gave the images another dimension. The traditional Tarot ideas and the *I Ching* had grown together into a new whole, and the cards would lose too much by removing their Chinese element.

You do not have to redesign the cards to encode meaning into them. The French esoteric tradition has developed complex and elegant ideas from the unaltered images of the classic Tarot de Marseille. The belief that such meanings exist in the cards spurs people to find meanings the original designers may never have intended (please note: *may* never is not the same as *never*). Once found, however, those meanings exist, and the cards become a physical embodiment of a vast, organized, and coherent system of laws and structures. And once we have found (or constructed) that system in the images, the cards become an instrument of it.

For the Tarot Kabbalist, the dynamic image of the Magician, with his wand and tools and his robes, represents a Hebrew letter, all the symbolic meanings around that letter, a pathway on the Tree of Life, the training for an actual magician, the rituals and other mystical acts that a magician performs, the mental state needed to perform those acts, what it feels like to experience those acts, the energy a magician draws on to perform his or her magic, and more. The same image will represent a principle of science, a moment in the early history of creation, particular qualities of the physical world, light and its properties, the investigative mind, maleness and masculinity (in a pure sense, not simply cultural), and ideas and qualities even more specific and detailed. And all this in a four-color playing card, with seventy-seven others alongside it. Most important, the card does not simply summarize all those ideas, but actually *contains* them. The card becomes a means to experience the things it symbolizes. An actual magician can use the picture to enter these states, move along the Tree of Life, and understand how the divine light expresses itself.

A number of contemporary researchers into the Tarot's origin have suggested the pictures derive from the Renaissance tradition of the Art of Memory. This art consisted of training the mind to construct an overall image, such as a palace, with every item that the person wants to remember

Magician

*The Magician from the Shining Tribe, Brady,
Marseille, and Rider decks*

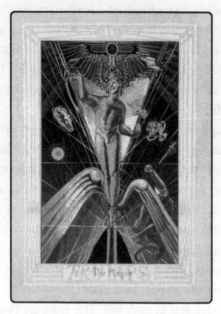

The Magician/Magus from the Thoth deck

represented as an object or place in the palace. The person who wanted to remember, or keep distinct, some vast system of thought would move through the palace in their mind, with every detail or concept seen as a window or a statue or a step on a vividly imagined staircase. (This idea was brought brilliantly to life in the TV show *Sherlock*.)

The Art of Memory did not simply form a vast filing system the way we might keep track of business expenses. The adept used it to memorize a network of correspondences—that is, precise connections—believed to exist between heaven and earth. This network included extensive disciplines such as astrology, alchemy, and the vast hosts of angels, demons, and other such beings thought to rule over every aspect of nature and every human enterprise. If you wished to do something—say, propose marriage, or maybe turn lead into gold (the outer purpose of alchemy)—you needed to know the correct phase of the moon, the best configurations of the planets and stars, what angels to ask for help, and so on.

At the heart of all these correspondences lay a famous doctrine from *The Emerald Tablet* of Hermes Trismegistus, "As above, so below." (This sentence is actually a paraphrase of a longer statement.) Creatures and events in the ordinary world reflect divine existence and the laws and structures of the greater universe. Such an idea intimately connects human life and daily experience with the vastness and beauty of heaven. We could know and experience God through a proper understanding of the physical world.

Here is a simple example. If you stand with your arms straight out to the sides and your legs apart, you form a five-pointed star, or pentagram. (A pentacle, which is a pentagram within a circle, became one of the four suits of the Tarot, introduced by the Golden Dawn as a replacement for the older suit of Coins.) Thus, the pentagram, famous as a magical seal, represents the human body.

The pentagram appears elsewhere in nature as well. Starfish have that form. Certain flowers, including wild roses, have five petals. If you cut an apple in half across the middle instead of up and down, you will discover a perfect five-pointed star in each half. This links the plant world with the human body and more. If we follow the path of the planets from our view-point here on Earth (rather than working out the actual path around the sun), they all seem to move in intricate loops within an overall motion around the

Earth. They may take several years to complete an entire cycle. Over eight years, the planet Venus forms a perfect five-petaled flower in the sky.

This is why Aphrodite, Goddess of love, whom the Romans called Venus, lies on a bed of roses or holds an apple. It also is one reason why Europeans identified the "fruit" in the Garden of Eden as an apple. The human body, the star in the apple, roses, the planet Venus, and the love that animates our lives all belong to the same giant web of meaning summed up in the simple image of a five-pointed star.

The network of correspondences did not depend on individual symbols. An entire view of the universe supported it. As we saw earlier, until Copernicus demonstrated the likelihood that the Earth moved around the sun, and not the other way around, people assumed the Earth rested in the center of a series of concentric spheres. Earth itself was a sphere (contrary to popular beliefs about Columbus, no educated person thought the earth was flat), and beyond it, with each layer enclosing the previous ones, turned the spheres of the moon, the sun, Mercury, Venus, Mars, Jupiter, and Saturn.

These seven planetary spheres themselves turned against the more stately motion of the stars, and beyond even the stars lay heaven, the realm

of God. The smallest sphere of all, far smaller than the Earth, was a human head, seat of consciousness. To be born inside a human body, a soul left the divine realm and traveled through each sphere successively to reach the fetus. At the moment of the soul's passage, each planetary sphere stood in a certain position against the background of the constellations. Depending on its position—the moon in the constellation of Virgo, say, or Mars in Aquarius—the soul would take on a particular quality. Astrology was fundamental to the system of correspondences, for it contained the entire system in each person and every moment.

The purpose of the Art of Memory was more than knowledge. If you remembered it all, if you could place every precise detail of every correspondence in your memory structure, then you would gain mastery over existence. You would become a magician of creation.

This is very like the Golden Dawn view of the Tarot. The symbolic pictures externalize the memory structure. You no longer have to keep the whole thing in your head, you just have to learn what each card contains and how they fit together. A house—or a palace—of cards. The Tarot is an instrument of our wisdom because it contains the intricate details of creation, but also the method to use all that information. Occultists refer to the Tarot cards as keys, by which they usually mean something that will unlock secrets and magical power. We also can compare them to the keys on a musical instrument (seventy-eight, ten less than the piano). The keys of an instrument are distinct notes, and you can do very little with an instrument until you learn what each key does. Such knowledge, of course, is only the beginning. The individual notes combine into melodies and harmonies, played in varied rhythms. The symbols on the individual Tarot cards also combine to produce complex systems of ideas and beliefs.

For much of the nineteenth and twentieth centuries, the occult interpreters of the Tarot agreed on the overall structure of the instrument. It was Kabbalist, astrological, alchemical, and Hermetic. They only disagreed about the details. These disagreements were intense, for if you believe that the cards are as precise as the notes on a piano, and you want to play the instrument, you need to know just which key on the piano is middle C. It won't do any good to know that a song begins, say, C-G-F, if you have not learned where those keys are.

To switch metaphors, if you have a ring of keys to unlock a row of treasure chests, you need to know which key goes in which lock. And so different occult groups or teachers would use logic or tradition or magical practice to prove that they alone understood the true structure of the Tarot instrument and how to use it. We can shift metaphors yet again and say that they indeed saw the Tarot as an instrument, but a scientific rather than a musical one, as precise as a telescope that reveals the far reaches of the heavens.

In the last third of the twentieth century a great change occurred in Tarot. People did indeed begin to see it as less scientific and more akin to music. When interpreters showed how you could map the Tarot onto many spiritual systems and at the same time historians demonstrated that the cards did not originate in ancient Egypt or the secret conventions of sorcerers, but as a popular game, people began to see how we ourselves code the meanings into the cards. And so neither Crowley nor Waite were right and the other wrong; they had simply created slightly different instruments. Each instrument worked according to the rules used to set it up.

The Tarot is a formal system, developed for a game that perhaps in itself mimics life. The formal system of twenty-two trumps and four suits must come from some deep symbolic level (even if an unconscious one), or it would not have proven itself so adaptable to so many traditions. Why should this be? Well, for one thing, the form itself has basic meaning. Let us take, for example, the number four. When we think of four, Tarotists might immediately call up the four medieval elements that were considered the basic qualities of existence: Fire, Water, Air, and Earth. In fact, most interpretations of Tarot assume a connection between these elements and the suits, though not everyone agrees on which suit goes with which element (see above, *Tarot of the Holy Light*). As well as the elements, the Kabbalist interpreters of Tarot might look to the four worlds of creation, each with its own Tree of Life containing ten sephiroth, just as each suit in the Tarot contains cards Ace–Ten.

In fact, the numbers four and, for that matter, ten are much more basic to human experience than their use in any particular symbolic system. Human beings have two arms and two legs, to make four limbs. Stand with your arms out to the sides and you create four literal directions: before, behind, right, and left. If you extend your fingers and thumbs, you have the number ten. You also have ten toes that touch the ground. If you keep your feet together you form a cross, with four points (compared to the pentagram formed with the legs apart). The number four also links us to the Earth, for just as our bodies naturally create four directions, so does the planet. The Earth rotates on an axis, and this produces a north and south pole, but also an equator around the middle, and east and west.

Every day at the equator—and elsewhere on the two equinoxes (spring and autumn)—the sun rises due east, shines for twelve hours, and sets due west to produce twelve hours of darkness. Not only does the Earth's rotation on a (tilted) axis produce four directions, it also creates four distinct moments in the year, the two equinoxes of equal day and night, and the summer and winter solstices. At the same time, the daily change between day and night provides that other fundamental symbol, the duality, or "twoness," of light and dark.

The Tarot arises from such basic principles of our existence. Just because it did *not* originally illustrate some specific doctrine doesn't mean we can't encode almost any coherent system into its wonderfully flexible structure. Once we encode this wisdom into it, we can play (or work) this instrument to give us back that wisdom in meaningful ways, like the Renaissance memory palaces.

Vicki Noble and Karen Vogel did that with their *Motherpeace Tarot*. They mapped the history and practices of Goddess worship onto the Tarot and created an instrument that has allowed hundreds of thousands of people around the world not only to learn about the Goddess, but also to bring that wisdom into their daily lives.

A more recent deck, *The Dark Goddess Tarot* by Ellen Lorenzi-Prince, incorporates female deities from all over the world. *The Ghetto Tarot*, created by a Haitian artist collective with Tarot guidance and photography from Alice Smeets, has brought the Tarot images powerfully to life.

The Tarot is an instrument of our wisdom because we can encode entire systems and traditions into it. It also is an instrument because we can do things with it to deepen our personal awareness of those traditions. If you establish that the Tarot you are using contains the Kabbalist Tree of Life then you can use the cards to move through the sephiroth and pathways.

The Priestess of Wands from the Motherpeace deck

You can travel on the Tree by entering the cards in specific meditations; you also can see how these sephiroth appear in your daily life by doing readings and paying attention to the Kabbalistic meanings. Readings also will give you fresh ideas and insights into the Kabbalistic wisdom because they will bring together unusual combinations of cards. For example, suppose you chose two cards at random from the Golden Dawn Ritual Tarot, and they came out Justice and the Seven of Swords.

What might you learn about the Seven of Swords, called Unstable Effort, if you paired it with the masked figure of Justice? Swords is the element of Air, symbol of mind and conflict. How does Justice act in the Tree of Air?

 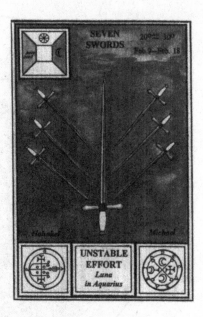

Justice and Seven of Swords from the Tarot of Ceremonial Magick

The occult tradition tends to see the Tarot as a *scientific* instrument. Author Lon Milo DuQuette writes about his *Tarot of Ceremonial Magick,* "The Tarot is the DNA of the Qabalah. Properly decoded, it reveals not only the mysteries of the Qabalah but also those of Ceremonial Magick and all other Qabalah-based systems." This is the grand Western esoteric tradition. DuQuette, however, is of his time, and so he adds a comment the old occult masters would never have included: "It is not our intention to lure you away from any Tarot deck you may currently fancy, but to help you understand the incalculable power and significance of whatever deck you may be using."

A scientific instrument is precise, carefully designed and calibrated to produce exact effects. Many modern Tarotists see the cards more in the manner of a musical instrument. We approach it with a spirit of play, with an openness to the wonder we might draw from it. We know that we need to practice, whether our goal is knowledge, meditation, or readings, and the more we practice the better we get, though there always will be masters who can dazzle us with their ability to play and interpret it.

There are different kinds of music as well. To look at Tarot in the Kabbalistic Golden Dawn tradition forms the equivalent of classical music—highly structured, complex, layered, and with fixed meanings. To learn that system may take many years. The rewards (and the promises) are many, for you will learn a framework of ideas and images and train yourself to magical power and awareness. Some people even say you can change your molecular structure.

But like a classical musician, you must also give yourself to a fixed set of meanings and beliefs. The BOTA (Builders of the Adytum) deck comes in black and white so that you can personalize it by coloring it yourself. However, the course gives you precise instructions for what colors to use, for in the Kabbalistic tradition every color affects the psyche in precise ways, and to use an unintended color is not an aesthetic choice but simply wrong. Similarly, if a classical musician strays outside the score of a work by Brahms or Rachmaninoff, they have not made a creative decision, they have made a mistake.

At the other end of the Tarot's uses, we might think of basic fortune-telling as the folk music of Tarot. As with folk songs, no one really knows the precise origin of the formulas used in fortune-telling: the "journey by water" or "a messenger brings sad news" or "a good outcome in a legal matter." Different sources give slightly different versions, in the way a song like "Barbara Allen" will have varied tunes and lyrics. Like folk songs, fortune-telling formulas are simple and compelling. They are easy to learn, often uncanny in their usefulness, but very limited in their wisdom. They may show us what will happen, but not what it means.

A great deal of contemporary approaches to Tarot focus on complex original interpretations. Readers and others who study the cards seek to discover new meanings, from the way the cards show up in readings and from a constant fresh look at the pictures. They may improvise a great deal as they create new meanings on the spot, from a reading, or in art, such as a drawing or a collage they've decided to make of a particular card. In other words, they are playing Tarot jazz. Like the best jazz musicians, who always know the tradition, they ground themselves in a thorough knowledge of the Kabbalah and other Tarot systems. But then they take off from there. The motto of the legendary avant-garde music group the Art Ensemble of

Chicago could easily apply to such Tarot jazz musicians as Mary K. Greer and Robert M. Place—*Ancient to the Future*.

If ever there was a Tarot classicist, it was Arthur Edward Waite, who designed the world's most popular Tarot deck, the Rider pack, painted by Pamela Colman Smith. Though Waite allowed himself some radical touches, such as the redesign of the Lovers card, he considered his deck a "rectified" Tarot, and the One True Key. Ironically, many of the improvisors have used the Rider cards as their primary instrument. I have worked with the Rider deck for well over fifty years, and it still amazes me with the ability to inspire fresh interpretations. I suspect Waite would have disliked this (just as he probably would have considered jazz music an abomination). But perhaps I'm being unfair, for in fact, while Waite says that it is a mistake to think of the Minor cards as having a "higher" symbolism, he goes on to say (in his book, *The Pictorial Key to the Tarot*) that "the field of divinatory possibilities is inexhaustible," and "the pictures are like doors which open into unexpected chambers, or like a turn in the open road with a wide prospect beyond."

The Six of Swords and the Four of Wands from the Rider deck

The deck's use as a jazz instrument comes from Pamela Colman Smith's paintings. They appear like illustrations in a story without words. Smith's friends called her "Pixie," and like that playful spirit, she took the Tarot and played tricks with it that forever opened up the cards' possibilities.

We have looked at the Tarot as a scientific instrument to unlock the secrets of creation or a musical instrument that we can play in different styles. There is another way the cards act as an instrument of wisdom, a very simple one. We can ask them questions.

Anytime we do a reading, even if we just ask, "Will Mickey ask me to the prom?" we absorb some measure of the Tarot's symbolic teachings along with the answers. We may learn about Mickey's plans but also some small confrontation with our own passivity. We may learn to seek greater self-knowledge. *What keeps me from finding someone?* or *Why do I fall for the same kind of person over and over?*

But why ask only about ourselves or other people? Are we so import-ant we only want to know about our own destiny? With such a powerful instrument, why not ask direct questions of spiritual wisdom? Some years ago, at the annual class I teach with Mary K. Greer, I decided to ask for knowledge of the soul. Mary and I had chosen "soul-making" as the year's theme, and it struck me that rather than ponder what the Tarot cards teach about the subject I could just ask them.

So I did a reading in which I asked a series of questions around the theme "What is the soul?" The deck was the *Shining Woman*, my own creation, now revised and republished as the *Shining Tribe*. The reading follows.

The Ace of Birds (traditionally the Ace of Swords)—the answer to "What is the soul?"—derives from an ancient Egyptian plaque. It shows an owl at night, with bright piercing eyes that stare right at us. Owls are strong creatures that hunt at night, able to see and attack their prey in the darkness. Special qualities of their wings allow them to fly in complete silence. We can say that the soul hunts truth and meaning in the mysteries and darkness of life. The soul does not announce itself, not even to our own conscious minds. Instead, it soars to high places and dives after what it needs to grow and be strong.

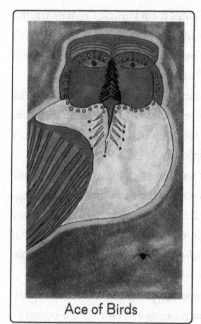

Ace of Birds

What is the soul?

Place of Rivers

How do we make soul?

Awakening

What does it demand of us?

Knower of Birds

What does it give us?

Many of us think of owls vaguely as absent-minded professors. This image comes from Walt Disney and other children's cartoonists or writers who have diminished a very ancient idea. The owl's reputation for wisdom comes from an ability to turn its head completely around so that it can look in all directions. Symbolically, it can see into the past and the future. The owl became the animal familiar of Athena/Minerva, Goddess of wisdom, but also of fierce commitment. We might describe wisdom and commitment as qualities of soul. The Algonquin people of North America describe the owl as the perfect soul-bird.

Compare the Ace of Birds with its traditional equivalent, the Ace of Swords. Swords symbolize the intellect that can cut through illusion and derive abstract principles of existence. While the suit of Birds in the *Shining Tribe Tarot* represents the mind, it focuses less on intellect than on creativity, art, prophecy. When we pursue these things we become like the owl, hunters in the darkness of existence.

The term "soul-making," the title of Mary's and my class that summer, comes from the psychologist James Hillman (who himself borrowed it

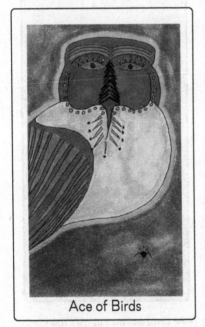

Ace of Birds

ACE of SWORDS.

The Ace of Birds from the Shining Tribe Tarot and Ace of Swords from the the Rider deck

from the nineteenth-century poet John Keats). Hillman liked to say that spirit goes up and soul goes down, meaning that spirit is the quality in us that ascends to unity with divine consciousness, while soul moves us into hidden depths and complexity. Now think of the owl who soars *down* from the night sky, and compare this to the Rider Ace of Swords, where the blade points *up* and penetrates the crown of material reality to reach pure mind.

The other cards in the reading further deepen (a good Hillmanesque word) our awareness of soul. "How do we make (create) soul?" gives us the Place of Rivers (Page of Cups in traditional decks). A figure sits in meditation by a deep pool of water. One way we enrich our soul is the simple willingness to look deeply into the unknown depths and darkness of our lives, and to do so with peace and acceptance. The Page of Cups in the Rider pack evokes a similar quality, with its picture of a young man who peacefully watches a fish rise from the cup he holds. (In recent years, I've become fascinated by the idea that the fish is actually talking to him, as in fairy tales.)

Place of Rivers

PAGE of CUPS.

The Place of Rivers from the Shining Tribe Tarot and the Page of Cups from the Rider deck

When we ask what the soul demands of us, we get card twenty in the Major Arcana, called Awakening in the *Shining Tribe Tarot*, and Judgement in traditional decks. The card usually shows the biblical Last Judgement, where the angel sounds his horn and the dead rise from their graves. In Christian doctrine the dead truly receive Judgement, with a few sent to heaven and the majority to hell. In the Tarot card Judgement, however, all rise up joyously. Over the years I have taught Tarot, I have seen many people become disturbed at that word *judgement*. This was one reason I changed the title to Awakening. The soul demands of us that we awaken. We must acknowledge our true selves, our connection to divine joy, and we must share it with others. For this reason, we see an urban setting in the card. The buildings show twenty-two windows, while twenty-two rays of light shine around the head of the spirit. (Both of these correspondences were accidental and arose without conscious plan.)

The final card, for what the soul gives us, returns us to the Birds suit, with the Knower (equivalent to the Knight of Swords, though in fact more mature in its wisdom). The card depicts Tsang Chieh, the legendary Chinese creator of the *I Ching*. If we are willing to look deep into the mysteries, to sit quietly, and to awaken, then the soul will give us wisdom and inspiration. In the myth, Tsang Chieh created writing when he saw images fall from the sky and combined them with the tracks of tortoises and birds. The story involves oracular visions. Tortoises and birds are divinatory animals. They represent the systematic side of oracles, for people study the flight patterns of birds and the marks on tortoise shells for divinatory clues. The images from the sky signify the prophetic or visionary aspect of the seer. The soul gives us both knowledge and inspiration.

This was the first experiment in what I came to call Wisdom readings. Notice that it does not ask for personal information, but for understanding about an important issue. We could make a personal spread from the question. We could ask, "What is *my* soul? What does it demand of *me*?" But with such a powerful instrument, why ask only about ourselves? Artists and interpreters have spent centuries pouring knowledge and ideas and visions into the cards to make them a true instrument of wisdom. Why not let them speak to us about issues beyond our own circumstances?

We should remember that the ancients considered Wisdom an actual being. The Bible names her Hokhmah, a name later adapted for the second sephirah on the Kabbalah Tree of Life. The Greeks named her Sophia; she remained in Christianity as Hagia (Saint) Sophia. When we envision an abstract quality as a person, we make it more real. To call the Tarot an instrument of wisdom allows us to see ourselves in direct communication, through the cards, with Hokhmah/Sophia. Our study, meditation, and readings become more intense when we allow ourselves to visualize Wisdom in this way.

Several days after "What is the soul?" I decided to ask another question. "What is Tarot?" The answer was the Six of Trees (Six of Wands in traditional decks). The picture shows a jaunty cartoonlike woman walking through strange, distorted trees with painted trunks. There are varied meanings for this card, such as the ability to defuse a dangerous situation by moving through it with great confidence. When we consider that people very often read the cards in times of fear or pain or anxiety, we can see the Tarot as a guide through unknown and fearful territory. Think of all the people who say Tarot scares them.

Sometimes, however, the most significant meaning of a card lies in the literal image. The paintings on the trees contain owl eyes (the picture derives from a series of five-thousand-year-old carved bones dug up in Spain). Owl eyes appear in the air, and an owl face with other symbols lie under the ground where the woman walks. If the soul is an owl, then these woods become a forest of souls, and the Tarot, as the title of this book says, is "a walk through the forest of souls."

We are each a mysterious creature, unknown to ourselves as much as to others. We are hunters, fierce in our desire for meaning and love. Together we form a complex and dangerous landscape. The Tarot helps us move through that landscape. It teaches us at the same time that it helps us find our way. It allows us to look at ourselves, to see how lives fit together, and also what possible meaning lies behind, or inside, events. If we choose, we can use it to look at those deeper mysteries under the surface of our everyday lives, the symbols that lurk under the woman's confident feet.

The two readings, "What is the soul?" and "What is Tarot?" began the practice of Wisdom readings. In this book we will take that practice to some memorable places, including questions about how we talk to God, and even how God created the world. For if we personify Wisdom as the Goddess of all truth, why not ask her the things we really want to know?

Five years after these early readings, I was teaching a small class of Tarot readers when Caroline Jerome, a brilliant esotericist and diviner, asked, "Does God have a soul?" I would not dream of trying to answer a question like that on my own, not when the instrument of our wisdom lies close at hand. So I suggested Caroline ask her cards. She mixed them with trepidation, and the card that came out, from the Thoth deck of Crowley and Harris, was the Three of Staves (Wands).

The Three of Wands/Virtue from the Thoth deck

The subtitle of this card, Virtue, indicates the purity of the question (and the questioner). The picture actually gives a strong answer, for according to Caroline it shows the movement of spirit into physical form. The Kabbalist tradition links Staves with *Atzilut*, the first of the four worlds of creation. This is the element of Fire, closest to God's pure essence. Card Three in each suit represents *Binah,* the third sephirah, or energy level, on the Tree of Life. Binah translates as Understanding, and it harmonizes the first two sephiroth. Can we describe the soul as that which harmonizes and understands? Astrologically the card represents the sun in Aries (we see this by the sun symbol at the top of the central stave and the Aries symbol at the bottom). This symbolizes spring and the beginning of new life.

For Christians, the three bright staves can symbolize the Trinity, for Goddess worshippers the Maiden, Mother, Crone of the Triple Goddess. In both these religions (and many others), the oneness of divine energy takes on distinct form by expressing itself in terms of three. Caroline Jerome commented that this picture shows the three highest levels on the Tree of Life as they create *Da'ath* or Knowledge, a sort of invisible sephirah that connects the three with the seven lower levels that are more accessible to human comprehension. Knowledge allows us to cross the barrier. Can we describe soul as the knowledge that joins physical experience to sacred truth? Taken all together, God's "soul" comes to us as the form given to sacred energy. The Three of Staves implies that "divine soul" means the ways in which we ourselves can understand spiritual truths.

Four

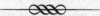

The Two-Part Question: A Reading on Divination

S ome years back, the late-night TV talk shows used to now and then feature a comic named "Professor" Irwin Corey, who would parody bombastic academic speeches, saying nonsense in a grand manner. He wore his hair rumpled, and he dressed in a shabby and too large tuxedo, with cheap, black basketball shoes. (This was before the days of Nike and other high-end sports shoes.) When Corey had finished his act and sat down, the host—Johnny Carson or whoever else—would ask him, "Why do you wear sneakers?"

The professor would draw himself up and in his grandest tones say, "You pose a two-part question! 'Why?' has plagued the greatest minds throughout the centuries. Philosophers, theologians, and scientists have all pondered this ultimate question, why. Far be it from me in the short time allotted to me to try to answer 'Why?' Do I wear sneakers?" Pause. "Yes."

I think of Irwin Corey when people ask me "How does the Tarot work?" I want to answer, "You pose a two-part question . . . *How* has mystified the greatest minds for millennia. Does the Tarot work? Yes."

Nevertheless, we can consider various theories. The oldest answer actually predates the Tarot itself by several thousand years. What I call the "archaic" view of (aleatory) divination assumes that Gods or spirits direct our hands so that the cards (or sticks or shells or whatever other objects we might use) fall in the correct order.

Similar to this view, only expressed in modern language, many people will say, with great assurance, that the person's "higher self" knows the future developments, knows which cards will best express those developments, knows where those cards lie in the deck before the shuffle, and knows just how to mix the deck (as well as how to control the hands) so the correct cards emerge in the correct order. Just what this higher self is remains a mystery, except that it belongs to you rather than some supernatural power outside you.

The Theory of Correspondences (as above, so below), which somewhat aligns the aleatory Tarot with fixed divinatory systems, suggests that the seemingly random pieces of information in some way "yearn" to align themselves with the person's life and destiny. Shuffling allows this to happen.

A more cynical view insists that the Tarot or any other divinatory system in fact does nothing at all. The symbols are vague enough that we can impose any meaning we like on them and tailor our interpretation both before and after events to give the cards a veneer of prediction. When Tarot readers describe some of the amazing things they've seen in readings—the sexual affairs they've discovered in their friends' cards, the warnings of danger from a lawsuit, the prediction of marriage for lifelong spinsters (all from my own experience)—the cynics, who call themselves rationalists, state confidently that if you do enough readings, you will score some lucky hits.

What always interests me about such people is their expectation that I will argue with them. I cannot speak for other Tarotists but, for myself, I have no quarrel with this point of view (though it does not match my experience). What concerns me is meaning, and the discovery of spiritual awareness, not knockdown predictions and secret revelations. In fact, such predictions can sometimes sidetrack us from the deeper mysteries we might find in the cards. And if we *impose* meaning, if the cards simply give us the opportunity, or inspiration, to see our lives in new ways, I personally have no objection. And yet—something I, and many other readers have observed—when the need is most urgent, the life situation dire or simply significant, the cards speak with unmistakable messages.

There are other approaches. In *Synchronicity*, the psychologist Carl Jung and the physicist Wolfgang Pauli made the first moves to a scientific explanation for divination. They posited an "acausal" principle they named synchronicity. (*Acausal* means "without a direct physical cause.") Defined as meaningful coincidence, synchronicity seeks to explain how people and events come together in odd ways and how oracles seemingly predict the future. Unfortunately, unless we can explain just how this principle functions or measure its effects, "synchronicity" means little more than an impressive title. We might compare it to gravity. When Newton put forward the laws of gravity, the concept seemed almost as bizarre as divination. (Newton actually devoted more of his life to astrology and alchemy than he did to gravity.) How could the sun affect the motion of the Earth when ninety-three million miles separated them? Newton named his action-at-a-distance "gravity," and then worked out its exact mathematics so that people could not deny its reality. So far, no one has done this for synchronicity.

In recent years, explanations for Tarot and other divination systems have tended to focus on quantum theory, the branch of physics that deals with the behavior of subatomic particles. These particles often act in very strange ways, and some of those ways suggest an acausal connection. For example, particles sometimes seem to appear out of nowhere or even to move backward in time. Michio Kaku's book *Hyperspace* describes an experiment in which a positron and an electron, two particles with the same qualities but opposite charge, collide with each other and explode. It seemed, however, that the very energy of the explosion reached back to cause the original two particles to come into existence. It would seem they had given birth to themselves.

Tarotists do not look to quantum physics for an actual theory of divination so much as a demonstration that cause and effect are not as simple as they appear and that a connection can exist between two things that seemingly have nothing to do with each other, such as randomly mixed Tarot cards and the events in a person's life. To this end, some Tarotists find the concept of "entangled particles" very exciting. Entanglements occur when two particles become powerfully connected, as when physicists split a single photon (the basic particle of light) into two identical photons. You can separate two entangled particles, move them miles away from each other, and they will behave as if in instant communication. If you set up an experiment where one photon has to choose between two paths, the other one will make the same movement at the same exact moment. Notice that last phrase. The most sophisticated instruments detect no time at all between the two movements. Thus, two things with no direct communication behave as if they are physically connected.

Albert Einstein found this situation disturbing. He called it "spooky," and argued that the particles only seemed to behave together. They acted in similar ways, he claimed, from what he called "local causes." In other words, it's just coincidence—the same argument used when Tarot cards predict some unusual event. Since Einstein's time, the evidence has become so strong for entanglement that the military and corporations now plan to use such particles for unbreakable "quantum codes."

Quantum physicists often stress that what happens in the subatomic world of elementary particles bears no relation to ordinary reality, that we cannot use entangled particles to bolster arguments for telepathy or divination. But consider identical twins. Like entangled photons, they begin (in the womb) as one embryo, then split into two exact genetic copies of each other. Identical twins who become separated at birth and then meet many years later often discover that they've acted in concert all their lives, for example marrying people with the same name on the same day. A good friend of mine is an identical twin, except that she is right-handed and her sister is left-handed. In other words, they are mirror images of each other. My friend told me once that if she stubs her right foot, she later will find out that her sister stubbed her left foot at the same moment.

Another favorite source for explanations of the how question is the Chinese spiritual philosophy/religion called Taoism. "Tao" refers to a flow of energy through all existence. If you move or rest in harmony with the Tao, all things become possible. If you resist the Tao, you accomplish nothing. When we shuffle cards for a reading, we give up conscious control of their order and so allow the Tao to sweep them up and direct their fall. They do not predict so much as show us how the energy flows.

We find a similar view in the West African divinatory and spiritual system known as Ifa. According to Stephen Karcher in *The Illustrated Guide to Divination*, Ifa does not foretell events but instead "dissolves resistance" between the person's inner self, how they act in society, and the spirit world. This is similar to many contemporary approaches to Tarot, which look at what blocks the person and how they can "break through" the block. (Notice the Western emphasis on force—not "dissolve," but "break.")

We have looked at theories mythological and scientific, mystical and psychological, all for the ancient question of "How?" But why stop with our own theories when we possess another resource for our investigations? For if the Tarot indeed works, and if the Tarot can become an instrument of our wisdom, why not ask it about itself? I decided to draw three cards, without specific questions other than the overall question of "How?" Once again, I used the *Shining Tribe Tarot*, my own favorite instrument of wisdom.

The three cards were the Chariot, Tradition (called Hierophant in most modern decks), and the Speaker of Rivers (King of Cups).

The Chariot is a card of the will. The Tarot works partly because we will it to work. This is not the same thing as saying that we only think or pretend that it works. The Western esoteric tradition has long recognized the importance of will in the creation of magic. Writers on the Golden Dawn sometimes define the entire enterprise as the training of the magical will.

A similar idea appears in quantum physics. Here it is not really the will, but simply the observer that determines reality, that actually brings reality into being. Classical physics considered the observer outside the experiment, and ultimately outside existence. The "New Physics" of the early twentieth century changed this. The famous uncertainty principle of Werner Heisenberg demonstrated that our presence always affects an experiment, or really anything else that we observe.

More recent ideas describe the conscious observer as basic to reality itself. The universe and all its parts do not exist in fixed states, but in a wave of probabilities. The moment consciousness observes something, the wave collapses into the solid condition that we think of as the real world.

The Chariot card shows this powerful observer. It even contains the image of a wave, in the spirit river above his head. He reaches into that wave and brings down physical existence. The Chariot is card seven of the Major

Speaker of Rivers

Chariot

Tradition

The Speaker of Rivers, Chariot, and Tradition from the Shining Tribe Tarot

Arcana. The cards before it show principles and archetypal experiences, such as light and darkness, parents, nature, society, and love. The Chariot is the card that brings all this together to form a life.

In quantum physics, the observer usually plays a passive role. It simply notices, and probabilities collapse into reality. Because the Chariot is a card of the will, it suggests that in divination deliberate intention is involved. We must direct our will for meaning to emerge. This does not mean a conscious decision, in the sense of "I will now create reality out of a wave of probabilities." The very act of mixing the cards and trying to see what they mean is a kind of statement of intent.

The Tarot works because we use our will (even if unconsciously) to reach into the river of probabilities represented by all the cards and draw out exactly those cards that will describe the most likely developments. It works because we look at the various cards and pull them all together to produce a meaningful story of a person's life.

Potentially the Tarot can go further than that. It can help us become conscious of our hidden intentions. For example, it might help us see the ways in which we destroy our relationships and the hidden experiences from childhood that might cause us to do such a thing. Tarot readings can help free us from our conditioning and past patterns. This allows us to become more conscious creators of our life's reality.

The use of quantum ideas gives us a scientific vocabulary to describe what the Chariot tells us about how the Tarot works. We can say something similar in spiritual terms if we describe the heavenly river above the Charioteer's head as the flow of divine energy that moves through all existence and gives life to what otherwise would be a dead universe. When we do a Tarot reading, and do it with serious intention, we reach into that flow of energy—the Tao, to use the Chinese term—and draw out images of reality. The random shuffle of the cards allows us to bypass conscious beliefs and information in order to bring up the best images (like the appearance of the Chariot in this reading).

In any Tarot reading, the card itself is actually only half the answer to a question. The other half lies in the way we interpret it. This too involves the will, for we must will ourselves both to explore what the card can mean and then apply what we get from the card to the actual questions or situations.

The second card, Tradition, reminds us that the Tarot works partly because we draw on various traditions to establish what the cards mean to us. On the most direct level, we rely on the traditions of fortune-telling. The various formulas—the famous "tall dark stranger" or "journey by water"—connect our reading to a kind of world all its own, a sort of artificial universe that we lay over the real one. The fact that people have used these formulas for centuries gives them power.

How does that artificial world of fortunes connect to the real one? The picture shows five spirits disguised as rocks. Lines pass through them. Inside the circles, the lines are golden, to symbolize understanding and awareness. Outside, the lines are green to represent growth in our daily lives. Is it possible that the cards and their traditional meanings act as a kind of electrical transformer to connect real events, including future events, to a way we can understand what they mean? Transformers step down the raw energy of electricity to a useful form. In the Chariot we will ourselves to reach into a river of pure energy. The card of Tradition shows us how the physical cards and their traditional meanings break that energy down into simple statements that we can understand and use in our lives.

Tarot cards have another kind of tradition, one that is more complex than fortune-telling. Since Antoine Court de Gebélin in the eighteenth century, the cards have carried various sacred doctrines, most notably Kabbalah. The ideas and beliefs put our intuitions and emotions about the cards into a meaningful framework. Like the green lines transformed into gold, the metaphysical traditions of Tarot transform our questions and worries into awareness of our lives' purpose.

We have become more theoretical than we might have expected. The Speaker of Rivers, a variation on the King of Cups, brings us back to a more direct answer. This is the card of the storyteller, and when we ask how the Tarot works, it answers that the cards invite us to tell stories about our lives. We see the pictures, read the meanings or examine the symbols, and then weave a story of past and future, of who we are and what we can become. The Speaker of Rivers is the element of Water, symbol of emotions, especially love. People ask more love questions than anything else, and this card reminds us to speak of our feelings and desires.

While the three cards suggest some fascinating possibilities, they do not really answer the question of how the Tarot works, at least not in any scientific cause and effect way. They imply that we ourselves create the meaning in the cards by making stories about them from traditional ideas, and then willing them to be "true," that is, of value and significance. Does this make them meaningless or a trick? Only if you consider your own life patterns meaningless and the discovery of who you are a trick.

Five

Some Jewish Thoughts on Tarot

Why Jewish? If you believe the Tarot portrays the Kabbalah, cleverly disguised for centuries as a game—sort of like Superman dressed up as Clark Kent, then it makes sense to examine Jewish ideas, since the Kabbalah originated with Jewish mystics. Even if you do not accept the Kabbalah as the origin of the Tarot, occult interpreters of the cards have developed such a strong Kabbalist tradition, we might as well extend it by looking to other Jewish concepts and seeing what they might tell us about Tarot or divination.

There is another reason to consider Jewish thoughts on Tarot (beside the fact that I happen to be Jewish). Jewish tradition does not really rest in the Bible but in the interpretation of it. Over many centuries, in the Talmud, in the story tradition known as *midrash* (stories and speculations about characters and situations in the Bible), and in the Kabbalah itself, rabbis, mystics, sages, and ordinary Jews have debated, meditated on, pondered, and played with the Bible, especially the Torah, the five books of Moses that contain the law, and the history of creation. Judaism therefore gives us a model on how to discover meanings in a mysterious work.

The Tarot certainly is a mysterious work, whatever its origin. Our sense of it, and its truths, does not come only through the pictures but also through the ways people have interpreted them. Antoine Court de Gébelin with his Egyptian images, the Golden Dawn and then Aleister Crowley with their Kabbalistic and astrological structures, modern interpreters, and recent decks that have brought in non-European, LGBTQ+, and people of different body types and abilities have all built wondrous castles on the original pictures.

In Jewish explanations of the Torah, you can take off in unexpected, even outrageous directions, as long as you can point to a biblical "proof text" that supports you, whether it's a whole passage or just a single phrase. In Tarot we do something similar. We allow people to make any number of claims about the cards, even far-fetched statements about their origins, so long as they can match their ideas to something in the pictures and their symbolism.

A Talmudic tale illuminates the radical claim to interpret. It actually uses a proof text that warns *against* interpretation. In Deuteronomy, Moses speaks to the Hebrew people about their obligations to follow God's commandments. So that they cannot say the law is too hard for them to understand or too mystical or too removed from ordinary experience, Moses tells them, "It is not in heaven or across the seas, but in your mouths and in your hearts that you may know it." (Abbreviated from Deut. 30: 12–14.)

And now the story. Four rabbis were debating a point of Torah, three on one side and on the other a certain Rabbi Eleazar. The three made their points with greater and greater eloquence, but Eleazar stubbornly held his ground. Finally, he said to them, "If I am right, let these walls prove me right." At that, the walls of the study house began to buckle and would have caved in had not one of the other rabbis commanded them to stop. This proves nothing, the three said to Eleazar. In that case, he said, "If I am right, let the waters prove me right." When the rabbis looked outside, they saw that a nearby stream had begun to flow uphill.

It proves nothing, the three insisted. Now Eleazar cried, "If I am right, let the Holy One Himself prove me right!" At that, the day became dark, and a voice shook the study house. "WHY DO YOU CONTEND WITH MY SON ELEAZAR? SURELY HE IS RIGHT IN ALL THINGS!"

Now there was a long silence. Finally, one of the three rabbis cast his eyes upward and said, "And what has this to do with You? Does not Your own book say that it is not in heaven but in our mouths and in our hearts that we may know it? So? Let us know it." Now the darkness withdrew, and Rabbi Eleazar finally agreed to respect the majority.

Later that day, the prophet Elijah was walking past the Heavenly Throne when he saw God smile. When he asked the source of God's pleasure, God said to him, "My children have corrected me."

So as we explore the Tarot, with all its wonders and intricacies, let us remember to do so with our mouths—sharing what we discover—and with our hearts—with deep feeling and commitment to emotional truth.

You Don't Have to Be Jewish . . .

Way back in the 1960s, a bread company named Levy's decided to reach out to a greater market for its rye bread. Ads on billboards and in magazines showed people of various ethnic groups with sandwiches and a big smile, and the slogan "You don't have to be Jewish to love Levy's Real Jewish Rye."

In that same spirit, I want to assure Pagans, Christians, Muslims, Buddhists, atheists, and everyone else that you do not have to be Jewish to enjoy "Jewish Thoughts on Tarot." I do not offer these thoughts in any attempt to give the Tarot a Jewish cast, and certainly not to claim a Jewish origin for the cards. (After all, one of them is called the Pope). I have only taken two traditions and brought them together to see what we might find in them.

At the same time, I also mean no offense to any religious Jews who might be shocked at such a conjunction. Though I take the Tarot seriously as a "sacred text," I do so in that spirit of serious play, that "what-if" approach. Unlike some occultists, I see no need to insist on the Tarot as a direct revelation and no problem with the idea that it began life as an allegorical game. I do not believe we should look at the Tarot in the same way we look at the Torah, or the Gospels, or the Qur'an, or magnificent Goddess images found in prehistoric caves and temples. I do, however, believe that the cards have evolved into a work of great wisdom, and if we experiment with ways of looking at it, we can dream that evolution onward.

THE TAROT WHILE STANDING ON ONE FOOT

For our first Jewish exploration, we turn to a famous legend about one of the great sages of Jewish history, a rabbi named Hillel, who lived around the same time as Jesus. Hillel was one of the founders of the rabbinical tradition of interpretation, famous in his lifetime as a great teacher. The following is a version—the first one I heard—of the origin of his most famous comment on meanings.

One evening he was studying alone when a group of vandals broke into his room. They had not come to steal or destroy, only to taunt the man who had devoted his life to subtle interpretations. They ordered him out of his chair and demanded that he stand on one foot. While he balanced himself, they insisted that he teach them his entire Torah before he could relax. Hillel looked hard at them and said, "Whatever is hateful to you, do not do to another. The rest is explanation." Then he put his foot down.

(My friend Bart Lidofsky, a man of great knowledge, has told me what is probably a more historical version of this story, but again, this is the one I have heard, and more important, the one that inspired the thoughts below.)

As time went on, people became fascinated by the question of a statement you could make about the essence of Torah so short and perfect you could say it while standing on one foot. About fifty years after Hillel, the great Rabbi Akiva ben Yosef took up the challenge. A big full-bearded warrior of a man, Akiva not only led his people in a rebellion against Rome, he also was a legendary astrologer who helped found the mystical tradition that in later centuries developed into Kabbalah. When Akiva considered a one-sentence definition of Torah, he chose the commandment from Leviticus, "You shall love your neighbor as yourself." Jesus, a rabbi after all, had made a similar choice when he stated that "love your neighbor" was "the whole of the law."

A rival of Akiva challenged him. What if you didn't love yourself? Then you would treat your neighbor badly. He chose instead God's statement from Genesis, "Let us make man in our image." When we recognize that we, and everyone else, exist in the image of God, we have no choice but to love ourselves and each other.

Now, the idea of the image of God is an interesting one. People who take it very literally assume God must look like a man, and so we get the famous *image* of God as an old man on a golden throne, which is a nice picture for a story (though very sexist), but causes no end of trouble when people treat it as a statement of fact. However, if we take it that we contain the essence of God, it becomes a much deeper concept. The very core of Judaism, like Islam after it, lies in the idea of a God beyond any fixed definition, beyond all the images we attempt to place on the divine.

We are approaching Tarot now, because the Tarot works entirely in images, seventy-eight of them, that all the volumes of explanations can never pin down. Remember the description of the Tarot as keys. Maybe we can say that rather than unlocking ready-made secrets, the Tarot keys unlock *us* from all our definitions and limited conceptions of ourselves and the universe.

A contemporary Jewish prayer puts the image paradox nicely. (We will return to the Tarot in a moment, promise.) The prayer was written in response to a problem. Every morning religious Jews say a series of blessings to thank the Creator for life and all its wonders. A blessing that men alone say offends many modern people, for it seems to express the most extreme male chauvinism. In its usual translation it goes, "Blessed are You, Lord, King of the world, who has not made me a woman."

Sexism is not the only problem in this prayer. The word *Lord* is a euphemistic translation for the four-letter name of God that appears in the Bible. *Lord* is not just patriarchal; it's also misleading, for the actual name is a mystery. Tradition describes it as unpronounceable, a symbol that God's true state lies beyond our mental definitions.

Kabbalists sometimes describe this name as a formula of creation, while Tarotists often compare the four letters to the four elements of Fire, Water, Air, and Earth, and therefore both the four suits of the Minor Arcana and the four Court Cards (King, Queen, Knight, and Page). The four letters actually appear on some Tarot cards, most notably the Wheel of Fortune in the Rider cards. We see them on the Wheel itself, interspersed with the letters *TARO*.

The Wheel of Fortune from the Rider deck

The fact that we cannot pronounce God's most powerful name is a paradox similar to the idea that a God without a fixed image has made us in God's image. Some contemporary Jews honor the mysterious nature of the name with many different translations, for the divine's many qualities. Examples include "Infinite," "Compassionate," "Parent," and "Creator." Thus, in place of "Blessed are You, *Lord*, who has not made me a woman," the prayer book for the Reconstructionist movement offers, for both men and women, "Blessed are You, the Imageless, who has made me in Your image."

With all this in mind (!), why not consider what we might say about the Tarot while standing on one foot? The first thing to realize is that if you stand on one foot you create the image of the World card.

The World is the last card of the Major Arcana, the card of spiritual attainment. This gives the posture a more powerful emphasis than in the Jewish story. You might want to try acting this out. Stand up (on both feet) and take a few deep breaths to center yourself for balance. Feel your legs planted on the Earth for a strong connection. Hold your

 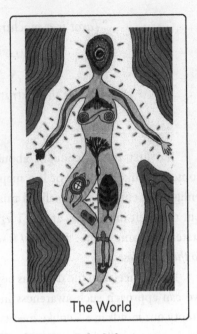

The World from the Marseille and Shining Tribe decks

arms out slightly to the sides and, when you can trust your balance, lift your left leg and cross it behind the right. Breathe deeply and, as you hold the posture, open your mind to any thoughts or images about the essence of Tarot.

Here are a few examples of people's ideas about Tarot at its root:

"Tarot is the DNA of Qabalah."

—LON MILO DUQUETTE

"Tarot is a dream that stands still."

—JOANNA YOUNG

"Tarot is an atlas of the heavens."

—ALAN MOORE

"Tarot is a machine for telling stories."

—ITALO CALVINO

"Tarot is the instrument of our wisdom."

—MYSELF

The first time I thought about this, I came up with a sentence something like "The Tarot is a map of the soul's journey from birth to enlightenment." Then I realized this might describe what the cards do, but not their inner core, and so I let myself go deeper and the following statement came to me: *The Tarot is seventy-eight images that are gateways to the Imageless.*

If we conceive of the divine as beyond any fixed idea or form or image, we can approach such awareness in (at least) two ways. We can try to empty our minds in a Zenlike meditation, where we peacefully release all the images that flood our thoughts. Or—we can try to move through the images themselves, enter their depths and subtleties until we can sense the mystery that lies within them. The Tarot images give us a special opportunity to do this. On the one hand they have inspired spiritual thoughts and mystical doctrines. And yet, after all the exhaustive interpretations, all the systems and confident ideologies, the pictures always remain. They came before the doctrines, and they will remain after, even in decks specifically designed to illustrate a set of ideas.

The Rider cards of A. E. Waite and Pamela Colman Smith demonstrate this perfectly, especially in the Minor Arcana. Here are the meanings Waite gives for the Six of Swords: "Journey by water, route, way, envoy, commissary, expedient." Reversed: "Declaration, confession, publicity; one account says it is a proposal of love." Now look at the picture.

We can feel an intense silence in this picture, as the ferryman poles the boat through the calm water, with what seems a shrouded and bent woman and her huddled child as his passengers. Where are they going? What is the purpose of this "journey by water"? And why the swords, so upright in the boat?

The Six of Swords from the Rider deck

Some people interpret the Minor cards Kabbalistically, and will say that the picture illustrates the sixth sephirah of the Tree of Life in the mental element of Air. Waite himself discouraged this. "The variations are not to be regarded as suggestions of higher and extraordinary symbolism." Instead, he recognized that "the pictures are like doors which open into unexpected chambers."

Loving the Images—or, What You Love Loves You

Some years ago, I described my approach to Tarot as "loving the images." This means, first of all, that we stay with the pictures rather than rush to say what they mean. So often when we get a card in a reading and decide to seek its meaning, the first thing we do is look it up in whatever book we use. Or else we plug it into a system, such as the Tree of Life. We approach the symbols as a problem in algebra, X = Y. The Magician = consciousness, the masculine principle, will, etc. When we become more "advanced," we may decide we no longer need to look it up; we see the card and we automatically "know" the meaning. We may even get annoyed at someone who sees something different in the picture. After all, we've learned the "correct" meaning, what does this beginner know?

But when we love the images, we do not run away from them. We really *look* at them, see what goes on inside them, for us, right at this moment, as if we face a new picture each time we look at it. We remember that the card of the Magician does not show solar consciousness or the male principle, it shows a *magician*, with his face in a particular expression, his body in a certain posture, flowers at his feet. And we remember that there is not one Magician, but a vast number of them in all the different decks—and the image really consists of the whole range, not just any single version.

Let's pause for a moment to consider some comments of the anthropologist Claude Lévi-Strauss (no relation to Éliphas Lévi). Lévi-Strauss argued that a myth, any particular myth, consists of all the different versions known, even modern ones from literature or psychology (for instance, Freud's interpretation of the Oedipus myth alongside the stories from ancient Greece). "Our method," Lévi-Strauss wrote, "eliminates a problem . . . the quest for the true version, or the earlier one." And, "There is no one true version of which all others are but copies or distortions. Every version belongs to the myth" (from "The Structural Study of Myth" in *Structural Anthropology*).

So it is with the Magician or any other Tarot card.

There is another level to loving the images, and that is to approach them with passion and excitement. The artists who've painted them, the mystics, mythmakers, or psychologists who write about them, the readers and psychics who seek truth in them, they all come to the images with a desire to take them to some deep place. If we remember this and work—or better, play—with the pictures in this same spirit, they can carry us, any one of them, to a place of wonder beyond all our limited definitions.

A card in the *Shining Tribe Tarot* demonstrates this idea of loving the image. In most decks the Lovers card depicts Cupid or an angel above two or three people. In *Shining Tribe*, it shows an angel and a human in passionate embrace.

The Lovers

The Lovers from the Shining Tribe Tarot

The picture suggests many things, including, of course, relationships and sexuality. At some level, however, it symbolizes our relation to the Tarot itself. If we approach it coolly and rationally, we will get a certain kind of knowledge. If we look at it as a device for fortune-telling, and see that only as a way to find out secrets, we probably can do some remarkable things. But if we embrace the cards, in all their many facets, if we allow the cards to embrace *us*, if we love the images and allow them to love us back—to teach us and inspire us, to reveal themselves to us—then they can lift us to great heights.

Another modern Jewish prayer, actually a translation of a biblical phrase, can illuminate this vision of Tarot as a lover. It also can open our ideas about readings and destiny. From the same prayerbook mentioned on page 72 comes this address to God: "And as for me, my prayer is for You, Gentle One, that it be for You a time of desire." *Gentle One* is yet another translation for God's four-letter name. The statement reads like words to a lover, which may shock people raised in traditional religion. (Pagans may find such a vision very comfortable, but not expect to come across it in mainstream religion.) Though I did not discover it until long after I had drawn the Lovers card, the two go together perfectly. But where does it come from?

The book said it was a translation from a biblical phrase, so I asked a scholar friend to help me track it down. To our surprise, we discovered that the word translated as "desire" is the word usually translated as God's "will." Now, *will* and *desire* are very different, so we dug a little deeper and discovered that the root of the Hebrew word indeed originally meant "desire." Not an implacable will that will crush you if you resist, but a desire that the world, events, and our lives move in a beneficial way. Just what we want for or from our lovers. The Bible, in fact, contains a surprising amount of erotic imagery for the relationship between God and humans and not just in *The Song of Songs*.

How does this affect Tarot? Some people worry that Tarot readings and divination will take away free will. The Tarot shows us our fate, and what can we do about it? An old-fashioned way to say this might be that divination—remember, the word comes from *divine*—reveals the will of God and so leaves us helpless. What if instead of *will*, a reading revealed *desire*? Or maybe even *invited* desire? What if when we read Tarot we do not just reveal the forces that shape our lives, but embrace them? Suppose we see Tarot and the readings we do as a way to say to the sacred forces that shape our lives, "May it be for you a time of desire."

But love cannot go in one direction only. We cannot expect anyone to desire us *if desire does not come from us*. And so we see that we ourselves must approach the cards with desire; we must embrace them, play with them, search into their inner soul as we would the soul of a lover.

The Hillel Reading

We return one more time to Hillel, to see if another famous statement of his can give us any ideas for Tarot. The sage once wrote, "If I am not for myself, who will be? If I am not for others, what am I? And if not now, when?" We can turn these questions into a Tarot reading about our responsibilities to ourselves and to other people. The reading can be used for troubled relationships, questions about divorce (especially with children involved), ethical issues at work, or problems in the care of aged parents. Here are the questions:

❖ In what way do I need to be for myself?

❖ In what way do I need to be for others?

❖ What do I need to do or look at right now?

Here is a sample reading, from a woman who worked in a large religious organization. She joined the organization through idealism and a desire to explore the mystical side of Christianity, but over time became disillusioned with what she considered hypocrisy. As a result, she had more and more taken on a role of provocateur, challenging the ministers' smugness and even outright lies. Unfortunately, she'd also become isolated, with work a source of great strain.

For the reading we decided to use the *Sacred Circle Tarot*, a deck based on Celtic mythology and developed with elegant computer art. The cards are shown on page 80.

The Chariot, first of all, represents firmness of purpose. To be for herself, she must believe in herself. She must take the reins of the Chariot, symbol of her challenges, and drive it with confidence and skill. The picture in this deck actually shows the female warrior queen Boadicea, who led the British in rebellion against Rome.

Kabbalist Tarot tradition associates two special qualities with the Chariot: speaking and will. The woman considered it her job, almost a mission, to speak bluntly. The card reminded her that she did this for herself and her own integrity.

The woman was a Tarotist herself and she pointed out other approaches to the card. Christian esotericists consider the number of the Chariot, seven, a sacred number. In most older versions of the card, the Charioteer does not hold the reins. To her, this had always symbolized giving her will over to God. Traditionally, both the Magician and the Chariot signify the quality of will. For her, the Magician meant being a conduit for divine purpose; the Chariot meant such purpose in action.

How she needs to be for herself

How she needs to be for others

What she needs to do now

In this card, however, she had to take the reins herself. To drive the Chariot, she needed to control the black and white horses. They symbolized ambivalence to her, uncertainty about what she really wanted, especially if she should stay in her job or leave it. She could not expect to solve this problem. To be useful, either to herself or to any higher purpose, she had to use her ambivalence as a driving force in her life, the force that would power her Chariot.

The second card also was a seven, the Seven of Disks, with the theme title of Prudence. The Golden Dawn originally introduced the idea of named themes for each of the numbered suit cards, and Aleister Crowley first printed them on the cards. Many modern Tarotists dislike theme titles for fear they will inhibit interpretation. Some even cut the borders off from all the cards, even the titles on the trumps. For myself, I often find theme words useful.

In this case, Prudence made sense as something she needed to do for others, especially if the issue involved speech. To stand up for herself, she needed to speak with the determination of the Chariot. To be useful to others, however, she needed to speak in a way that would help them, and that meant a kind of prudence. She needed to rein in the horses.

The book for the *Sacred Circle Tarot* points out that the seventh disk does not fit into the neat pattern of the other six. The woman saw that as a description of herself at work, and in much of her life. She did not fit into any social slot. This actually seemed to her something she did for others, to act as an outsider and look at situations differently. Prudence would aid this position, for if she became too aggressive, or even just moved too far outside the social patterns, people would not take her seriously.

The Lovers card addressed the question of what she can do now. On a symbolic level, it suggests that she move toward an embrace of the people around her rather than a confrontation. This is because the Lovers moves away from the warlike stance of the Chariot. (We could say that the reading revives the old 1960s' slogan, "make love, not war.") Since in the Major Arcana, the Lovers as card six precedes the Chariot as card seven, we can say she literally steps back from the Chariot. We might think of that outsider disk dancing with the other six.

This does not mean she should form emotional (let alone romantic) relationships with the people at work. Instead, it describes a way to relate to people. What she must do *now* is speak honestly, but from what she called the "highest manifestation of my holy wisdom." This does not involve ideology about religion, but rather seeking "divine intent," awareness of what the divine wants from her. She pointed out that in the Kabbalist Tree of Life the sixth sephirah, *Tiferet* ("Splendor" in Hebrew), harmonizes and holds together the whole Tree. As a Christian, she considered this harmony to be "Christ-centered thought," or thought that moves beyond ego to the will—or desire—of God.

Though clearly very serious about her Christianity, the woman had begun to explore contemporary Paganism. She liked its playfulness and sensuality, its dedication to life. These qualities appear in the *Sacred Circle* Lovers card. Where the Chariot is stormy, and the Seven of Disks dark, the Lovers is bright and cheerful. It reminded her, she said, to have fun, enjoy herself. She called this a "divine but light touch."

Six

The Tarot before Creation

Let us continue a little further with Jewish ideas adapted to the Tarot. Among the more striking concepts in Jewish tradition is the suggestion that the Torah, the five books of Moses, existed before creation. Supposedly, God created the Torah before the universe and then consulted it in order to make the world. The Torah, therefore, is not just a *history* of creation, but in fact a *prediction,* a blueprint. And God did not simply set out a plan. God allowed Him/Herself to be bound by the Torah, so we might say that God gave up a measure of freedom when She/He gave life to the Torah. (The double pronoun is not just political correctness. The rabbis described God as hermaphroditic, partly because God could not have made men and women in God's image unless God contained male and female.) As we saw with the story of the rabbis who corrected God on the basis of a sentence in Deuteronomy, God cannot act arbitrarily but must follow the Torah.

Let us think about this for a moment in modern terms. The universe, and our life on Earth, exists in stable form because of a whole group of forces and interactions that work exactly right. For example, there are two forces in the nucleus, the "strong" and the "weak." If either one of them had been slightly greater or lesser, the Big Bang that began the universe would also have ended it, for the very particles of existence would have collapsed or flown apart. So we might imagine that even a divine Creator might have needed a blueprint.

Once again, I want to emphasize that nothing here endorses—or negates—any religious ideology. Using *Creator* here does not mean an all-powerful ruler sitting on a throne and waving their hands like a stage magician pulling rabbits from a hat. It simply is a way to personify ideas, a kind of shorthand for the mystery of how the universe came into existence, and what this can tell us about Tarot and about ourselves.

The myth of the Torah's preexistence does not have to lead to a rigid fundamentalism. First of all, we do not need to see any myth as literal fact to find wisdom in it. I would argue (and this whole book is really such an argument) that we can only begin to enter the depths and mysteries of myth, and Tarot cards as well, when we let go of a belief in these things as literal fact.

There is another reason why the story of the Torah opens, rather than limits, possibilities, and points to ways to look at Tarot. This is because the Torah is not a static document. Human beings interpret it. The very center of Judaism over the past two thousand years lies in this interpretation. *Turn it and turn it*, as the wonderfully named Rabbi ben Bag Bag said, "for everything is in it."

So it is with the Tarot. Whatever its origin, it has evolved and changed through the many different interpretations. In fact, it changes every time we do a reading, for whenever we mix the cards they form new relationships, new patterns, new discoveries. *Shuffle it and shuffle it . . .*

Now, of course, some people will point out that the Torah did not exist until the time of Moses (portions of it much later), just as the Tarot did not exist until the fifteenth century. Once again, a problem only arises if we tie ourselves in literalist knots. For when we say that the Torah existed before creation, we do not mean a rolled-up scroll of parchment, such as the High Priestess holds in her lap in the Rider Tarot and other modern decks.

Instead, we can imagine something alive, made of energy—"black fire on white fire," as Rabbi Akiva famously described it. Or as the Christian Gospel of John puts it, "In the beginning was the Word, and the Word was with God." The Torah that exists on parchment or paper is a human

The High Priestess from the Rider deck

extension of the divine Word that not only is with God, but *binds God's actions*. The myth would say that it came into the minds of the people who composed it because it already existed on a level beyond ordinary reality, beyond time. And again, once God brought it forth into being, God could no longer act arbitrarily but must follow the Torah.

Can we say something similar about Tarot? Can we play with the idea that the Tarot images that have proven so vibrant, so suggestive of so many systems and visions, actually existed before the physical universe? In this Tarot origin myth, the fifteenth-century allegorical pictures—and all the thousands of decks that have come after them—came into artists' minds because they already existed beyond the physical.

An interesting parallel to this idea comes from the traditions around the Chinese *Book of Changes*, the *I Ching*. A system of divination, the *I Ching* is also a book of wisdom, some say the oldest book in the world. Stephen Karcher, translator and interpreter of the *I Ching* (and a strong presence in these pages), describes it as the very center of Chinese spiritual teaching. Karcher translated a work called *Ta Chuan*, or "The Great Treatise," the earliest explanation of the *I Ching*, or "Change," as the ancients called it. In his commentary, he writes of the idea that Change existed before the people who made it. The idea is deliberately paradoxical, meant to shock us out of our beliefs that we understand how the world works. Karcher writes in his *Ta Chuan: The Great Treatise* (St. Martin's Press, 2009), "The Sage People used Change to create Change. It exists both inside and outside of time."

What do we get if we explore the idea that the Tarot existed before Creation? First of all, it brings us back to the Kabbalistic myth of the Tarot as a book of all knowledge and a representation of the Tree of Life, which Kabbalists do indeed see as a blueprint of existence, an "atlas of the heavens," as comic book writer Alan Moore calls it (*Promethea*, issue thirteen). So in this version of the myth the Creator sets out the Tarot as the actual plan for the universe. More than a plan, for physical existence itself came out of the Tarot images, and if we could discover the "original" pictures, and just as important, their (supposed) correct order, we would gain the key of keys and become masters of creation.

Here's another way to play with the same idea. The Creator used the Tarot to physically form the universe, the universe that eventually would give rise to the invention of Tarot itself. In the Book of Job, God says to Job, "Where were you when I laid the foundations of the world?" The question is rhetorical, without a real answer, for in fact God is saying, "Who are you to challenge me?"

Or maybe there is a deeper level here, maybe the question *is* literal and we need to ponder just where our *self*, our soul, was before it entered the limited form of everyday life—in other words, where were *you* before you had a body? Where were you before you existed? Or, as I once put it, *Where was your mother before the creation of the World?*

Regardless of the biblical author's intent, let's take the question seriously—or playfully—and suppose that the Tarot provides an answer. The Creator invented the Tarot as a tool to "lay the foundations."

This is a metaphor, and metaphors work best when kept in physical terms, when we follow them before we interpret them. So, to paraphrase Isaiah, *Come, let us imagine together.* Imagine that God has taken the four suits of the Tarot, set them out at the four "corners" of existence. The suits of the Tarot mark out the physical reality. And then God poured the spirit/

life energy of the Major Arcana into the physical vessel, so that the universe came alive.

Now what might this mean? For this is how we learn new things—we do not start with a set idea and try to construct the correct image or metaphor to express it, we start instead with a strong image and then look inside to find out what ideas we can discover there.

Obviously, the universe doesn't have corners, but it does have particular qualities. Tarot occult tradition describes the suits as expressions of the four elements, Fire, Water, Air, and Earth. (Other cultures have a similar idea, but different "elements.")

Maybe we can then say that the Creator laid the foundations of the world by creating four basic elements that combine to form all the myriad realities of the physical universe. The medieval theory of the elements (derived from ancient Greece) contained a fifth element, or "quintessence," called Ether. Although thought to be immaterial, Ether pervades all existence. It bore the same relation to the four physical elements—a relationship of spiritual life energy, the divine breath that flows through all things—as the Major Arcana to the four suits of the Minor Arcana. Many Tarotists describe the trump cards as the element of Ether.

For centuries, really until the beginning of the twentieth century, science considered the ether a physical reality, even after people learned that the other four elements were not basic properties at all, and even if no instruments could detect the ether. Scientists thought of ether as the medium through which light waves moved, the way sound waves moved through the medium of air. When experiments to detect the effects of ether indicated that it did not in fact exist, and that light was a kind of absolute, physics was thrown into confusion, out of which emerged Einstein's special theory of relativity. Einstein's most famous equation, $E = mc^2$, which was published a year after the paper for special relativity, is the understanding that matter and energy are not really two separate categories, but in fact the same thing in different forms. If we translate "matter and energy" to "body and soul," we get an important lesson, one found in many modern Pagan teachings: that the body is an expression of the soul and vice versa. (We will go into this issue in more detail in chapter thirteen.)

Once we know that the four elements do not really describe basic reality, does the metaphor of the Tarot's four suits lose its meaning? Suppose we consider the elements, and therefore the suits of the Minor Arcana, in modern terms as the various states of matter. It turns out they correspond remarkably well. The element of Earth (Tarot suit of Coins, Disks, Pentacles, or Stones) represents solid matter, like rocks or trees or bones and skin. Water (Cups, Bowls, Rivers) becomes matter in liquid state, such as water itself or blood. Air (Swords, Blades, Birds) signifies the gaseous state of matter, such as steam or the air we breathe. Fire (Wands, Staves, Trees) can signify the chemical combinations, changes, and transformations that can move matter from one condition to another. For example, ice is solid. Heat it and it becomes liquid. Heat it further and it becomes steam, that is, air.

Thus we can say metaphorically that the Creator used the four Tarot suits to set out the foundations, that is, the different kinds of existence, of the physical world.

The Four "Foundations"

Element	Fire	Water	Air	Earth
Modern version	Chemical reaction	Liquid	Gas	Solid
Suit	Wands (Trees)	Cups (Rivers)	Swords (Birds)	Pentacles (Stones)
Kabbalah Letter	*Yod*	*Heh*	*Vav*	*Heh*

And Ether? If light does not need a substance to travel through, then light itself becomes the quintessence, the fifth element that moves in that exact relationship to the four physical elements—spirit mixed in with matter—that the Major Arcana does to the Minor. The Creator set out the four suits and set the Major Arcana in the center to bring them alive. The Creator "laid the foundations of the world" and then declared, "Let there be light!"

The four elements (Aces) from the Rider deck

Metaphors do not just help us understand or envision life. They also give us tools. You can do a ritual of spiritual rebirth based on the myth that God used the Tarot to create the world. The ritual works best when five people give their concern and effort to the person who undergoes the transformation. It arose in a class I taught in a small town near my home that just happened to consist of five women.

One of the women had just broken up a long and painful relationship, an experience that brought into question the very *foundations* of her belief in herself. We did a reading on her and then I asked the other women if they would be willing to help her in a ritual. The woman lay down on the floor and I did a breathing meditation with her that helped her get a sense that she could release whatever limited or frightened her or left her helpless. Then the other four women, each with one of the suits, sat around her: the suit of Wands, for Fire, by the head, Cups for Water at her left, Swords for Air at her right, and Pentacles for Earth at her feet. Each one held the cards in front of her with both hands and the Aces face up. The Aces signify the purity of the element and the sense that it comes as a gift. We used the Rider Tarot cards, in which each Ace shows a hand emerging from a cloud with the emblem of that suit, as if to offer it from out of the Spirit world.

As they held the cards, the women imagined themselves as guardians of that life energy. Together, we all envisioned the woman lying down as both a ground of creation and an empty vessel. I then gave her the Major Arcana and told her to hold the twenty-two cards in both hands at her center. With all of us focused on her, she sensed the powerful spiritual forces of the trumps enter her and bring her to a new life. When the woman felt herself ready, we all consciously released the powers that we had brought into our circle and put the four suits and the trumps back together as a set of painted cards.

If God consults the Torah to create the world, then God gives up total freedom and must follow the Word. If the Creator consulted the Tarot to make the world, then once again Creation cannot come arbitrarily but must follow the plan revealed in the cards. We can look at this in terms of the Tarot as a structural diagram of existence, a blueprint. Or—we can say that God did a reading. Readings allow newness to emerge. We give up control in order to see the patterns that exist but also to give new patterns a chance to emerge as new possibilities.

After I had thought about the implications of the myth that God consulted the Tarot to create the universe, I decided I needed to test the courage of my imagination. I decided to ask the Tarot cards if they existed before Creation. I chose six questions, though two to five depended on a positive answer for the first. The questions were:

❖ Did the Tarot exist before Creation?

❖ How did God use the Tarot to create the world?

❖ Is God bound by the Tarot?

❖ What is our partnership with God?

❖ What is our part in that partnership?

❖ What is God's part?

When I first learned to read Tarot, the book I used said to mix the cards and then cut the deck into three piles and reassemble it with the bottom pile on top and the top pile on the bottom. Recently I've found it valuable, especially in Wisdom readings, to look at the bottom of each pile before I put the deck back together. I call these cards the "teachers" and consider that they have a message for me about the subject of the reading. We might consider the three teachers wise friends who advise us about the subject as a whole, rather than specific questions.

The reading, therefore, contains *nine* cards, not six. It ended up looking like this:

Teachers	A	B	C
Questions	1	2	3
	4	5	6

Ten of Birds

Place of Rivers

Nine of Birds

The teacher cards from the Shining Tribe Tarot

In this case the teacher cards, from the *Shining Tribe Tarot*, were the Ten of Birds, the Place of Rivers, and the Nine of Birds.

The Ten of Birds shows someone overwhelmed by everything in front of her. Ten birds, many of them with a fantastic quality, alight before her and she covers her eyes. The card reminded me that this question potentially can take me to some very deep waters, and if I were to look too closely, it might overwhelm me. The card recalls a famous Jewish tale (yes, another one), of four rabbis who enter "Paradise"—that is, by their meditation and spiritual practices journey to deep inner realms. Three of the four in one way or another allowed the experience to overwhelm them. One died from the ecstasy that flooded him; another went mad and died shortly after; the third took everything he saw too literally and lost his faith. Only the fourth, Rabbi Akiva (remember him, the one who described the essence of the Torah as "Love your neighbor as yourself"?) entered and left in peace. In other words, he stayed grounded and so could experience the visions and wonders and then return to ordinary consciousness. The Ten of Birds reminds me to enter and leave this question in peace.

The second teacher, Place of Rivers, in a way responds to the first, for it shows the attitude that works best here, to sit by the deep dark waters, look into their mysteries, and remain calm.

The final teacher, Nine of Birds, evokes the story of the four rabbis even more than the others, but for a special reason. Some years ago, I did a reading on the tale, and when I asked "What is Paradise?" I got the Nine of Birds. This card represents what I call the Land of the Dead. This does not mean literally where we go when we die, but an image of mystery, of the hidden links between death and birth, between creativity and sorrow. This card here teaches me that when I look into the soul questions, I look beyond the ordinary realm of our experience.

The picture shows a tomb out of which a Goddess emerges. The stark Goddess, with her exaggerated pubic triangle as a symbol of rebirth (colored gold in the card to indicate spiritual rebirth), comes from a carved bone figurine found in Bulgaria, around 6,500 years old. A symbol of new life, a drawn or carved vulva is far older, found on cave walls in Europe and elsewhere from tens of thousands of years ago. *Creation* can mean the origins of the physical universe, but it also can signify the origins of recorded history. The Goddess image on the card indeed reaches back far before the patriarchal cultures our history classes describe as the earliest human civilizations.

When I decided to ask the cards if the Tarot existed before Creation, I wondered how they might answer. What cards could convey either a yes or no? The card that emerged was the Ace of Rivers, an answer so clear it gave me that excited feeling we sometimes get of the hair on our necks standing up. Here it is, along with the other five cards (readers with a good memory will recognize the final two).

The Ace of Rivers means the source of all nourishment, literally a river that flows from a Goddess's or God's mouth. Sometime after I drew the picture, I became interested in the famous phrase, "Man does not live by bread alone," and discovered that the full sentence, in the Book of Deuteronomy runs "I gave you manna, which neither you nor your ancestors knew, so that you might know that humans do not live by bread alone, but by all that issues from God's mouth."

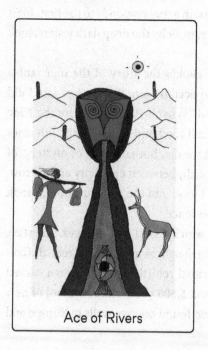

Ace of Rivers

Place of Trees

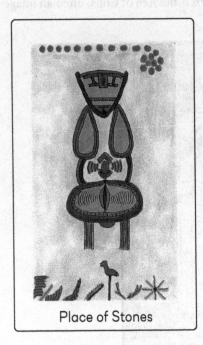

Place of Stones

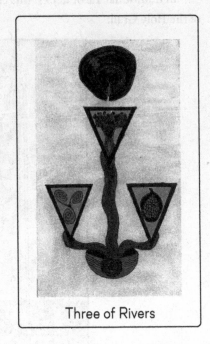

Three of Rivers

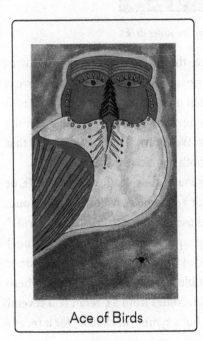

Ace of Birds

Six of Trees

In traditional Tarot decks, this card is the Ace of Cups, often an image of the Holy Grail.

The Ace of Cups from the Rider deck

The Grail symbolizes divine grace, the active presence in the material world of spiritual truth. The waters overflow the cup, for divine love is without limit. Many scholars of the Grail myth believe that it derives from older Celtic images of a cauldron of a benevolent Goddess, one that literally overflowed with food and good things. We return, in other words, to that idea of the source of all nourishment, both physical and spiritual.

I cannot think of a stronger yes answer to the question, "Did the Tarot exist before Creation?" And since we got a suitable answer to question one, we get to go on and ask, "How did God use the Tarot to create the world?" The Place of Trees. This card (roughly equivalent to the Page of Wands) shows a garden where two women, one of them perhaps a Goddess, honor an emblem of transformation, the double ax. The ax, found everywhere in ancient Crete (the picture on the card comes from a Cretan seal several thousand years old), was not a weapon but a symbol of change, for it recalls both the crescents of the waxing and waning moon and the wings of the butterfly, which emerges out of a lowly caterpillar. (The Greek word *psyche* meant both "soul" and "butterfly.")

Trees are the suit of Fire. This may seem paradoxical until we remember that trees grow through photosynthesis, a process that absorbs sunlight and turns it into food. The fire of the sun roots itself in the world through trees. For our purposes, this means that the Creative Source used the Tarot as the way to form laws of nature. These laws structure divine energy into forms that can take root and survive. At the most literal level of the card's title, God created a "Place," that is, a physical universe that could receive the Fire of life.

Is God bound by the Tarot? The Place of Stones. Stones is the suit of Earth, and the difference between Fire and Earth is the difference between the beginning of a project and its completion, between the flash of flame and the solidity of rock. The Place of Trees receives the first spark of Creation. It establishes the laws and structures. When we get to the Place of Stones, we come to the actual reality of the world. If we accept the idea that a divine intelligence created the physical universe, then the laws of that universe, once created, bind that intelligence as much as the lowliest inhabitants.

I realize this goes against what many of people will have learned in Sunday school that God made the universe and God can do whatever He wants with it. I do not ask any reader to cast aside their beliefs, but only to let themselves play with a different possibility to see where it takes us.

In fact, we do not have to accept the idea of a Creator intelligence bound by the Tarot in order to play with what the idea might mean for us. When *we* create something, we are bound by the reality of what we have made, but if the Tarot—and I'm using Tarot here to represent all the esoteric laws and correspondences the cards have come to symbolize—seems to limit us, it also liberates. This is because we can use it as an oracle, and oracles do not just reveal a fixed destiny—or a fixed beginning. We can use them in the spirit of freedom to open up new possibilities. We can use an oracle to understand how we came to be who we are, and thus free ourselves from what Stephen Karcher calls the "slavery" of conditioning. And more—we can use it to gamble with the Moon and expand reality.

Now the reading gets really interesting. When we ask, "What is our partnership with God?" we get the Three of Rivers, a card of the deepest possible partnership. The picture shows three streams of blood that pour together into a bowl that represents the Grail. In the traditional Ace of Cups, the Grail overflows with nourishment. Here we pour our life energy into the sacred vessel. So we might say that our partnership means that we give ourselves to God (to paraphrase twelve-step programs, however you understand the term *God*). The divine receives our energy, our lifeblood, and transforms it into spiritual joy.

There is a simpler, though maybe more radical interpretation as well. We can consider the streams on either side to be ourselves and the divine, while the stream in the center becomes a new thing that we make through our joining together. To people raised in traditional Western religions, where God is "Almighty" and humans insignificant, the idea of a real partnership with the divine may seem absurd. It suggests that God needs us as much as we need God, and even that in some way the world depends on this partnership. Pagans may find the idea less strange, for in modern Pagan belief, the energy of a God is not detached from the world but instead expresses all nature. Pagans often describe God/dess and humans as "cocreators."

We actually find similar ideas in Kabbalah. There we learn that God has both a female and male aspect, but these two have become separated. They can only come back to each other through the agency of human men and women who join together in physical love with the intention (intention is a concept very important in Kabbalah, as in Tarot) that they will embody— or channel, to use the current term—the divine male and female.

Divination does not involve sex (it can, but it usually doesn't), but we can look at similar viewpoints to the idea of unification or cocreation. The term *divination* ultimately means a conversation with the divine, whether we think of that as spirits, God, the higher self, the unconscious, or however you understand the idea. Usually people think of this conversation as one-way; that is, we look to the divine to reveal secrets to us. However, there also is a long tradition that considers it a genuine communication and that the divine needs us to reveal things that otherwise the Divine itself would not know. In Kabbalah we learn that God created the universe to have an "Other," a kind of living mirror, or in other words, someone to talk to.

Let's look at this another way. The mainstream religious traditions of the West describe God as all-knowing, with the entire universe and all history known, maybe even planned, from before the beginning. Children often find this confusing and ask such questions as, "If God knew Adam and Eve would eat the apple, even though He didn't want them to, why did He put it there?" Good question. Many people give up on the whole idea because of such questions.

But why do we have to believe in a God who knows everything? Maybe the more important question is, what do we get from such a belief? Do we think of ourselves as protected and safe? Or simply useless, of no consequence to a God who knows all in a universe where nothing really original can ever happen? No wonder so many genuine spiritual seekers turn away from traditional religion.

Consider an alternative. Consider a Creator that makes a world to watch it unfold and see what will happen, a Creator who does not know everything in advance and, in fact, needs humans to help discover its wonders. What is your visceral reaction to such an idea? Confusion? Fear? Excitement? Maybe it's satisfaction, as in, *Ah, now that makes sense.*

The concept of partnership and two-way communication changes divination entirely. Instead of a way to uncover secrets, it becomes a method for the spirits and ourselves to sit down and have a conversation.

People who spend a long time with myths and sacred art often come to a sense that sacred energy expresses itself in images and stories. As Jennie, the hero of my novel *Unquenchable Fire* comments, "God is made out of stories. Everyone knows that." Human beings, on the other hand, tend to express ourselves in actions, events, physical realities. So we have two kinds of existence: the spiritual and the practical, images and events. In divination systems, images describe events. The pictures in the Tarot describe such things as a crisis in a marriage or someone's dreams to become a healer. Divination acts as a bridge between the two realities of the human and the divine.

Now we go to yet another level, for when we ask "What is our part in this partnership?" we get the Ace of Birds, the exact card that came up for the original Wisdom question, "What is the soul?" This is an example of a principle in Tarot that gets too little attention, especially in books that give rigid definitions for the cards' meanings. I call this principle "accretion," and it works like this: You do a reading that results in a new meaning for a particular card. This may come from an answer to a specific question, such as "What is the soul?" Or it may happen through an interpretation. For example, someone told me once that the Seven of Swords means an affair. I immediately thought of the Rider Seven of Swords, where the man seems to be sneaking off with a satisfied smirk. The fact that he seems to have stolen five of the seven swords pictured on the card suggests that he has cuckolded the tent's master.

The Seven of Swords from the Rider deck

Since learning that, I have seen several readings where the card came up, and I asked the person if they, or someone in their life, was having (or thinking of having) an affair, and the answer has been an immediate *yes*.

So if we ask about our place in a partnership with God and we get the Ace of Birds, it tells us we must give our soul. We must hold nothing back. Hopefully we will not seem overly pious if we quote yet another famous statement from the Bible: "You shall love the Infinite, your God, with all your soul, and all your heart, and all your might." (Deuteronomy 6:5) Or, on a more playful level, the famous nightclub song "Body and Soul": "I'm all for you, body and soul." (Sarah Vaughn's recording of this has often struck me as a divine experience.)

Even without any reference to the previous (soul) reading, the owl here suggests that we must look deeply, seek the truth in the darkness and confusion of life. Notice, by the way, the owl perched on the tomb in the Nine of Birds, one of the three teacher cards. Perched on the rock it seems to preside over the emergence of new life in the form of the Goddess with her golden triangle.

If we have any doubts about the two questions—"What is the soul?" and "What is our part in this partnership?"—the final card settles it. The answer to "What is God's part?" was the Six of Trees, the exact same card that answered "What is the Tarot?" This is the card whose owl faces on the trees connected it to the Ace of Birds and gave this book its title. Now the same two cards have appeared and in a similar kind of relationship.

So is it God's part to *be* the Tarot? Can we say that God "hides" in the Tarot in the same way that God hides in the Torah and the Gospels and the Goddess symbols in the caves and stone circles, and all the sacred books, myths, and divinatory systems of the world? God *hides* in these things because we need to enter their inner levels, play with the words and images, explore under the surface to get the most profound meanings (when people read the Bible or any sacred book just on a literal level, we might say that God is hiding in plain sight). I might describe this book as an attempt to seek out where God hides in the Tarot. The idea also gives us another stand-on-one-foot description of the Tarot: God's hiding place. Mari Geasair, a Tarotist from Boulder, Colorado, put it to me this way: "God hides in the spaces between the cards."

There is a simpler way to look at the Six of Trees as the answer to the question, What is God's part in the partnership? We can say that God gave us the Tarot. To enable us to exist in some kind of partnership with divine energy, the Source of that energy gave us—inspired people to create—a game called tarocchi, whose images over time would gain greater and greater meaning until they would come to inspire spiritual awareness and become a serious tool of communication. If indeed no

Kabbalist, mystic, or witch designed the Tarot, if it began life simply as a game, doesn't that make it even more remarkable, like some special jewel found on a walk through a woods where the trees stare at you with the faces of owls?

Our part is to look deeply into the dark wonders of life and of ourselves. God's part is to give us the tools to do this, the seventy-eight suggestive images of the Tarot. Tarot here is a stand-in for all divination systems. They enable us to take a step outside the ordinary flow of events and return with knowledge and insights.

As with other cards, we can consider this gift in two ways. The more traditional idea would be that God gave us the Tarot so that we might learn secrets. Through study of the images and through readings, we go beyond our limitations to a better partnership with the divine. We also can look at this gift of Tarot in another way, which is that divine energy needs us to use divination to reveal things that even God does not know. Divination creates new possibilities, it *liberates the Creator* from a universe where everything is planned and known ahead of time.

We are the soul; God is the Tarot. If indeed a divine intelligence created a universe that holds together through natural laws, then maybe those laws need an escape clause. Tarot and other divinatory systems provide an opening for newness. *God*—whatever that term may mean—gave us the Tarot, the images that "issue from God's mouth," and trusted us to "look closely," as the Zohar says, so that we may create and play with ideas and wonder.

At the end of the reading, I cut the deck for one more card. Some readers consider such a practice risky, for the Tarot may tell you something you do not want to hear (in other words, leave well enough alone). In this case, the card was the Seven of Rivers.

Now, the primary meaning of this card is fantasies—beautiful visions that may not be anchored in reality. This is an example of something most readers discover, that the Tarot and other forms of divination have a sense of humor. (The *I Ching* is rather famous for this.) In effect, the Seven of Rivers says, "Come on, don't get carried away. These are beautiful fantasies, but that's all they are." Only—the joke is double-edged, for in order to accept this chiding about fantasies, we need to take seriously the idea that

Seven of Rivers

The Seven of Rivers from the Shining Tribe Tarot

the Tarot can speak directly to us about our questions. And if we believe that, then why not believe the cards that came before it?

The Living World—An Example of Accretion

Just as the Ace of Birds and Six of Trees gained extra meanings from their previous appearance, so the cards of this newer reading now carry their various special qualities. Sometime after the B.C. (Before Creation) reading, I was reading Stephen Karcher's *Illustrated Guide to Divination*. Karcher writes that the primary thing that happens to us in divination is that we establish a connection to a "Living World." (In the spirit of full disclosure, I should say that the expression comes originally from my own novel *Unquenchable Fire*.) Instead of some sort of giant machine that grinds along by mindless laws, the universe comes alive with meaning, excitement, consciousness.

I decided to do a reading for my own connection to this Living World. The reading bridges the gap between personal and Wisdom readings, for it asks "soul" questions, but in a personal way. I recommend it for anyone on a spiritual quest or who wants to discover what work with the Tarot can mean for them on a deeper level.

I decided to ask three questions: What connection can I make with the Living World? What will I learn or become if I make such a connection? What do I need to do to make the connection real? The cards were the Ace of Rivers, the Two of Rivers, and the Spiral of Fortune. Rather than set them out in strict order of one, two, three, I decided to place card three between one and two, as a bridge from the possible to the hoped-for actual.

Ace of Rivers	Two of Rivers	Spiral of Fortune
1	3	2

What connection can I make to the Living World? The Ace of Rivers. As the card of the Tarot before Creation, this picture now has special meaning. The connection I (or anyone) can make to the Living World is exactly a return to the very source of life. It shows the side of me that yearns for spiritual nourishment, that goes to the Living World in order to drink from the river that flows from "God's" mouth. Two figures go to the river, a woman and an eland (both images come from rock paintings, five thousand years old, found in the desert in Tunisia). The eland suggests impulse, when we just want to experience a moment of sacredness. We are like the eland when we close our eyes and listen to a Sufi chant or join the Wiccan Spiral Dance to celebrate spring or simply climb a hill to witness the red and gold flares of a spectacular sunset.

The woman, with her water bags to take away the precious liquid, symbolizes a more long-range approach to spirituality. When we study Tarot or do some kind of daily meditation or follow the yearly circle of Pagan seasonal rituals or the cycle of rites in "traditional" religions, we are like the woman bringing her bags to the river. So this is my key connection: to remember, in the middle of everything I do—my work, my relationships, the endless errands—to *go to the river and drink* and to take away water for other times.

The Two of Rivers flows naturally from the Ace (being, after all, the sequence of the suit). Inspired by the famous yin-yang symbol of black and white halves of a circle, the picture shows a dark and a light fish who follow each other's tails. The card seems very appropriate for a reading inspired by the ideas of Stephen Karcher, for Karcher is above all an expert on the *I Ching*, and the way it joins us to the Tao. We might describe the Tao as the subtle flow of energy in all existence, or that which makes the Living World alive. In Western culture, we tend to strive all the time, to meet life firmly, to go after what we want despite all obstacles. The Taoist view suggests that no single approach can serve all situations and at times we need to give way. But the Tao is not just about practicalities. To sense it, to move with it and let it carry us, this is exactly what it means to join the Living World.

The reading tells me that if I go to what nourishes me (for me this means friends, divination itself, mythology, art, and such simple things as the shadow of trees on snow under a full moon), then I will find that I can move with a sense of the rightness of the world, the Tao—at least for those brief moments. The middle card tells me how to do this. As with the others, it shows an ideal, or maybe a principle.

The Spiral of Fortune comes out of the traditional Tarot card of the Wheel of Fortune. In many decks, that card contains a great number of mythological references—the wheel of the year, the wheel of karma and reincarnation, the Goddess cycles of death and rebirth.

Most of these cards and references suggest a closed system. We go round and round while ultimately nothing changes. By contrast, the *Spiral* of Fortune shows a breakthrough. The main picture comes from a Native American rock carving in what is now the state of Utah. We think we go round and round in circles, but in fact every turn of the spiral takes us closer to the moment when we open up into greater consciousness. The spirals become the neck of a bird.

An actual circle encloses the spiral until the neck breaks through it. I call this circle "the limits of the known universe." It represents everything that holds us back, especially our beliefs about ourselves and what we can and cannot do. It recalls the Egyptian year of twelve months of exactly thirty days each that will not allow the birth of anything new. Maybe we can think of the bird that emerges as Thoth, for as we saw in the introduction, the Egyptians pictured the God of Knowledge with the long-beaked head of an ibis.

Thoth did not defeat the Moon (or, if Thoth himself is the Moon, the other Gods) in a battle. Instead, he gambled to win the five days. Gambling means risk. You take chances in life and you might lose. But how else do you win? Sometimes you have to take a risk to break free of a closed belief system, or to experience a world bigger and more wondrous than the one you were taught.

The Wheel of Fortune from the Rider and Thoth decks

In the year or so before I did this reading, the Spiral of Fortune came up very often not just in my own readings but the ones I would do for other people. It developed its own accretion for me as a card that signaled a way to go beyond whatever I believe to be absolutely true, about myself and even about the world. It applied especially to any beliefs that include the concept "impossible." The reading says to me that a breakthrough from such limited beliefs does not lead to mysterious powers or sudden success, but simply to awareness of that ebb and flow of energy, of light and dark, that creates a Living World.

Seven

God's Reading

If the Creator consulted the Tarot to create the cosmos, how did the cards come out? Can we say to the Tarot, "Show us the reading that God received in order to create the world"? Obviously, the question is fanciful, even absurd, but there is an interesting parallel, again from the Tarot's Chinese sister, the *I Ching*. Peter Lamborn Wilson, a writer on many esoteric subjects, told me once of a British expert on contemporary Chinese politics who needed to tell British intelligence whether or not China would invade India. Presumably he studied official documents and press statements, but he also went to the *I Ching* each day of the crisis. He did not, however, ask what China would do or what was in the minds of the Chinese authorities. Instead, he asked each morning, "Show me the reading you gave today to the Chinese generals." When he saw the readings, with a clear message, he reported correctly that the Chinese would back off.

The myth of the *I Ching* tells us that the spirits, called *shen*, gave it to humanity through the "sage-people,"—prehistoric wise figures from a long ago Golden Age, just as Thoth gave the Tarot to his human disciples and an angel named Raziel gave a "Book of Secrets"—the original Kabbalah—to Adam in the Garden of Eden. The *I Ching* is always the same book, no matter who uses it. The Tarot, however, is not one pack of cards, but literally thousands, each published deck with greater or lesser variations from a general pattern. So even within the terms of our myth—that the Creator, the Infinite, consulted Tarot to discover how to make a finite material universe—we cannot really ask to see the actual reading, for we would not know what images God used (or God's method of shuffling!). Then why pursue such an idea? The answer is that the Tarot works best as an instrument of our wisdom when we dare to ask it outrageous questions.

To do this reading required first of all a spread. Several times in this book I have given spreads and showed how we could apply them to personal issues (for example, in the What is the soul? reading). This time it worked the other way around. My friend and fellow Tarotist Jill Enquist wanted to do a Halloween reading with a spiral as the form. Halloween, or Samhain to give it its original name, is the Celtic New Year's Eve and a traditional time to do divination of any kind, but especially Tarot. Like many people, the Celts considered transitional moments both a danger and an opportunity. Transition means we have left one category behind and not yet entered a new one. Evening, between one day and the next, is such a moment, and so is the time between the old and new year. On Samhain, therefore, the "veil between the worlds" grows thin, and so we get ghosts but also a good moment to do divination.

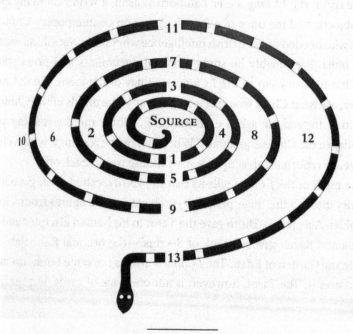

Jill wanted to do a spread with three turns around a central card, and four cards in each turn, plus one extra card at the end to begin a new cycle.

For the *personal* version of the spread, the center card, which we called the Source, signifies some core truth about you at this point in your life. The cards that follow form three levels, one-four, five-eight, nine-twelve. The first represents your inner self, including your emotions, desires, imagination. The second group indicates your dealings with the outside world, including work relationships. The third shows your spiritual or emotional "becoming," what you can grow into during the coming time.

Each group of four cards follows the same pattern. The first cards (one, five, nine) reveal some significant past experience. The second cards (two, six, ten) show how that experience has affected you, or what you've done with it. The third position (three, seven, eleven) shows what is coming into view in the near future. The fourth position (four, eight, twelve) indicates long-range possibilities. The final card, thirteen, represents a possibility for a new beginning.

Though Jill and I designed this reading for Halloween, you can do it whenever you find yourself in transition or simply want to discover your own spiral of meaning.

After Jill and I had tried out the personal version, it struck me that the spread might work very well for what I call "God's reading." I liked that the spiral suggested a snake shedding its skin, for snakes so often symbolize wisdom and even the life force itself. More, the ability to shed their skins to allow new growth seems perfect for this reading. Maybe we should title the spread *Shedding the Skin*.

Here is how the reading looks as what I call the Spiral of Consciousness. The spiral turns down because of the tradition that says the *spirits* descend into matter.

Here are the questions for the different positions in terms of Creation.

Source—this card looks at the origins of Creation, that which comes before the beginning.

First turn:

❖ One—this is a card of mystery, the first movement from the Source.

❖ Two—what first emerges, from a deep level.

❖ Three—the first spiritual ascent.

❖ Four—what results from the beginning.

Second turn:

❖ Five—the mysteries of physical matter.

❖ Six—what begins to emerge from the physical.

❖ Seven—Creation itself. The early stages of existence. (Note that Creation comes at the halfway point.)

❖ Eight—evolution.

Third turn:

❖ Nine—the mystery of what the universe can become.

❖ Ten—spiritual emergence to come.

❖ Eleven—higher possibilities.

❖ Twelve—what will happen.

The final card:

❖ Thirteen—return to divine mystery.

• • •

On the following pages are the cards that came out in the reading, once again from the *Shining Tribe Tarot*:

❖ Source—Seven of Birds.

❖ One—Ace of Birds.

❖ Two—Six of Stones.

❖ Three—Tower.

❖ Four—Emperor.

❖ Five—Magician.

❖ Six—Six of Birds.

❖ Seven—Gift of Birds.

❖ Eight—Place of Birds.

❖ Nine—Eight of Birds.

❖ Ten—Five of Rivers.

❖ Eleven—Two of Trees.

❖ Twelve—Awakening.

❖ Thirteen—The World.

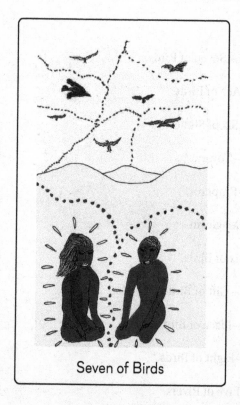

The Source, Seven of Birds

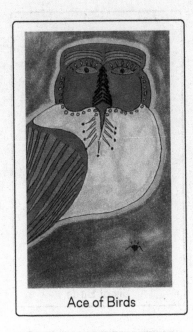

Ace of Birds

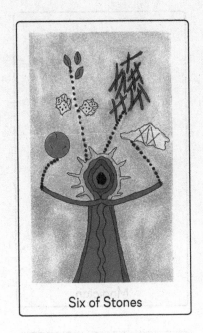

Six of Stones

Tower

Emperor

First turn: Ace of Birds, Six of Stones, Tower, Emperor

Magician

Six of Birds

Gift of Birds

Place of Birds

Second turn: Magician, Six of Birds, Gift of Birds, Place of Birds

Eight of Birds

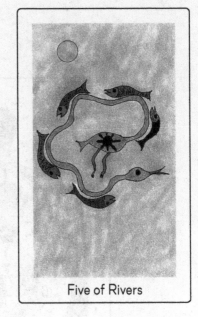

Five of Rivers

Two of Trees

Awakening

Third turn: Eight of Birds, Five of Rivers, Two of Trees, Awakening

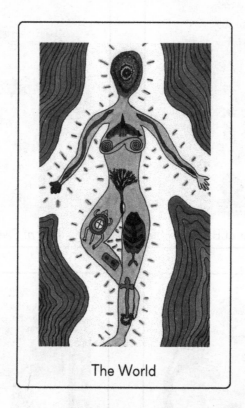

The World

The final card: the World

We easily could devote an entire book to this reading and still leave the topic wide open for future speculations. I invite everyone who reads this to explore it on their own. You might want to enter one or more pictures in meditation and see what comes to you through a kind of direct experience with the cards. I suggest that people try this spread out with their own decks and see what emerges. In the short space allotted to me here (as Professor Irwin Corey might say), I will try to point out the basic lines of the reading, along with some highlights.

The first thing we might notice is the dominance of Birds, six of the fourteen cards. The Birds suit, changed from Swords, embodies the element of Air and the quality of mind. Many esotericists consider Air the purest of the elements, furthest from solid matter, and therefore closest to Spirit. Scientifically, air consists of molecules, the same as rock, only fewer of them, with more space between them. And yet, air is quick and subtle and stretches to the boundaries of space. Unlike earthbound humans, birds can fly freely in the air. They also make beautiful sounds. These qualities have made birds messengers of the Gods and carriers of divination all over the world. In the *Shining Tribe Tarot*, the Birds suit signifies intellectual ideas but also art and prophecy. The many Birds cards in the reading give it qualities of intellect and prophetic wonder.

The next most common suit is trumps (Major Arcana), five of them. As we will see in more detail later, one way to look at the twenty-two trumps is the Fool (the journeyer) plus three groups of seven cards each. Two of the cards in this reading—the Emperor and the Magician—come from the first group of seven (trumps one to seven), and three—the Tower, Awakening, and the World—from the final seven (cards fifteen to twenty-one). That first group represents the basic issues of life, and therefore the reality that exists outside of us. The final seven reach beyond the self to universal energy. The middle seven grouping of Major cards eight to fourteen, the most personal and psychological cards, do not appear at all. Apart from the six Birds and five Majors, the other three suits—Trees, Rivers, Stones—all appear with one card each.

As we look at these cards, we need to keep in mind our fiction about them. They are not our cards, not even cards to teach us sacred mysteries. They supposedly represent the cards God drew in order to make the world.

The first card is in some ways the most interesting, for it brings us immediately into Kabbalist myths about Creation. The Seven of Birds shows two people sitting across from each other, with a kind of invisible border between them. Golden lines of energy radiate from them as they communicate with great intensity. They are almost, but not quite, identical, and they appear to be without sexual definition.

The picture was inspired by a description in Bruce Chatwin's book, *Songlines*, about the way some Aboriginal Australians maintain tribal boundaries. The tribe will map its territory in the form of a song that describes details of the landscape, both physical and mythological. For example, the song might describe a specific hill as a place where sacred ancestors once held a meeting.

Each initiated member of the tribe bears responsibility for a piece of the song map. When tribes meet at a border (unmarked, and certainly not "patrolled"), they will sit across from each other. For each pair of tribal opposites, first one then the other will sing the song of their tribe. In this way they actually join together to define the border by stating their own territory.

When I first read Chatwin's description, it seemed to me a wonderful metaphor for how people create and maintain good relationships. We function best with people when we don't try to tell them about themselves ("You know, you're very defensive. You need to face the truth.") but instead genuinely listen to people and then speak as honestly as possible about ourselves (for most of us, this is surprisingly more difficult).

The picture, however, can suggest far more than personal relationships. The great sixteenth-century Kabbalist, Isaac Luria, taught a myth of Creation that brings to mind this image of two people facing each other. Luria described God before Creation as filling all reality so that nothing existed that was not God. This prevented God from full self-knowledge, for not even God can truly know her/himself without some other figure to reflect back on them. So God "contracted," as Luria put it, to make room for Something Else, a created cosmos, with conscious beings to explore the Creator.

The Seven of Birds, as the Source of the reading, shows this separation and the communication that results from it. Before Luria, the Zohar described a male and female aspect of the One God. These are not meant to be literal but simply ways to begin to comprehend divine qualities and the ways human beings mirror those qualities. In the Seven of Birds, the androgynous form of the two people, so alike to each other, suggests a sacred consciousness beyond all categories.

When we look at the next card, we find ourselves suddenly back with an old friend. The Ace of Birds appeared first as the soul, then as our own part in the partnership with God. Clearly this card likes to show up in any reading about the sacred! Here, as the card of the first movement down from the Source, it emphasizes the mystery of Creation, for it looks deep into darkness. Since this is the first movement away from the Source, we can imagine the Infinite staring into the great Nothing created when the Infinite withdrew to make room for the universe.

From descent into mystery, the spiral turns up to see what will emerge out of this deepest level. The card that turns up shows the Tarot's sense of humor, for the Six of Stones is the card of divination itself. What emerges from the owl's stare is the desire to know things and the realization that knowledge does not always come from rational investigation, but sometimes from ways of knowing that bypass conscious choice.

Card three represents the initial upward turn of the spiral, the first move to Creation. The Tower may startle some people, for card sixteen of the Major Arcana often signifies destruction. For many people, the Tower means a violent release from material limitations, or from some kind of imprisonment. In normal situations, it might, for instance, indicate that a bad marriage may come to pieces in a painful way that nevertheless brings freedom. On a mythological level, the Tower suggests the Christian idea of an apocalypse that destroys the universe. So why does it appear in this reading at this point?

For one thing, some older decks call this card the House of God. Perhaps it means a structure that the Creator forms to hold the energy of Creation. In Kabbalah such a structure would mean the famous Tree of Life that so many modern Tarotists consider a literal description of the universe.

My good friend, and brilliant scholar, David Vine pointed out to me once that La Maison—Dieu does not mean the House of God. It's not actually a French construction at all. The French would be La Maison de Dieu. It would be the same as if card 16 was called in English the House-God. However, Maison-Dieu is a literal rendering of the Hebrew Beth-El, the place in ancient Canaan where Jacob had his dream of the ladder (actually the Hebrew means ramp, which makes a lot more sense) to Heaven, with the "angels" (messengers) going up and down. Beyond that, the city of Bethel, aka Luz, was a famous and prosperous town. David and I translated Oedipus some years ago, a wonderful project, and we talked about a book about Jacob wrestling with God (not an angel—the text is clear, if shocking) and also the ladder/ramp passage and all the ways people have seen those moments.

The card also means revelation, the sudden flash people call enlightenment. On his way to persecute the Christians, Saul of Tarsus was struck by lightning and transformed into Paul, who spread the Christian word to new communities. People in deep meditation will experience the rise of energy in the body that yoga calls *kundalini*. When the energy rises all the way, it seems to burst open the top of the head, and the person experiences the oneness of all existence. We will return to this idea for the final card, the World (and in more detail, in chapter thirteen). Here we need to notice that in the *Shining Tribe* version of the Tower, nobody falls to destruction. Instead, a single figure dances ecstatically in the flames.

Maybe we can best understand the Tower here if we return to Isaac Luria's Creation myth and compare it to modern scientific descriptions of the universe's beginning. Luria taught that God contracted to a single unknowable point, sometimes depicted as a dark dot above the Tree of Life. Cosmology, the branch of science that studies the origin and structure of the cosmos, describes the state of reality before the beginning as a "quantum singularity," an infinitesimal concentration of energy.

"Let there be light!" the Creator says in Genesis. Luria tells us that the light burst forth to fill the sephiroth, which Luria imagined as vessels, akin to clay pots. Only, the vessels were not strong enough to contain the energy and they broke. As a result, we live in a fragmented universe, and we ourselves are pieces of the Tree of Life, each with our own hidden light. The Tower, therefore, shows what Luria called the Shattering of the Vessels at the first moment of Creation.

In the scientific story, we learn that the singularity experiences a random fluctuation that results in an explosion. This explosion releases enormous heat and movement. It is as if the entire universe had been packed into a kind of cosmic egg and then burst forth all at once. The universe today still is expanding from the energy of that original explosion. The Tower, therefore, shows the Big Bang at the origin of the universe.

And what results from this first energy? The Emperor symbolizes structure and form. Ever since the rather harsh Emperor of the Rider Tarot, who wears armor under his cloak and scowls at us from his throne in a desert, many people have regarded this card as the oppressive rule of society. Other decks, however, see the Emperor in a grander role, as the laws that govern the cosmos. They may even compare him directly to a Kabbalist title for God, the Ancient of Days. The divine energy itself takes on a form after that first explosion of life.

The Emperor from the Rider and Marseille decks

In many older decks, the Emperor crosses his legs to form the number four. This is more than just the number of the card. In traditional symbolism, the circle represents the spirit, and the square with its four directions the material world. Four also refers to the four elements (and therefore the four suits of the Minor Arcana) and the four letters of God's unpronounceable Hebrew name.

Out of the Big Bang, the form and structure of energy must emerge or Creation simply will not survive. Physics identifies four forces that hold everything together: the strong and weak forces within the atom, plus electromagnetism and gravity. If any of these did not exist, or were even slightly different, the universe would have flashed out of existence as quickly and cataclysmically as it began. Card four appears in position four, as if to emphasize the point.

The first turn of the spiral starts up the universe and establishes its laws. Now the second turn will explain what those laws mean. Position five begins by asking about the mystery of physical reality. The answer is very direct. The Magician looks at the world as an ongoing act of magic, a great wonder. The universe is not really a onetime creation, with laws that run like an old-fashioned clock that once wound up ticks and ticks of its own accord until it eventually runs down. Instead, life, spirit, moves continuously into physical beings.

We see this in the Magician's stance. He raises one hand toward the river of energy above him. With the other he points down to a flower in a desert, as if he has made the flower grow with his magic. *Magic* here means that movement of spirit into matter. Artists and writers often pick this card as their favorite. This is because they understand the experience. Over and over, artists say that they themselves do not really create a poem or a portrait. Something moves through them, and they become vehicles to allow that to happen. This is the mystery of Creation, and it goes on at every moment, and for every one of us.

Position six reveals "what begins to emerge from matter." Here we find a six, the Six of Birds, set alongside the Six of Stones (position two), as if to emphasize it. Both the Six of Stones and the Six of Birds emphasize ways of knowing that lie out of ordinary consciousness. Because Stones are solid, knowledge in the Six of Stones comes from the use of physical objects as tools of divination. The suit of Birds is mental, and the image for this Six evokes dreams. The sleeping woman on her bench depicts a carved figurine found in an underground Stone Age temple on the island of Malta. Archaeologists assume the room was used for "dream incubation," the use of ritual and prayer to evoke a powerful dream, usually for healing, divination, or guidance.

What begins to emerge from matter is dreams, for dreams come from the material world, the brain, yet take us beyond matter to remind us we can experience things that clearly are not physical. The Tarot almost seems to instruct the Creator (remember our story here, that we are eavesdropping on the reading the Infinite did to create the universe) to construct a firm physical universe but not to forget a window beyond it. That window is dreams.

With card seven we arrive at last at full Creation, the world as we know it. We find another Birds card, the Gift of Birds (equivalent to the Queen of Swords but more positive and dynamic). Creation is indeed a gift; how else can we view it, even if we consider it self-created or a result of pure luck (the viewpoint of those who do not accept the idea of a conscious creator)? This particular gift, however, is the gift of art. The picture shows a flute floating down from the sky; people most likely created flutes and other lyrical instruments in imitation of birds. So Creation, the very cosmos, is not a machine that will tick along without meaning. The Tarot has told the Creator to fashion the cosmos as a gift of art.

Card eight, the final card in the second turn of the spiral, will show us evolution. We find yet another Birds card, the Place of Birds. Equivalent to the Page of Swords, this card actually comes earlier in the deck than the Gift. In this reading, however, it shows a fully developed universe that emerges from the initial gift. The picture shows a vast labyrinth formed across several mountains, and made out of trees, caves, streams, pathways, and even living birds. Peer closely and you will see only the details. When you take the very high perspective of the Birds, then the total picture takes shape. This holds true for our "evolved" universe. The more we look at it as a whole, the more we discover its incredible structures and beauty, the more we can see it as a magnificent work of art. Not for nothing do scientists consider beauty an essential quality in a scientific theory.

The final turn will tell the Creator about what can develop beyond the evolved universe. As it turns down, it asks what the universe, this work of art, can become. Like the Tower, the Eight of Birds is an explosive image, a volcano. The Creator must not make the universe so stable that change becomes impossible. But the card also deals with knowledge and recovery of lost memories. A woman casts stones before a volcano. Through the divinatory stones (remember the Six of Stones in position two), the woman seeks forgotten truths. A house opens in the volcano, with an eye on the door to signify memory. In this card the created universe becomes a kind of puzzle. Explosive truths lie inside it for those with the courage to unlock the door. The image of the woman recalls the occult myth of the Tarot as the key of keys to reveal the secrets of existence.

Card ten shows a spiritual emergence yet to come in this grand work of art. The Five of Rivers concerns consciousness that can emerge from loss. In other words, through sorrow we gain new understanding. The fish adapt themselves to follow the bends of the river downward. At a certain point, however, the river changes and becomes the neck of a bird. As in the Spiral of Fortune (both cards come from Native American art), what seems random change produces new awareness. No one can escape the fact that we live in a universe of loss. People die, moments of love and beauty fade away. And yet, the very pain can lead us to "spiritual emergence" and deeper knowledge of the meaning within existence.

The woman in the Eight of Birds (also a Native American card, inspired by the work of the contemporary Muskogee/Creek poet Joy Harjo—twice poet laureate as I write this) wants to unlock mysteries. Part of the process demands that we accept sorrow as a path to wisdom. Does such sorrow involve only God's creatures and not the Creator? Christians refer to Christ as a Man of Sorrows, and one of the modern translations for the Hebrew four-letter name of God is "Compassionate," a term that means to share the suffering of others.

Card eleven stands at the highest point of the reading, and so it indicates the higher possibilities from a future stage of the world's development. The Two of Trees gives us the picture of a gateway into a new reality. A woman stands between two trees that part then curve toward each other, as if to create a gateway for her. She wears a tattered dress, for material wealth does not concern her. The sun shines on the river, and the path of the light makes it look like it surrounds the woman's head.

What might all this mean? Maybe we can say that the "higher possibilities" for the physical world make it a gateway for consciousness to experience/embrace divine light. Remember the idea that the Major Arcana signifies the absolute state of light, while the four suits embody the four aspects of physical existence. For those who like to read sacred texts, an early Kabbalist named Joseph Gikatilla (1248–after 1305) wrote a book called *Gateways of Light*. Long before that, in ancient Egypt, the set of papyri and pyramid writing usually called the Book of the Dead, actually bore the title of *Pert Em Hru*, a phrase that means "coming forth into light," or "awakening in light."

To some people, this may sound like an old view of the physical world as some sort of prison or punishment and the light of Spirit as a release. Pagans have waged a campaign against this idea for a long time. The physical world in Paganism is a place of wonder, beauty, and spiritual truth. To me, these cards, and the Two of Trees in particular, embrace that idea. We do not escape or deny the world, but we move through it. We allow it to reveal wonders beyond our current understanding.

And what will happen? This is the question of card twelve, and the answer comes through very clearly: Awakening. As described before, this card takes the place of the usual trump twenty, Judgement. Judgement shows the Christian myth of the Resurrection that will come at the end of the world. This might have given the reading a specifically Christian or apocalyptic direction. It would have said, "What will happen out of the Creation? The world will come to an end, and the dead will rise up to meet the Judgement of the Lord."

Luckily—for I find such an expectation much too literal, and much too negative about the world—the *Shining Tribe* card is not called Judgement, but Awakening. There is no destruction or "release" from material existence, only an understanding of our own truth and destiny, and the true nature of existence that currently remains beyond us. A spirit appears in a city. People at last recognize and celebrate the divine wonder in everyday life. We see more than one person, for this is not an isolated revelation, but a hope for all of us.

The final card turns the spiral down once more, for a return to divine mystery. Now we see something really remarkable. The previous card, Awakening, is card twenty, the next to last card in the Major Arcana. The card that shows up here, as the last in the reading, is the final card: the World. As the humorist Dave Barry used to say, I'm not making this up. These cards did indeed come from a random shuffle.

The World card shows the cosmos as a single perfect being. The spirit light no longer shines Out There, but inside the self. At the same time, the world does not become reduced to a homogenized unity. Instead, the universe shines in all its splendid detail. Animals, stars, human constructions, abstract symbols, stories, they all come together to form the dancing Goddess, who is in fact hermaphroditic, all things. (The World card as a hermaphrodite is an old tradition. Usually the picture shows a woman with a sash over the groin, so we cannot see the genitals. Some decks show the alchemical figure called the Crowned Hermaphrodite. Here, the tree at the genitals suggests both male and female imagery.) In the Place of Birds, we gained an aerial view of existence, as if seen from a high place. Here, the overall view, where everything becomes part of a greater truth, lies within as well as without.

The reading began with an image of two, the Creator's need to separate into a double in order to become aware of itself. It ends now with a return to oneness, with a consciousness beyond all ordinary knowledge.

◆ What is the...

Eight

Easter, 2001:
A Reading for the Resurrection

By the vagaries of work time, I happened to type the passage above,
God's Reading, on Easter Sunday. In the middle of the day, it
struck me that I should take the opportunity to see what the Tarot
might have to say about the essential Christian mystery, the sacrifice and
resurrection of God become man. The reading became another one of
those amazed hair-stand-up experiences and a further example of just how
well the Tarot can adapt itself to any spiritual tradition.

I decided to ask seven questions, a number that evokes the premodern
cosmology of the heavens. As described in the section on correspondences,
ancient peoples saw seven movable "planets" in the sky: the sun, moon, Mercury, Venus, Mars, Jupiter, and Saturn. Since the rainbow contains seven
colors and the body seven chakras, the number seven unites the heavens and
the human world. In Christian theology, Christ too unites God and humanity.

We saw earlier how all the heavenly bodies seem to move about the
Earth so that people envisioned concentric planetary spheres spreading
outward from the Earth in the center, with the divine origin beyond the
outermost sphere. Mythically, Christians might say that Christ left his
home in the perfection of the "kingdom of heaven" and traveled through

the seven spheres to become human and sacrifice himself in order to save humanity. To take souls with him to the divine kingdom means to raise human consciousness through the seven planetary spheres

For all these reasons, seven struck me as a good number for the reading. Here are the questions:

❖ What is the message of sacrifice?

❖ What is the meaning for God?

❖ What is the meaning for humanity?

❖ What is the experience of resurrection?

❖ What does it give us?

❖ What does it ask of us?

❖ Where does this experience take us?

I should point out that just as you don't have to be Jewish to find wisdom in Jewish ideas, you do not have to be Christian, or believe in the literalness of Christian ideas, to appreciate the Tarot's willingness to express them in such fascinating ways. I myself am not a Christian; I'm just willing—indeed, happy—to ask Christian questions. No disrespect is intended toward any Christian readers who may take both the Gospel stories and Christian theology much more literally than I do.

Since this reading followed in a way the Creation reading, I once again used the *Shining Tribe Tarot*—and also because I'm partial to it! Before looking at the cards for the reading itself, I cut the deck into three piles and checked the bottom of each one to see the "teachers," (the idea of teacher cards is explained in chapter six). This time I also looked at the card underneath each teacher card for a further comment (we could call the card underneath the "teaching"). In fact, though I looked at all three teachers, I actually looked at only two of the *teachings*. I confess that this was an arbitrary decision, governed only by what seemed especially interesting. Something I've learned over the years I've worked with Tarot is to give myself permission to break the rules, even the ones I make up myself.

Because the teacher and teaching cards stand outside the formal questions of the reading, it seems to me they give us some leeway. With the addition of the (three) teachers and (two) teachings, the reading actually looked like this.

Teacher A		Teacher B				Teacher C
Teaching						Teaching
1	2	3	4	5	6	7

The first teacher immediately made it clear how directly the cards would address the questions. The card was the Lovers, and below it the Seven of Trees.

 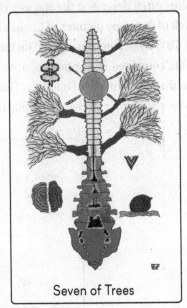

The Lovers   Seven of Trees

Teacher A: The Lovers. Its Teaching: Seven of Trees.

The Lovers embodies some basic Christian ideas. "God so loved the world that He gave His only son," runs the theology. Jesus is said to embody love itself. In this version of the Lovers, which depicts an angel and a human embracing, we see the Christian concept of love as a dynamic force, a genuine passion. Rather than a one-way love, the picture shows that humans need to respond, to give ourselves to the divine embrace.

As well as the idea of God loving humanity, the picture can represent the idea that in the figure of Christ, God incarnated as a human being and that this too happened as an act of love. The divine embraces the human. It takes on human form with excitement and sensuality.

We can think of this outside the specific Christian myth as a demonstration of our own origins and incarnation. The soul does not take on a body as a punishment or a test or a learning experience. Instead, it does so in order to love the physical world and be part of it.

Below the Lovers, we find the Seven of Trees. The card gives us a graphic image of psychological and spiritual openness. We see a spinal column with the sun shining at the level of the heart. In the Middle Ages, Christian symbolists often described the sun as a representation of Christ. We also might think of the many pictures of Christ's heart in pain for the sadness of humanity. To truly become human the divine had to take on a body, with the energy of life contained in a spinal column, but also to open the heart to the sorrow that fills so much of our lives. (For a detailed description of the Seven of Trees, see chapter twelve, "Opening the Heart.")

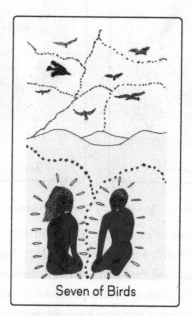

Seven of Birds

Teacher B: The Seven of Birds

The second teacher card amazed me as much as the first, for it turned out to be the Seven of Birds, the exact same card as the Source in the reading I was typing, God's Creation reading. Christians certainly would describe Christ as the *Source*. The connection with the previous reading also implies the Christian idea that the very purpose of Creation, its Source, was to provide the setting for Christ's death and resurrection. When the Tarot adapts itself to a particular tradition, it certainly does so with enthusiasm!

The image of two figures who sit across from each other suggests the idea of dialogue with the divine. In the Lovers, the human and divine embrace; here they communicate with the same intensity. One thing we might say is that we get the same message in both cards—spirituality does not come only from the divine down to lowly humanity. It must go both ways. It is not sameness, for my understanding of Christian teaching is that Christ's incarnation was unique—"God's one and only son," as I believe the Gospels say—but a kind of radical equality with God. We must make ourselves *present* for God truly to come to us.

We ask about the resurrection of Christ and we get a teacher who tells us that we are directly involved. Most people who grew up in traditional churches will think of this idea as heretical at best, or more likely just outside Christian beliefs. I suspect, however, that those who go below the surface of traditional doctrine will recognize the concept of humans and God as equal partners in both the creation of the world and its salvation.

The final teacher was Death, with the Moon as the teaching.

Death certainly is what we would expect in a reading about Easter, for even more than the actual resurrection, Christians consider the center of their religion to be the willing death of Jesus. The Moon under Death emphasizes mystery. The journey through death that leads to resurrection is not anything that comes with a simple explanation, even if theology or biblical prophecy or holy vision describes what is supposed to happen.

Death followed by the Moon is also a sort of wink at Pagan qualities in the Christian story. The gospels state that Jesus died on Friday and rose three days later, on Easter Sunday. This is the period of time that the moon remains dark, hidden from human sight, and so we find traces of lunar Gods and Goddesses in this Christian holiday whose very name in English of *Easter* derives from *Eostre*, a German fertility Goddess.

Death   The Moon

Teacher C: Death. Its Teaching: the Moon.

The seven cards (below the teachers and teachings) came out as shown on pages 136–137, reading horizontally across both pages.

1. What is the message of sacrifice? Tradition. At the first level, this card suggests that we have to understand biblical accounts within religious and mythic traditions. This may be difficult for some Christians, whose whole *tradition* emphasizes that Christ's death and resurrection were historical events. Nevertheless, the *message* of this world-changing event comes as a story. This is the case if you accept that story as an actual event that happened two thousand years ago. "The greatest story ever told," as Christians say. After all, most of the events that happen in our current world—elections or the life and death of famous people—come to us as stories in newspapers or on television or the internet. And this particular story of the sacrifice and resurrection of Christ also comes with two thousand years of theology and popular tradition.

The older Tarot decks title this card the Pope. If we'd been using the Tarot de Marseille, we would have to point out that the "official" Church has controlled and directed what message its followers learn from the

Christian mystery. France, from where the Tarot de Marseille derives, is, of course, historically a Catholic country. But this is not the Tarot de Marseille, and we can look for aspects in this particular card that do not appear in standard versions of card V.

In the picture, five spirits disguised as rocks surround a flower, something delicate and beautiful that needs protection. We might think of our own belief in life as such a flower, always in danger from the harshness of existence. Christians might say that the message of the sacrifice is that we are protected. Christ suffers in order to protect humanity.

Lines go in and out of the circle, changing color as they do so. When we asked "How does the Tarot work?" and got this card, we looked at the circle and the lines as suggestive of a kind of electrical transformer. The cards with their symbols took pure spiritual energy and "stepped it down" to a level our human consciousness could comprehend. We could say something similar about the resurrection of a divine being. Such an event, or story, channels divine energy into a form we use in our lives. Put another way, when Jesus dies, his humanity dissolves back into the divine consciousness in the center of the circle. When he returns, he emerges back into the world of human awareness, but transformed.

Another interesting detail, a sign of Tarot humor—an aspect of the cards that is very underrated but very real—is the fish emerging from the water. In the book that accompanied *Shining Tribe Tarot*, I described how the water is meant to represent the Dead Sea, and the fish a demonstration that the power of the spirits can bring life out of death. The Dead Sea, of course, is in the Holy Land, not far from Jerusalem. The Dead Sea Scrolls were found in caves along its shore. From the beginning of Christianity, its followers have seen their God symbolized as a fish who brings life out of death. The fish coming out of the Dead Sea literally sums up the *message* of Christ's resurrection.

We can look at this card in still another way. "God," or divine consciousness, lies outside of time. Through the incarnation, death, and resurrection of Christ, God enters time, and indeed, *tradition*, for Jesus very much came out of the Judaism of his age. "I do not come to change the Law, not one iota of it," Christ says in Matthew 5:17.

Tradition

1. "What is the message of sacrifice?"

Ace of Trees

4. "What is the experience of resurrection?"

Eight of Stones

5. "What does it give us?"

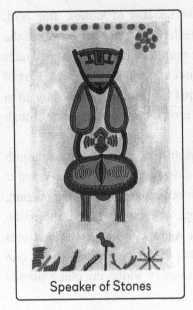

Speaker of Stones

2. *"What is the meaning for God?"*

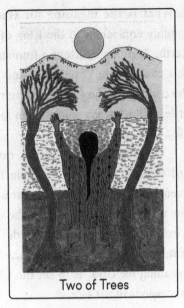

Two of Trees

3. *"What is the meaning for humanity?"*

Justice

6. *"What does it ask of us?"*

Ten of Rivers

7. *"Where does this experience take us?"*

2. What is the meaning for God? The Speaker of Stones. This card, roughly equivalent to the King of Pentacles, expresses the power of the Earth. Through death as a human and then resurrection, God becomes able to *speak* the experience and wisdom of the material world. Part of the concept of the Christian trinity is that God had to become human in order to know true compassion for the mortal beings who suffer through life and then die.

The central picture in this card, taken from an engraved mammoth tusk found in the Czech Republic, is the oldest in the deck, carbon dated at twenty thousand years. By contrast, Christianity is a very young religion, one tenth that age. However, the concept, or experience, of resurrection is extremely old, going back to the Stone Age and its images of Goddesses of rebirth. The ancientness of the Speaker of Stones reminds us that one "meaning for God" is to set the Christian story within the oldest human expressions of the sacred.

I am aware that Jews, as well as Christians and many others, may reject the idea that we can ask such a question, as if we can use a pack of printed cards to interview God. I do not intend this a kind of statement of fact, but rather a guide to exploring meaning. Tarotist Mary K. Greer has described Tarot reading as an "outlaw profession," and I sometimes describe my "religion" as heresy. From this point of view, what is the Tarot for, if not to ask questions?

3. What is the meaning for humanity? The Two of Trees. Once again we see a card from the previous reading. There the Two of Trees showed up as the future stage of world development after creation. This is certainly the Christian view: that the death and resurrection of Jesus forms a new stage in human experience, a complete break with the past.

We also can look at this card simply in terms of the picture. The image shows a kind of opening or gateway. The meaning of any religious or mythic breakthrough is to open new possibilities for human consciousness. Notice that in the picture sunlight shines on the river before the woman in such a way that it appears as a halo around her head. Resurrection creates holiness and the possibility to become like God (not God, but *like* God).

Does this mean that the picture shows heaven or some other concept of a world beyond the body? The woman's dress is slightly ragged to indicate the lack of importance she gives to material conditions. Is the body, then, just a ragged suit of clothes that we cast off in order to follow Christ into heaven? Is this the gateway formed by the two trees? This is the same issue we looked at before (and it will come up again, for it is central to occult ideas about Tarot). Once again I would answer no. The picture actually celebrates the body, for along the line of the mountains we find the words "Blessed is the Mother who has given us shape." The term *shape* means physical existence.

It seems to me that when Jesus speaks of entering the Kingdom of Heaven, he does not mean some literal place after death but rather a radical change of consciousness. (We have looked at this idea before as well.) If we are willing to enter through the gates, we can do so right now, in this world.

Any time the image of two trees appears in a context of Christian or Jewish beliefs, we can consider the idea of the lost paradise of Eden, with its Tree of Knowledge and Tree of Life. In Genesis, the gates close to Adam and Eve, and the two trees, Knowledge and Life, become lost. Part of the Christian concept of the resurrection lies in the idea of what the poet John Milton called Paradise Regained. Through Christ's sacrifice, the gates open once more and human beings return to a pure state. In the time of Jesus, a mystical line of Judaism had developed that focused in part on finding the way to the Garden, not in another world or after death, but right now, through techniques of intense meditation and visualizations. (These techniques are the source of the story of the four rabbis who enter Paradise.) This return to the Garden is one way to look at the gateway formed by the Two of Trees.

4. What is the experience of resurrection? Ace of Trees. From the dualism of the Two of Trees, we go to the directness of the Ace. So the simplest answer to question four is that the experience of resurrection takes us through the gateway and back to a sense of unity, the same kind of intense unity we once experienced in the womb. "Except you become as a little child," said Jesus, "you will not enter the kingdom of heaven."

The question for this part of the reading—"What is the *experience?*"—implies something that we can know in ourselves, compared to a message or a religious doctrine. So let us see if we can make the grand idea of resurrection more accessible to our ordinary lives. We can say that resurrection, in the form of a psychological rebirth, becomes possible when we allow ourselves the possibility to let worn out aspects of our lives die away. Maybe we can go even further. Maybe we experience rebirth when we look at life in a new way, as something wondrous and sacred. Maybe all we need to do to experience resurrection is to allow the world to open up, like the Two of Trees, and reveal the divine within the "shape" of physical existence.

The picture for this card, inspired by the *Brain-Heart Tarot* of Dirk Gillabel, shows a baby—actually a fetus—a wonderful image for resurrection. We experience resurrection exactly this way, as a return to a pure state when the whole world becomes as new as the universe of a child.

The baby's umbilical cord opens out to become a Tree of Life—not the Kabbalistic diagram, but a living tree. Through spiritual resurrection we discover that the basis of our lives no longer seems outside ourselves, in the way a traditional doctrine comes to us from priests or schools or books. Instead, it grows from our most essential nature.

Once again we can discuss the Genesis story. Adam and Eve lost the possibility to eat from the Tree of Life because of their arrogance when they ate from the Tree of Knowledge. In the Gospels, the cross of Jesus' crucifixion becomes the Tree of Life, as the sacrifice of Christ brings life. But of course, it also acts as a Tree of Death, since Jesus dies on it. Here we see a genuine living tree, for it grows from the resurrected child.

5. What does it give us? Eight of Stones. This card carried a special resonance for me. Once, on Christmas day, I was chatting on the internet with a friend from Denmark, and we decided to each do a reading. When I asked "What is my gift to God?" I got the Eight of Stones. So we might say that in this reading God offers us back the same gift.

The primary meaning that has emerged for this card over several years of readings is something I call paradoxical thinking. We see a winged horse, made of stone but with live hair. Delicate butterfly wings lift up from its back, while above it broken chains seem to burst from around the sun, as if all the impossibilities have liberated the light that perhaps was trapped in logic and doctrines.

Paradoxical thinking means the possibility to think in nonlinear, even impossible ways. The notions that the Tarot might have come from the future or might have existed before the creation of the world illustrate this way of thinking. Through resurrection we can see the world in completely new ways. Here's another nice Christian touch in this reading: Christmas brings God into the world as a baby, and so the Magi (a Persian word from which we get "magicians") bring the child gifts. From my personal reading came the idea that as humans we give the divine *our* gift of a willingness to think beyond normal limits. Myth, insight, and vision all come partly from this willingness. Easter, however, reverses the gift, not from us to God but from God to us, and so the card appears again. This is only fitting, for Christians consider the crucifixion and resurrection God's ultimate gift to humanity.

6. What does it ask of us? Justice. Before we can have the renewal of the Ace of Trees, we must follow the path of Justice. This does not particularly mean good works, as in acting morally, helping others, and so on, though certainly that plays a role. Instead, Justice calls on us to be totally honest and recognize who we are. Beyond ourselves, we need to act with complete integrity, a commitment that demands more of us than simply following the rules of social morality.

(Here is a nice bit of synchronicity. Just after writing the previous sentences, I got up from my desk and turned on the radio to the news and feature show *All Things Considered*. A folk singer named Scott Miller was pouring out the anguished cry, "There's room on the cross for me.")

We will look much more closely at Justice in chapter twelve, "Opening the Heart," but for now we can realize that it occupies the exact middle of the Major Arcana. This makes it a crucial point—either a barrier or a gateway depending on how we approach it. This, then, is what resurrection asks of us: that we give ourselves to Justice so that we can, as Jesus describes it, enter the Kingdom of Heaven—not in some distant future, not in some vague place up in the sky, but right now, right here.

7. Where does this experience take us? Ten of Rivers. The first and simplest thing we can say about this picture is that it shows us happy. We see a man and woman holding hands with their outside arms up, as if in celebration. Beyond them we see a house and a dovelike bird. The experience of resurrection takes us to simple joy. We could describe it as recognition of the love that gives our day-to-day lives spiritual value.

And yet, as we find so often with the Tarot, this card is not as direct as it first appears. For one thing, different people see it in different ways. In readings, some people will describe the two people as waving goodbye to the house. They have made peace with the past and now want to move on. Resurrection takes us to a place where we can release the past and claim a new existence.

Does this mean that we forsake the world? Once again, I can see that as a possible interpretation, but not a necessary one. What changes is our attitude to the world, our very perceptions. Every moment, every object, can become a source of joy and celebration. We can think of the two people as Adam and Eve, but from the realistic style of their clothes and the contemporary look of the house, they also are real people, right now. The man and woman stand in the waves. Maybe we can imagine that they have let their old selves dissolve in the great sea of consciousness and have now come back to their ordinary lives with new understanding. This, too, is a kind of death and resurrection.

In Christian imagery, the dove that flies above them symbolizes the Holy Spirit. This is the most mystical aspect of the Christian view of God, yet here it appears as an actual bird. Resurrection takes us to a place where we can recognize the presence of the divine in every creature and Paradise in every moment.

• • •

I offer this chapter, in deepest respect, to Jim Sanders, Helle Agathe Beierholm, Geraldine Amaral, and Darcey Steinke.

Nine

Some Kabbalist (and Dream) Thoughts on Tarot

"Most books and articles on the Kabbalah are about explaining and simplifying, which is all well and good, but there has to come a time when the explaining stops and the dreaming begins." These remarkable words, a sort of manifesto in one sentence, come from David Rosenberg's small and astonishing book, *Dreams of Being Eaten Alive: The Literary Core of the Kabbalah*.

Rosenberg, a poet and translator of the Bible, gives us a Kabbalah that is more about mystery than explanation, more about the soul's yearning for the sacred than any point by point listing of the "higher planes" of knowledge. Rosenberg approaches Kabbalah like a dream, one of those in which you wake up and lie in bed hardly able to move, and you can't explain it so much as just experience it, a well of meaning that goes deeper and deeper with no end.

Of course, I am not just talking about David Rosenberg and Kabbalah, I am talking about Tarot. It has long seemed to me that we approach the Tarot best as a kind of dream, "a dream that stands still," in the wonderful words of my friend Joanna Young. Even dreams often fall prey to what I call the Empire of Explanation: all those people so eager to explain, classify, and make safe all our experiences. But do we really want to make everything safe? Some experiences, if we stay with them, can truly open up our world and give us the awareness—not information or doctrines but awareness—that the world is bigger and more wonderful than we ever knew.

Think of all the dream books you've seen in recent years. Think of how many of them promise to explain each and every "symbol"—as if everything has to represent something else; nothing in a dream, or even life, can exist for its own sake. As if explanations were not enough, the books then go on to instruct you how to *control* your dreams, even program them ahead of time, the way you might plan to watch an uplifting video on your phone. I mean no disrespect to people who work directly with their dreams. You can do remarkable things with lucid dreaming. And yet, it often seems to me that we need to leave some aspect of our experience outside our conscious control. When the Empire of Explanation takes over dreams and myth—and Tarot—*how will we ever know what we don't know?*

Books that explain dreams are not a new phenomenon. They go back at least to Artemidorus in ancient Greece and beyond. Here are some delightful explanations listed in a *Dream Book* from Egypt, approximately 1275 BCE. They come from Peter Lamborn Wilson's book *Shower of Stars: The Initiatic Dream in Sufism and Taoism* (Autonomedia, 1996).

Each begins "If a man sees himself in a dream," and then continues with the specific instance.

Killing an ox: Good. It means the removal of the dreamer's enemies from his presence.

Seeing a large cat: Good. It means a large harvest is coming to the dreamer.

Drinking blood: Good. It means putting an end to his enemies.

Copulating with a pig: Bad. It means being deprived of his possessions.

Seeing his face over a leopard: Good. It means gaining authority over his townsfolk.

Besides indicating that the Egyptians had some unusual dreams, the book demonstrates how much people have always desired to make things useful.

(A divinatory moment: I happen to be writing these words on a plane from New York to Copenhagen. A moment after I wrote the above sentence, I glanced to my side. The man next to me had a magazine turned to an ad that read "Fly your dreams on our wings.")

The fact that people approach Tarot—and Kabbalah—exactly the way they approach dreams should make clear that all three carry similar qualities. All three are wonders. They take us to realities that daily life ignores, even when they seem to deal with ordinary concerns. All three work through images. Even if the Kabbalist images, such as the sephiroth on the Tree of Life, at times seem highly ordered and abstract, the Kabbalist in training cannot make use of the knowledge so long as it remains intellectual. They must contemplate the sephiroth as images, emanations of sacred splendor, to truly comprehend them.

The Kabbalah is so much more than diagrams of sephiroth. Similarly, all the thousands of pages that carefully lay out the meanings of the Major Arcana (yes, I include my own books here) cannot give you the true experience of Tarot unless you allow yourself to enter the pictures. I do not mean a formal guided meditation, but simply an openness to really look, to let the pictures go inside you by your going inside them.

The Tarot works on us so deeply exactly when we allow it to be like a dream. Dreams shift shape constantly—one moment you are walking down a dark street, the next you're playing your grandmother's piano—and so does Tarot. It shifts shape through all the many decks, and even more, through shuffling, for each time we mix the cards they emerge in a different order. The Tarot is malleable. It fits itself to any genuine tradition, that is, a tradition that attempts to open the heart. (For more on this idea, see chapter twelve.)

In dreams, every moment possesses a sharp reality even if they make no rational sense. When we really look at Tarot, each card grabs us with that conviction of deep meanings just beyond our conscious ability to explain them. Court de Gébelin's announcement of the Tarot as the Book of Thoth was a kind of dream statement, made with such conviction (and no evidence) that it has seized hold of people ever since. We might say that we all have entered Antoine Court de Gébelin's dream.

We often try to explain Tarot in the same way we try to explain dreams. We analyze the cards, symbolize them, look them up in a reference book, all to make the Tarot rational and safe. We try to pin it down, to give it an origin—Kabbalah, Paganism, card games, processions—all to take it out of its dream state and land it safely in history. We don't have to treat Tarot this way. In fact, we can use Tarot and its dream playfulness to *remove* the pins that hold down all those other traditions. If we say, for instance, that Tarot equals Kabbalah, then we can use the strange and ultimately silent pictures of Tarot to liberate Kabbalah from that endless list of explanations.

A personal story. I once was staying in a youth hostel in the Galilee, in Israel, not far from the hill where Jesus gave his sermon on the Mount. Three of us decided to walk there and arrived at the lovely small church on top of the "mount" in midafternoon. We stayed there for some time, imagining the hillside filled with people, watching the nuns as they moved about the church. Toward the end of the afternoon, a tour bus rolled up to the parking lot. The guide hurried the people off and crowded them outside the door to the church. There was no time to go inside, he said, so he recited all of two sentences from the sermon (I remember thinking that the whole thing was not very long) and then ordered them back on the bus with the unforgettable sentence, "We have to get to Bethlehem before it closes." What might have happened if this group, probably Christian pilgrims, had spent some time without their guide? Might they have entered Christ?

Guided meditations are a mainstay of Tarot, and indeed of Kabbalah. Some dream therapists will lead you through a replay of your dream to produce a more desirable outcome. That is, they will tell you to close your eyes and repeat the dream sequence of events out loud, but to do something different, perhaps more assertive, than you did in the original dream. (I have sometimes done this, but only after a Tarot reading has opened the dream to new possibilities.)

Too often the guide in a guided meditation will not trust the person or the experience and will direct them very closely, with every detail carefully described. "You stand before a black tree with yellow leaves. A red door opens in the tree. You feel afraid but you decide to enter." (Yes, these guided tours will even tell you what to feel.) "You see a long wooden table and on it a silver bowl with a gold key." Now, this might be an interesting story, but it won't be your story. With everything so laid out, you never get the chance to experience your own journey.

Tarot, Kabbalah, and dreams are all dangerous. Dreams can frighten us, especially if we take them too simplistically. You may dream of attacking someone close to you or sex with a family member and believe the dream reveals a genuine desire. Simply the intense energy of our dreams may disturb us.

Kabbalah is more dangerous than dreams, for Kabbalah involves deliberate practices to invoke the dreamlike states that we leave when we wake up. And because Kabbalah is communal, people can misuse it. In the seventeenth century, a "false messiah" named Sabbatai Zevi misused Kabbalah doctrines and almost split Judaism in two. This probably is why study of Kabbalistic texts and practices became restricted to married men over the age of forty with children. This was not always the case—Isaac Luria, whom many consider the greatest of the Kabbalist masters, died at thirty-eight. Here, too, there is a parallel in Tarot, in the swindles sometimes practiced by storefront fortune tellers. The vast majority of people doing this work read cards with a desire to help. Occasionally, however, someone will use the reading to scare someone into giving over a great deal of money. The scam may involve the reader "discovering" from the cards that some jealous person has put a curse on the client.

Kabbalah, it seems to me, is dangerous for more immediate reasons than manipulation. First, you may stir up energies you do not know how to handle or go to some deep place and not know how to return. Another reason concerns literalness. You can get confused, to say the least, if you take statements in the Zohar, or other texts, as literal statements of fact. You can fall prey to superstitious beliefs or the idea that you have learned the secret laws of the universe.

Most dangerous of all, you may discover that you have gained a kind of power that other people do not know about, and if that happens, you may start to think of yourself as superior to ordinary people or that other people are simply insignificant compared to you. This attitude is seductive but dangerous for anyone on a spiritual path.

Many myths describe this danger, and the hero's ability to resist it. Two examples come to mind: one light and the other profound. The first comes in *Star Wars*, when Darth Vader tells his son Luke to use the dark side of the Force to get what he needs. Luke knows, from his father's evil, how corrupt the dark side will make him, and so he refuses to give in.

A much deeper example appears in the Christian Gospels, when Satan stands with Jesus on a mountaintop and offers to make him the ruler of all the world. Christian tradition rightly calls this a temptation, for if Jesus had accepted, he would have lost his spiritual path and given way to ego.

The way people interpret this story can say a good deal about their own approach to mystical experience. Some Fundamentalists insist it happened exactly as told. Those who consider Bible accounts—and Kabbalah—and Tarot—as fantasies treat the story as a metaphor or intellectual idea. Both approaches seem to me to take us away from the actual story and what we can learn from it.

The Reverend Bruce Chilton, in his book *Rabbi Jesus*, has suggested a middle way: that Jesus indeed experienced this temptation, but at an inner level of reality. Chilton describes Jesus as deeply involved in the mystical journeys and meditations that later would develop into Kabbalah. Through this work, similar to shamanism, Jesus had gone to a very high place. There he faced great danger, for the magical and mystery traditions of the world all teach us that we can fall as high as we climb.

Another Christian myth teaches a similar lesson, this time from someone who failed the test. Lucifer, the bringer of light, was an angel of great beauty, closest to God. When he gave way to ego, he fell all the way into Hell and became Satan. Many people raised as Christians reject this story because they know how the literal idea of Hell has been used to frighten people into obedience. But there is much to learn from the myth once we overcome the doctrine of sin and punishment.

We who work with Tarot (or indeed, Kabbalah) face far less danger, for we make no claim to anything like the level of Jesus or Lucifer. But danger does exist, for whatever level we reach. In Tarot, we can become so good at reading that we come to believe that we possess psychic power and knowledge beyond those of ordinary people, and that this makes us superior beings. Doing so we can become lost, not only to others but to ourselves. Remember the Tarot card of the Magician? His posture with the one arm raised to the sky and the other pointed to the Earth tells us that our personal power does not bring the light into the world; instead, we make ourselves a channel, an open passage for power to pour through us. Indeed, this is how most Tarot psychics experience what they do.

Still, if we do readings with Tarot, we face the danger that we will come to believe that we have special powers. If we see the Tarot as a blueprint for secret knowledge, we may think ourselves above the mass of people who don't know what we know. Both approaches may stir energies in us that we do not know how to handle. For there is power in the cards, just as there is power in all deep symbolism: the power to awaken us in barely charted ways.

The idea that we can fall further because we have climbed higher shows up in the Major Arcana of the Tarot. The Devil does not come in until card fifteen, following after Temperance.

Temperance and the Devil from the Marseille deck

Temperance signifies a high degree of awareness. In the card before it, Death, we let go of whatever does not really matter in life, so that in Temperance we can discover our "angelic" nature. The danger, however, is that we believe we have gone all the way to divine consciousness, that we have in fact become God—not part of God, but a sort of replacement. This may sound fanciful, but sadly, the history of religion and esotericism includes many examples.

People often say that the Tarot scares them. They may laugh out of embarrassment when they say it, but usually they mean it. They may have gone to a Tarot reader as a game or an experiment, only to find their lives laid out before them, not just secrets or future events, but possibly some inner truth of the heart. So they laugh and say, "Oh no, I'm not doing that again. That stuff spooks me."

Some religious fundamentalists express a more lurid fear. Somewhere the idea arose that Satan sat down at some fiery pit table and invented Tarot cards as a trick to lure confused humans away from the true path. I once read a pamphlet that explained that Tarot cards do indeed "work" (predict the future) but only because Satan feeds people the answers. The point, apparently, was to make people think that Christ was not necessary or that maybe humans possessed supernatural powers and could replace God.

Both these reactions express similar fears, just in very different mental frameworks. The Tarot does indeed seem to contain a power, and they do not understand it and want to keep it away from them. Part of that fear lies in the outrageous idea that a pack of cards can actually reveal future events and/or a person's inner state of mind. But it is more than that. It may feel as if a dream had followed us into the waking world. Or worse, as if the dream had run ahead of us, and was lying in wait around the corner.

Here is a story of the way Tarot can seem to seize hold of someone: If you travel south along the highway near the coast in Tuscany, Italy, you will suddenly see brightly colored statues towering over the fully grown trees. In vivid rounded shapes covered in bits of mirror and polished ceramics, the statues belong to the Tarot sculpture garden of the great artist Niki de Saint Phalle (1930–2002). Like a vision of another world—a dream world— the garden contains all the Major Arcana. It took Saint Phalle some twenty years to create this project, during which she lived on-site, literally inside the body of the Empress, which she depicted as a large-breasted female sphinx. Each day, the whole crew would arrive to pour concrete into steel frames or to carefully glue pieces of color and mirror fragments onto surfaces. At night, however, they all would leave, and the artist would find herself alone with her statues.

Toward the end of this great work, it all began to get to her. During the time she worked on Death, a dear friend became ill, and Saint Phalle feared he would die, as if under a spell. The friend in fact survived his illness, but to her horror a heart attack claimed one of the workers. During this period, Saint Phalle took a break to take care of family business in Paris, where by coincidence I had gone to visit a friend. We met and she asked if I would do a reading about her sense of the statues as an overwhelming presence that had begun to frighten her.

I do not remember the specific cards, but I remember very well the message. The reading told her that she needed to release the statues. She needed to give up the belief that they belonged to her because she had designed and built them. Like a parent who lets a child live its own life once it reaches a certain age, she needed to consider the statues as independent of her. Paradoxically, this would return them to being statues, rather than creatures who lived inside her head.

When frightened of the power of Tarot or Kabbalah, we might think of an old Russian expression, "What is to be done?" One thing many people do is define and name that power in order to create an illusion of control. Like Adam counting the stars, they make lists. "The Magician contains such and such qualities. It belongs to the planet Mercury. If symbolizes the masculine principle." And so on. When David Rosenberg writes "Most books on the Kabbalah are about explaining and simplifying," we could easily substitute "Tarot" for "Kabbalah" and get a good description of what goes on in so much of Tarotology.

As Rosenberg says, "explaining and simplifying" are "all well and good." We need books and classes that transmit the centuries of wisdom people have encoded into the cards. Explanations are useful because they give us an entry into the pictures, but we need to be careful not to confuse a description with the thing itself.

Sometimes in a class or a reading, a person will get a card that they don't understand or find disturbing. I will say to them, "What do you see?" If they answer with symbolic ideas or traditional "divinatory meanings," I may say, "Those are ideas. What do you *see?*" Then they might pick it up, hold it in front of them, and start describing it in ways completely original, and meaningful to them, in that moment.

Rosenberg again: "We can try to disarm the other side" (the fearsome dreamlike images and stories that well up from deep places) "with knowledge and more knowledge. But there will never be enough knowledge." Like Kabbalists, we attempt to disarm Tarot with knowledge. Often it's the same knowledge, the lists of correspondences, the Tree of Life, the astrological correlations, the pathways and their precise signs. We correlate, enunciate, enumerate. We need to remember, however, that knowledge is not an end in itself.

However, knowledge can be a vehicle. On the Tree of Life, "Knowledge" is actually the title of the invisible sephirah, Da'ath, the energy that will carry us across the "Abyss" that separates the outer way of explanations and definitions from the inner way of direct experience. The term *knowledge* here means more than our usual sense of it as information. It means an awareness that lives inside us. In Tarot, that can only come by spending time with the images and not just the lists of what they're supposed to mean.

The Woman with the Lion

What will carry us across the Abyss is not just information but openness. If we want to discover the secrets of Tarot, we must expose our own secrets. By *secrets*, I mean first of all the deep places in ourselves, our fears and desires. Without such honesty we cannot go forward, certainly not safely, for if we suppress some part of ourselves at the same time that we attempt to explore the wonders of the Tarot, we can disturb the psyche.

Exposing secrets does not mean that we must beat our breasts or tell all our friends. It certainly does not mean that we must track down any awful thought or action we have ever done and denounce ourselves, for that is shame, not openness. It does not even mean actual hidden things.

Instead, it just means that we accept ourselves, become at ease with who we really are, every part of our lives and character and desires and fantasies, whether luminous, fearsome, or simply absurd. (Admittedly, not an easy experiment!)

Strength from the Rider deck and Force from the Marseille deck

The Tarot gives us a wonderful image of such acceptance. We call it Strength (or Force or Fortitude, depending on the deck).

In the traditional imagery, the woman does not control or dominate the lion. She does not cage it or whip it into submission. Instead, she embraces it.

Some older Renaissance versions of the card showed the famous mythological scene of the Greek hero Hercules killing a lion. Some people have taken this image to mean that we must battle and even kill our passions the way a warrior kills a wild beast. However, some two hundred years later than the Visconti-Sforza, the Tarot de Marseille, shows us the woman holding, perhaps taming, the lion. She seems to open the lion's mouth, as if to make it give something up, maybe reveal secrets. Does it tell us the hidden truth of the cosmos? Or does it in fact release the very passions that Hercules sought to destroy?

Fortitude, from the Visconti-Sforza deck

The image of a woman with a lion is in fact extremely old, far older than Hercules and his thick club. In fact, the Hercules story might have represented the need of the warrior Greeks to subdue an older, more indigenous culture, one centered on a Goddess. The image of a female deity with big cats goes back at least eight thousand years, to a small statue excavated in Turkey. A powerful woman sits on a chair and gives birth, without struggle, while leopards lie on either side.

The Babylonian Ishtar appeared with lions in stories and iconographic art. The Greek myth of the sphinx was a combination of a woman and a lion (not to be confused with the famous Egyptian statue, whose human aspect is male). In India, we find the warrior Goddess Durga with lions. And out of Turkey, from exactly the same area as the anonymous statue, only some five thousand years later, Cybele, the "Great Mother" of the Gods, traveled to Imperial Rome in a chariot drawn by lions (thereby combining the Tarot cards of Strength and the Chariot).

The partnership does not end there. At the end of the eleventh century, in France, the Zohar describes the Shekhinah, the female aspect of God, with lions at her side. And some five hundred years after that, the Tarot de Marseille's woman and her talkative lion replaces Hercules as the standard image.

Rather than produce an explanation for this partnership, I suggest you spend some time with the partners. Try to imagine yourself first as the woman and then as the lion. Let yourself begin to experience the card from inside. And if what you find is a lion who does not remain gentle, but who turns and attacks you, let yourself experience that as well. Not for nothing does David Rosenberg call his book *Dreams of Being Eaten Alive*.

The Woman with the Veil

The occult tradition refers to the Tarot cards as "arcana," or secrets. When we consider the word we often assume it means secret information, like some classified document kept under lock and key (or as the cliché goes, locked in the basement of the Vatican). If not information, such as a formula of some sort, then maybe revelation. Or contemplation. At any rate, *secret* seems to imply "knowledge."

Consider the card on the next page of the High Priestess in the Rider Tarot (we might look at many other versions, and in fact we will see at least one more in a moment, but the Rider imagery speaks most directly here).

Dressed in the robes of the Goddess Isis (remember her, the one who got Thoth to help her bring Osiris back from the dead?), she sits before a veil, as if to block the entrance to her temple. Veiled Isis is a symbol taken from the mystery religions of the Hellenistic world (the world of Hermes Trismegistus). Author Madame Helena Blavatsky (1831–1891), cofounder of Theosophy, a nineteenth-century movement that influenced the Golden Dawn, titled one of her massive works *Isis Unveiled*. She called her other primary work *The Secret Doctrine*. We are definitely in High Priestess territory here, even shown by the fact that Blavatsky published two works, each originally in two volumes. So the veil hides the secrets, and we may assume, with the example of Blavatsky's many hundreds of pages, that the secrets are extremely complicated.

The imagery of secrecy continues in the rolled-up scroll in her lap. Marked TORA (a variation of Torah, the Hebrew scripture, but also an anagram for *taro*), it lies closed, as in forbidden or esoteric. If open, it would signify the "outer," exoteric Torah, read in synagogues on Saturday mornings. Closed, it suggests an inner truth. At the same time, Kabbalists often describe this esoteric level as the meanings that lie in the space between the visible letters. In other words, the rolled-up scroll does not say, "I know things you don't know and you're not allowed to know them," but rather "The world contains more wisdom than appears on the surface. Learn to look at the spaces and you will discover wonders."

The High Priestess from the Rider deck. On the left we can see how the symbolism of this card creates the Tree of Life.

The veil stretches between two pillars, one black and one white, and labeled *B* and *J*. (Perhaps the most common of the many questions asked of me in workshops is "What do the *B* and *J* stand for?") The symbolism derives from Freemasonry, that bastion of complicated secrets. Boaz and

Jakin were the names of the pillars erected by the entrance to the Temple of Solomon in ancient Jerusalem. Portrayed on the card, the pillars symbolically recreate the entrance. This is the Masonic spiritual goal—to rebuild the Temple, not of actual stone and wood, but rather a psychic construction on "the astral plane," or "a higher vibrational frequency," as occultists like to say. (My deep apologies to Freemasons if I have distorted their goals and practices.)

Is Freemasonry the secret? Are the teachings of Blavatsky? The initiation rituals of ancient Egypt or of Hellenistic Alexandria? Maybe the secret lies buried in the Temple Mount of Jerusalem or perhaps in one of the two great mosques that now stand on the same spot—more twoness, and I am sure it is no accident that one gleams with a golden dome and the other with silver. Or maybe the Bible contains the secret, concealed in God's instructions to Solomon on how to build the Temple. Though all these doctrines have led to wonderful constructions, in stone or philosophy or allegories, they are still doctrines and not the secret itself.

The pillars do not just create a reference to Solomon or Freemasonry. Black and white, they symbolize all the duality, all the twoness, of our human existence. Light and dark, positive and negative, male and female, conscious and unconscious, action and stillness, birth and death, comedy and tragedy, beauty and ugliness, hot and cold, dry and wet ... and on and on. This is the universe as we know it—or rather, as we perceive it, since in reality none of these absolutes exist.

But wait. There is a third column in the picture. The High Priestess sits between the two pillars. Just by her quiet presence she embodies the middle column in the Tree of Life.

In Kabbalah, we find duality in the right and left columns, with the right as the principle of *expansion* and the left of *contraction*. Expansion includes the ideals of compassion and mercy, contraction those of severity and justice. Both are necessary, just as the universe could not survive without both positive and negative charges inside atoms. Too much contraction and everything would just collapse, too much expansion and it would fly apart. Any parent can tell you that much the same goes for raising children.

But what keeps the universe from wild swings between expansion and contraction? The middle pillar represents harmony, the principle of balance. And in the High Priestess we do not see this principle as a stone pillar or an abstract symbol but as a human being, a woman calm and confident. Now we begin to approach the kind of secret the card really shows us—not forbidden information, but a discovery.

As a living woman or man—or trans or intersex or nonbinary (but no one more so than anyone else)—you yourself can harmonize the opposites and conflicts of life. Learn the path of the High Priestess and you can sit calmly in the midst of turmoil. Similarly, learn the path of Strength and you can play gently with lions.

Is that all? Well, no. Don't forget the veil, the curtain hung with pomegranates and palm trees (the plants actually form an image of the Tree, with the pomegranates as the sephiroth and the trees as the right and left columns). It blocks the way to the temple so that we cannot see the wonders hidden inside. Or does it? Look closely at the picture. A gap appears between the curtain and the pillars so that you actually can see what lies behind, and what is visible is a pool of water. No carved stone tablets, no supernatural beings, no great list of formulas or equations. Just a pool of water. This is the perfect image of the Imageless, for water is powerful yet without form other than the container that holds it. Deep and mysterious as the mind, water is life itself, for the ancestors of all organic creatures, whether animal, plant, or microbe, originated in our Mother, the sea. The surface of the Earth is something like three-quarters water, and so is the substance of the human body. The blood that carries life through our bodies tastes of salt, just like the sea, just like the tears that express our deepest emotions, whether heartbreak or joy.

The *secret* of the High Priestess is very simple—no fixed rule defines existence, no absolute truth. To know reality we must flow like water and open our souls to the pulse of life. It's easy to say, perhaps, but hard, or maybe just frightening, to do. To truly experience such a reality we must let the fixed shape of our personality dissolve and flow away. We must give up our desire to count the stars and believe we control them. That is what makes it a secret.

Does all this mean that Water is the ultimate element, and the suit of Cups the one true reality? Clearly not, or the Tarot would come to us in a different form. Water in the Minor Arcana indeed symbolizes the formlessness of existence, but this is a particular point of view. We need to balance it with others in order to live in the real world. The suit of Water represents one of the four aspects of our experience.

Danish Tarotist Helle Agathe Beierholm describes the Minor Arcana as four ways to bring the spiritual principles of the Major Arcana into our lives. The idea really works in both directions, for the Minor suits also describe four approaches to discover such principles.

Beierholm describes the elements in terms of a child being born. The child lies in the water of the womb, which we also can compare to the original planetary womb of the sea. Fire brings to mind the way the body burns food for energy to stay alive and to grow. When the child emerges from the mother and must exist for itself, it begins to breathe in air for the oxygen that will feed its cells. Air is the suit of mind, an expression of the baby's fascination with its new universe. All this activity takes place in a body, and that physical form, the body itself, represents the element of Earth. The Major Arcana in this scheme signifies the body's soul, that which makes it both a living being and uniquely itself.

Ten

Becoming a Reader

We can look at the elements through a different lens if we think of how we work with Tarot. Once again, David Rosenberg tells us that we cannot fall back on knowledge if we wish to move deeply into Kabbalah, for knowledge can become a screen. This certainly is the case with Tarot. The more you think you know, the more likely you will gloss over what lies before you with a click of recognition on a mental list. "Oh yes, this means . . . "

Rosenberg makes the wonderful statement, "We must become more than knowledge bearers. We must become readers."

Now, he does not mean readers of Tarot cards, he means the qualities of someone who actually reads a poem or a story, in place of the person who explains it or categorizes it, even if only to themself. To really read something, you need to open yourself to it with heart and intuition as much as with intellect, and continue to do so, no matter how many times you've read it before. But even if Rosenberg did not think of Tarot, his words carry special meaning for us, from the double meaning of *reader* in Tarot. This is a microcosm of the odd relationship between Tarot and Kabbalah—Kabbalistic systems and ideas apply so well to Tarot that the two indeed seem made for each other.

The Moon from the Marseille, Rider, and Raziel decks

We must become more than knowledge bearers, we must become readers. To truly enter the cards, we need to do more than learn about them; we need to *use* them. Reading the cards allows them to take you places you never would think to go on your own. It involves risks beyond knowledge, for a knowledge system is just that, a known system, whereas when you gamble with the Moon—play with imagination to bring forth your deepest intuition—you never know just what might come to the surface. The Moon card of the Tarot illustrates this mystery in the form of the crab or lobster that crawls up from the depths.

What are the qualities of a reader? We can use the Tarot itself to reveal possibilities. Suppose we consider the four suits and their elements as different aspects of how to read the cards. With Fire we read with passion. We get flashes of insight. We must care deeply, and be willing to give ourselves to what we can sense in the cards, or it will never work. Like the Knight of Wands on his fiery steed, we ride into the reading with the joy of adventure.

There is a Christian story about the element of Fire that Annie Dillard quotes in her book, *For the Time Being*. In the early days of the Desert Fathers—real-life examples of the Hermit—a certain Abbot Lot came to see his teacher, Abbot Joseph. "Father," he said to him, "according as I am able, I keep my little rule, and my little fast, my prayer, meditation, and contemplative silence, and according as I am able, I strive to cleanse my heart of thoughts. Now what should I do?"

Knight of Wands from the Thoth and Tarot of the Spirit decks

The elder priest stood up and stretched out his hands to heaven. His fingers became ten lamps of flame. He said, *"Why not be totally changed into fire?"*

The spiritual quest—and Tarot readings are a kind of spiritual quest, as shown in the word *divination*—is not the place for false modesty. To get a real result we must give ourselves completely. We must allow the images to change us into Fire.

With Water, we receive subtlety and deep feeling. We let our intuition guide us, as if we float down a river. Water is the element of love, necessary to establish a true bind with the person who has asked the question—even if the person is yourself. Water brings *compassion*, a word that means to share someone else's suffering. Many people come to the cards because of some kind of pain. We tend not to consult the cards when a love affair goes well, but run to them when Mr. or Ms. Right no longer returns our calls. If you do not want your readings to become cold or even cruel, an egocentric display of your skills and prophetic power, then you need to remember that the reading does not exist to show off your insights but to ease the questioner's discomfort. You need the Water of Compassion for the person who has asked the question—even if that person is yourself.

Air brings intelligence. We cannot rely on feelings alone to understand what lies in front of us in a reading. Even if intuition can guide us to the point of a card, we still need to understand how it fits in with the others and with the life of the questioner. We also need mind, the premier quality of Air, to get the benefit of all the interpretations and scholarship done in the more than two hundred years since Antoine Court de Gébelin opened up the esoteric Tarot.

The element of Earth, material reality, reminds us that a reading deals with real things. People fall in love, they work at their jobs, they get sick, they travel or move house, they give birth. All these realities come into the wisdom we seek when we lay out Tarot cards. For many people this is all they seek in the Tarot. They have seen the movies with the "gypsy" fortune tellers or late-night television ads for psychic readers waiting to take your calls, guaranteed 98 percent accuracy, and now they come to the Tarot expecting to learn whom they will marry, whether a partner is cheating on them, or where to apply for a job. The Tarot reader may try to show them the spiritual lesson in the cards or the psychological issues, but they want to know only one thing: How accurate is it?

The concerns of Earth are real concerns, and we should not dismiss them as inferior to "higher truths." A truly valuable Tarot reading will combine the practical questions with the many layers of meaning that surround it.

Many of the older occult works exalt Air, and mind, as the element closest to the pure Spirit symbolized in the Major Arcana. Air is invisible, not bound to the Earth, the least physical and therefore (supposedly) most like the divine. The mind (supposedly) can free us from the limited perspective of our physical senses and therefore liberate us from illusions to discover the truth of pure reason. To understand this exaltation of Air, we need to look briefly at the history of spiritual ideas, and in particular, attitudes toward women.

It is no coincidence that those who wrote about the superiority of mind were almost all men, and that they considered sensuality and intuition female and rationality male. The dislike of the body and the physical world comes from a cultural history (going back at least to ancient Greece) that wished to deny the sacred possibilities of women and exalt the qualities of men. Why should men associate women with the body and consider both inferior? Very simply, all of us, men and women, come from our mothers' bodies. Many early expressions of religion, such as Stone Age art and temples (sometimes constructed in the shape of a woman's body) celebrate this female capacity to give forth life. In reaction to this very powerful fact about our existence, the (male) Greeks and others treated physical existence as not just separate from spirit but inferior to it, even its enemy. They described spirit as literally imprisoned in the "gross matter" of physical reality. Supposedly our minds can free us from the prisons of our bodies. We might notice here that *matter* derives from *mater*, the Roman word for "mother."

Much of the prejudice against the Water qualities of instinct, intuition, and emotion turned almost completely around in the 1960s and '70s. Suddenly, people considered the *mind* the enemy of true existence. If we would just get rid of our thoughts, if we could act instinctively, like the animals, we could "blow our minds" (explode ourselves out of our own thoughts). We would return to nature and rediscover our true selves, or even our divine selves. We also would discover great powers. In the movie *Star Wars*, Luke cannot guide his spaceship into the heart of the evil Death Star as long as he tries to do it consciously. "Trust your feelings, Luke," his teacher tells him. Only when Luke bypasses his mind can he contact the Force and let it carry him to his goal.

Why should we consider one element superior to another, one clean and another dirty, or one trustworthy and another false? In the Tarot all four suits have the same numbered cards, Ace–Ten, and the same characters, whether we call them Page, Knight, Queen, and King; or Daughter, Son, Mother, and Father; or any of the other variations. When we do a reading, we mix all the cards together, because this is what we find in life: a complex stew of qualities, each with its own flavor and nourishment, and each with its own excesses and dangers.

The contemporary Goddess and Pagan movements began in the 1970s and '80s. (These were not new ideas, but they became widely known at that time.) These movements honored both the female and nature, with a sense of the physical as sacred. Awareness of the environment began in that same time, and with it a fascination to learn the sacred ways of indigenous peoples, whose greatly varied traditions sometimes get described together as "Earth-based religions." In Tarot, this time period saw the emergence of Goddess decks, Tarots honoring different cultures, and Pagan/Wiccan decks.

It may seem at first that if the earlier occult ideology placed Air and reason above all else, and the hippies made supreme the feelings of Water and the impulsiveness of Fire, that the Pagans simply exalted Earth above all else. Happily, this has not been the case. Pagans and Goddess worshippers have their one-sided people like any other group, but overall they have made the balance of the elements an important goal.

Maybe this sense of balance has come partly from the importance of Tarot in the Pagan revival. Many Pagans make sure to read the cards at festival times, especially Samhain (Halloween), the Celtic and Wiccan New Year, which they consider an opening between the "mundane" world and the world of the Spirits. Others choose a card in the midst of rituals. They might walk a labyrinth laid out on the ground and in the center come to a veiled priestess with a fanned-out deck of cards who invites them to choose one card for what they need to release and one for what they want to take with them.

Some Tarot occultists and Kabbalists have dismissed readings as trivial when compared to the study of the cards as a memory system for the laws of existence. When you do this, you can choose certain cards or elements as superior, or "higher," than the others. You can designate certain cards as evil or misguided. But when you make readings the center of your spiritual Tarot work, you learn that life shifts all the time and some quality or idea that serves you well at some point may hold you back at another.

Suppose at the center of your labyrinth you've received the Sun for what you must leave behind and the Devil to take with you.

The Sun and the Devil from the Marseille deck

Do you panic or decide to dismiss them as a mistake? The fact is, the Tarot never compels us and we can always refuse its advice. If you interpret these two cards as "Give up happiness and become a devil worshipper," you probably would do well to turn them down. But if you have made a commitment to take the Tarot seriously, you might consider that simplicity and pleasure do not always serve us in every situation and sometimes we need to enter our inner darkness to liberate whatever hides or is held prisoner. And some, of course, will see the Devil as sensuality.

In all this balance of the elements, what of the Major Arcana? The first thing to say is that it brings the element of Ether, the spiritual, into the play of Fire, Water, Air, and Earth. Here again, readings teach a valuable lesson, for when we mix the cards we cannot hold them apart, as superior to the suits. The spiritual becomes inextricably mixed into daily life. Over the decades of esoteric Tarot interpretation, writers and teachers have sometimes dismissed the Minor Arcana as trivial compared to the lofty truths of the Major. Books of hundreds of pages have not mentioned the suits at all or given them only the most cursory of meanings. The prejudice has carried over into readings. People get excited if they get many Major cards in a reading and disappointed or *insulted* if most of the cards turn up Minor. But, as I hope the readings in this book have shown, the instrument of our wisdom uses all seventy-eight cards. Truth issues from their individuality and the way they fit together. Just like life.

Three Levels of Tarot, Three Levels of Reader

As mentioned before, in my work with Tarot I have found it valuable to look at the Major Arcana as the Fool plus three groups of seven cards each: the Magician to the Chariot, Strength to Temperance, and the Devil to the World. We will come back to these groups several times more in this book, with different views of how they work together. Right now, however, we will consider what they might tell us about how we become readers.

The image of three strikes very deeply into the mythological mind. We can find threes in so many religious trinities, from the Triple Goddess of Maiden-Mother-Crone to the Hindu Creator-Preserver-Destroyer to the Christian Father-Son-Holy Spirit. Three also shows up in modern mythologies, from philosophy (Hegel's thesis-antithesis-synthesis) to psychology (Freud's id-ego-superego). Three comes from two basic sources: the need to go beyond duality and, more fundamentally, the triad of mother-father-child. Because we all come from a mother and a father, three is built into our psyche. As a result, we organize time as past-present-future and the world of experience as body-mind-spirit. Tarot author and teacher Mary K. Greer has told me that when she teaches two-card readings, people keep wanting to add another card. Show them two sides to an issue and they will immediately seek a resolution. She points out that sometimes we can gain a great deal by staying with the dilemma.

It becomes natural, then, when we consider any important topic, to look at it in three levels. The Major Arcana gives us a perfect model for a journey to three worlds. As the Fool travels first to the Chariot and then to Temperance and finally the World, we discover different issues and life challenges. For our final "dialogue" with David Rosenberg's views on Kabbalah, we will look at suggestions he gives for three kinds of treasures people seek in Kabbalah and discover something very similar in Tarot.

Rosenberg labels his three approaches practical, creative, and frontier. Practical describes the people who want to use Kabbalistic formulas, magic, and meditation to benefit their lives. When I first wrote this book, at the start of a new (calendar) millennium, Kabbalah was seeing a great surge of popularity. Movie stars extolled its power, Tree of Life necklaces were sold in New Age gift shops, and books appeared that promised the reader financial success, perfect health, and better sex, all through Kabbalah with its divine truths. Even before that, you sometimes could find small tables with brightly colored books on Kabbalah and all it can do for you in train stations or airports.

In Tarot, we certainly find no scarcity of practical approaches. Most people who go to a reader expect answers to specific questions, usually about love, sex, career, or health. (A mass survey of Tarot readers on what questions they get, and the frequency of various topics, might reveal much about what people want in life.) Sometimes the questioner will conceal the question to test the reader. A woman once came to me for a reading and, when asked what she wanted to look at, said she had no specific issue, she just wanted to see what the cards might tell her. When I laid out a spread for her, the eight cards included the only three in the *Shining Tribe* deck that dealt with babies and pregnancy. So I asked her the sensible question, "Is there any chance you might have a baby in the coming year?" She became very excited and said that that was what she had come to find out.

The fact that Tarot can do such things amazes and sometimes scares people so much they cannot see anything else in the cards. It would be a mistake, however, to dismiss such expectations as shallow. This "Chariot level" of Tarot looks at some of the basic issues of people's lives. The cards can teach us a great deal as they reveal answers to questions about love or work. We can learn to see ourselves and our patterns. The cards can help us to build our lives. We can think of it as creating our own Chariot, a vehicle to carry us through life's challenges.

Most "serious" books on Tarot, ones that try to correct that lurid image of the fortune teller, actually approach the cards from the Chariot level, only in a fuller way, truer to what they consider people's genuine needs. Teachers and readers will describe how they work with a person who wants the cards to tell them if someone loves them, or even how to make someone love them. (The newsletter for the American Tarot Association once quoted a letter that asked, "How can I make Mikey go to bed with me?") Usually the reader will suggest that they turn the question around to the person's own issues about love, with such questions as "What do I want from a relationship?" or "What is my pattern in relationships?" and "How do I block myself from love?" and "What will help me break through my blocks?" Anytime Tarot readers or books speak of blocks and break-throughs, we are riding in the Chariot.

Rosenberg describes his second category as "Creative Kabbalah." Here the person seeks a spiritual transformation. Study and deep meditation lead the seeker to shed outer concerns and discover a spiritual center and awareness of the sacred. We find these themes very strongly in the middle level of the Major Arcana, the seven cards that end with Temperance. The person finds the Strength to turn away from the Chariot's success, to reverse previous values and seek the Death of the ego in order to find a calm and balanced inner angel. Ego reversal, the discovery of true values, the release of spirituality—to most of us these would seem the ultimate goals of any quest. And yet, in the Tarot, another seven cards remain, a whole new level.

Rosenberg writes that he did not doubt the sincerity of those who followed the creative path, yet something left him uneasy. He finally understood when he realized the entire quest concerned the self. Every invocation, he writes is "in service to the human."

Even the vast universe somehow becomes an entity made for the benefit of human beings. If you spend any time in New Age circles, you probably have heard people say things like "Put out to the universe that you need a new job," or "The universe will give you the perfect relationship." We can easily see such statements as Chariot acquisitiveness. But what of the person who meditates on the lessons learned from universal law or who insists on a benevolent universe created to lead us to enlightenment? Does the universe really exist as a kind of homeschooling system for human consciousness?

In recent years "the universe" has become an even more common expression among Tarot readers, spiritual seekers, and psychics. It has often struck me that *Universe* substitutes for *God* for people who have rejected the harsh or dogmatic religion of their childhoods. People might say, "The Universe always wants what's best for us," or, "The Universe never gives you a challenge you can't overcome." Clearly, the word means something different here than it does in astrophysics!

When we mistake the Temperance level for ultimate reality, everything becomes a lesson, a metaphor. Nothing exists just for itself, with no need to teach or give us anything. We start to believe that every event in life, every card in the deck, exists only to help us advance. Whether we study the cards' symbolism or figure out the spiritual message in a reading, we do not allow the pictures to remain a mystery, a thing of wonder. This is why I so often insist that we must love the images. How else can we let them escape the cage of explanations we build around them?

And how else can we let them *love us*? One of the phrases that came to me years ago—I tend to believe I made it up, but at this point I do not actually remember—is *What you love loves you*. If you approach the Tarot with love, it will open itself to you, reveal wonders and mysteries, guide you and show itself to you.

Rosenberg titles his third level "Frontier Kabbalah," a term he borrows from ecologists who seek to recognize the frontier that exists in nature beyond human control. The Frontier Kabbalist does not follow a set explanation for every sephirah, does not give all their attention to the Tree of Life or any other predetermined knowledge system. The frontier becomes the place where we become more than knowledge bearers, we become *readers*. So then, let us come to the final cards of the Major Arcana, not for their doctrine, but for their story. In fact, we will look at one story in particular, a tale most readers will have known since childhood.

Devil

Tower

The Star

Cards 15–17 from the Rider and Shining Tribe decks

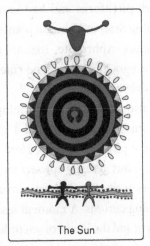

Cards 18–20 from the Rider and Shining Tribe decks

Tarot, Tarot, Let Down Your Hair

On the surface, cards fifteen through twenty-one of the Major Arcana follow a definite plan, even a simple one. Let's call it the liberation of light, for it moves from darkness in the Devil to the lightning of the Tower, then starlight, moonlight, sunlight, on to the light of the spirit in Judgement/Awakening, and finally the cosmic light discovered within the self in the card of the World.

But if the plan is simple, that does not mean it does not contain complex ideas.

We can begin at the level of story. The angel of Temperance descends into darkness to liberate the light. Occult tradition identifies the angel as Michael (in Hebrew *Micha-el*, meaning "Who Is Like God"—a statement, not a question), the divine champion who according to Christian myth flung Lucifer down into Hell. Lucifer was not just a scary bogeyman who tortures souls with pitchforks and bad contracts. Lucifer was the Light-bearer, the Morning Star, or Venus, a planet the Pagans considered a Goddess, whether Venus, Aphrodite, Inanna, or Ishtar. Lucifer gave up divine light for pride, ego, and so became ruler of what the poet John Milton called "darkness visible."

But the Star card also signifies the mythological planet Venus (the aspects of Venus as an image in the sky, and a story, as opposed to any factual examination of the physical planet). Here we see her in her Goddess aspect. As a result, Venus actually appears twice, on either side of the Tower: Venus in darkness as the Devil, Venus revealed in the Star.

Now here is something curious. A moment ago, we made a distinction between the Venus of myth and the Venus of scientific knowledge. Because of Venus's lovely light in the sky ancient people pictured the planet as a glorious figure, a Goddess or angel, and a bringer of love. When late twentieth-century scientists sent probes, however, they discovered that Venus actually suffers from an extreme greenhouse effect. Thick clouds cover the planet. They produce intense surface pressure (the strongest probes could only last a short time), illusions and distortions (if any conscious being could survive long enough to look around), and immense heat, the hottest planet in the solar system. Doesn't that sound a good deal like Hell?

The Devil, the Tower, and the Star from the Marseille deck

And yet, there still is the other Venus, the figure of beauty and hope—the image liberated from the physical facts. Venus is not visible throughout the year, and in many places her reappearance signaled a time to plant, that is, a return of the Earth's fertility. This is why the various Goddesses associated with her were almost always sexual figures, for the ancient peoples saw a deep bond between human sexuality and the Earth's ability to bestow plants. The Devil, then, becomes Venus hidden from sight, the time of infertility, or sexuality trapped, while the Star shows Venus returned and life once more restored and vibrant.

The story of the last seven cards is simple, yet we can map onto it almost as many myths, philosophies, and even scientific theories as the Tarot itself. The Gnostics saw in the Devil's darkness and the liberation of light their own favorite tale of the soul imprisoned in dark matter. We can find in these cards all the stories of Gods and Goddesses slain and taken down into underworlds, then rescued by a loyal lover.

We can view the Devil as a perversion of love, love with chains, for the Devil's number, fifteen, reduces to six, the number of the Lovers (15 = 1+5 = 6). A. E. Waite made this explicit by redesigning the Lovers card so that the Devil ends up looking like a distortion of the Lovers.

The Lovers and the Devil from the Rider deck

In the *Shining Tribe*, the connection with the Devil becomes more subtle, though just as strong. There, we see the Lovers as a passionate couple freely embracing in the sky, while the Devil appears as a solitary figure locked in doorways, with their sexuality highly concentrated from being repressed.

To liberate the Devil's light means to liberate love. Remember the idea of the three levels in the Major Arcana? Each one presents its own task, and we look to the final card as the result of meeting those challenges. The Chariot level shows us personal challenges in the outer world. The Temperance level brings us to a personal transformation. The third takes us beyond the self to a kind of divine experience. It moves from the Devil to the World, darkness to ultimate light. In mythic terms, the purpose of Temperance is not just to carry us beyond ego. Temperance actually prepares us for the great task of the third line. We become Micha-el and find the divine champion in ourselves, not to cast Lucifer into darkness, but in fact to liberate him. In other words, we must enter the darkness in order to discover the light and release it to the world.

This is one story we can find in the cards, the liberation of the light. There are many others, countless others. We will look at one tale in particular that may at first seem a surprise.

In the Brothers Grimm fairy tale of *Rapunzel*, a sorceress named Gothel (not a "witch" in the original text but the darker and more powerful figure of a sorceress) imprisons her adopted daughter in a tower with no door. According to William Irwin Thompson, in his book *Imaginary Landscape*, "Goth-el" means "bright God." And yet, like Lucifer, she becomes a figure of darkness. This sorceress/God wants to control love, like the Tarot Devil with his chains, keeping Rapunzel from any contact with creatures other than the sorceress herself.

The anonymous prince, like a reverse Orpheus, the Greek poet/singer who descended to Hades to bring his lover Eurydice back to life, hears the eerily beautiful song of lonely Rapunzel and climbs up the "ladder" of her body—her hair—into the tower. Gothel discovers them and in a rage flings them from the window and into a bleak wilderness of lost love. This is the exact image of the Tower, two people flung out a high window of an edifice with no door.

The Devil and the Tower from the Marseille and Rider decks

Now we need to play a little, switch two cards around, and put the Moon before the Star. At least we will find ourselves in good company, for the Golden Dawn switched the order of Justice and Strength, and Crowley swapped the Hebrew letters for the Star and the Emperor. The card of the Moon, with its wolves and mysterious crayfish and lack of humans, can signify the plight of the prince, blinded when he fell from the window onto thorns, and so, reduced to an animal, he feels for food and dodges wild beasts.

Years go by, and then—he hears the song. After that long night, he once more thrills to the strange barely civilized song of his beloved, who after all had never heard the music of human culture but had to teach herself to sing in her loneliness. The prince comes to her, helpless and weak.

Seeing her lover's state, Rapunzel weeps. The water of her eyes tumbles into the dead sockets of her lover and, miraculously, he heals. Is this not the very image of the Star—naked, uncultured, pouring out her waters without cease? She is once again Venus, the Morning and Evening Star who in the form of so many Goddesses heals her slain or damaged lover.

Restored, the prince sees a wondrous sight, not just his blessed Rapunzel, but a boy and a girl, twins. Despite all Gothel's attempts to make her daughter an extension of herself, Rapunzel has brought children into existence. This image of twins is also the exact picture of the traditional Tarot card of the Sun.

The final two cards bring us to the happily ever after. Judgement, with its mother, father, and child, can signify the reunited family (with one child rather than twins). It also suggests love made whole, the original vision of the Lovers that the Devil corrupted. And the World card reminds us that this simple fairy tale, which we have discovered in pictures as well as words, contains more truths about the world than we ever suspected.

Is it just fanciful to see the Major Arcana in the fairy tale? Maybe, but is it any more fanciful than the "discovery" that the cards contain the secrets of creation? And maybe we might accept such a connection more easily if we thought of Rapunzel as more than a light bedtime story (pun intended—*puns* intended, for we could play wonderful games with *light*, and *time*, and *story*, and even *bed*, had we the time, and space, to do so).

The Moon, the Star, and the Sun from the Wirth deck

The Devil, Judgement, and the World from the Marseille deck

Thompson, in his essay on Rapunzel, reminds us that *rapunzel* is a plant, a kind of lettuce known as rampion in English. (Shortly before I wrote this passage, I stayed with Anne Gentner, a Wise Woman teacher in Germany; one evening her husband served us a wild salad made with rapunzel.) In the story, a peasant couple lives next door to Frau Gothel's garden, where they can see her beds of rapunzel lettuce. When the woman becomes pregnant, she craves the lettuce so intensely that her husband crawls over the wall to get her some. Unfortunately, Frau Gothel catches him and forces him to promise that, in exchange for all the lettuce his wife desires, she can take their child when it is born.

The wild rapunzel plant contains two interesting qualities. First of all, like many plants, it can self-fertilize, effectively cloning itself if no insects come to pollinate it. To induce pollination, however, the plant sends up a towerlike stalk. If the tower does not draw insects; it splits into two stems which curl around each other, "like braids or coils on a maiden's head," as Thompson says. This brings the female tissue into contact with the male pollen. There is more, for to aid in this fertilization, the tower stalk grows "collecting hairs," and so we have the exact image of Rapunzel setting out her hair to bring the male into her otherwise sterile tower.

Self-fertilization actually suggests a throwback to asexual reproduction, before evolution created males. Frau Gothel's walled garden represents that very early world, when creatures simply divided in two, and a mother became two daughters. Her imprisonment of Rapunzel in the tower becomes a kind of experiment in evolution in reverse. Can she make Rapunzel an exact copy of herself, can she keep away the outer world? As so often happens, sex overcomes all attempts to block it, and the perfect world of the tower comes undone. Sex is the great agent of change, the bringer of new possibilities. Each child forms a unique and fresh opportunity for life, but even without children, sex undoes ego, it shows up our illusion that we can control ourselves or other people, let alone the world.

Some Tarot decks show the Sun card as two boys rather than a boy and a girl. Paul Huson, in his unjustly neglected Tarot study *The Devil's Picturebook*, links the image to the myth and star constellation of the twin heroes Castor and Pollux. Alexandra Genetti, in the book for her *Wheel of Change Tarot*, describes the card as the rebirth of the sun in midwinter, with the twin brothers as the Sun God and his shadow, who will take over after the summer solstice, when the light begins to wane. (Genetti, in fact, identifies the second child with the Devil.)

The Sun from the Wheel of Change Tarot

I personally prefer the image of a boy and girl for two reasons. First, it suggests the introduction of sexuality and therefore evolution. Second, it finally brings together the opposites set up all the way back in the Magician and High Priestess, where the Magician signified light, maleness, the sun, and consciousness and the High Priestess darkness, femaleness, the moon, and the unconscious. In the Sun, male and female join together, and, in Judgement, they produce a child, the new consciousness that will come to full awareness in the World.

When we discover the same images—two people falling from a doorless tower and twin children—in both Rapunzel and the Tarot, we realize that both tell the same story. This does not mean that the Tarot originated in the fairy tale. Both come *from the same source*, the mysteries of evolution and spiritual consciousness.

And the mysteries of the heavens as well, for the second special quality of the plant rapunzel is that it contains a five-petaled flower. Like the star in the middle of Eve's apple or the five petals of Aphrodite's wild rose, rapunzel's flower joins it to the planet Venus and the pattern of a five-pointed flower it forms in the sky over its eight-year cycle. Ancient people considered certain kinds of wild lettuce as aphrodisiacs. Middle Eastern myths of the Venus Goddess often place her dying and reborn lover in beds of lettuce. (Apparently, salad bars back then were not just health food!)

The ancient astronomers who tracked the patterns of the planets (the knowledge goes back to the Stone Age) did not only look at the individual patterns, but the way they moved together and their connection to earthly life in the seasons. If you look at Venus and Mars together over a period of time, they seem to dance around each other in a passionate movement, like lovers. The planetary signs for Mars and Venus also signify biological male and female. (♂ and ♀ respectively). In some Tarot decks, the Empress bears a shield with the Venus sign on it. It identifies her with femininity, but also with the planet Venus and the Goddess of love.

Most Tarot decks with astrological attributions follow the Golden Dawn system, in which cards one to four signify Mercury (Magician), the moon (High Priestess), Venus (Empress), and Mars (Emperor).

An alternative that would make sense is Sun, Moon, Venus, and Mars. That would give us the ideal principles of male and female in Sun and Moon (symbolized in the Magician and High Priestess), followed by the realization in Venus and Mars (Empress and Emperor). The cards do show that kind of relation, with the Magician and High Priestess as principles, such as light and dark, while the Empress and Emperor move the principles into less abstract qualities, such as nature and society or passion and control.

And what of the actual cards titled Sun and Moon? Without worrying for the moment about astrological correlations (the point is not to set up a new system but to suggest new ways to look at the cards), we could say that the Magician and High Priestess represent Sun and Moon as ideas, while the cards of the Sun and Moon show a point where these ideas become real experiences, within our own lives, our own bodies. That is why they appear so late in the sequence.

Thompson writes that ancient peoples titled the complex dance of the two planets "the courtship of Mars and Venus." They did not consider this simply a saucy tale acted out in the heavens. Venus returns to visibility in the sky at the beginning of spring, and that meant more than an indication to plant crops or when to watch for new flowers. The courtship between Mars and Venus, the return of Venus into light, indicated a correlation between heaven and Earth, between the great movements of the planets and the facts of our own survival through the food we eat, as well as the surge of our own sexuality when the leaves appear on the trees and color bursts up from the dull ground. Mars and Venus taught the ancients the miracle of existence.

(Special note—I am working on this on May 1, May Day, in older times a celebration of joy, sex, and fertility, which in the year I am writing this, 2021, comes on Friday, that is, the Goddess Freya's Day, dedicated to the Planet Venus.)

The modern world has largely stripped away the sense of the miraculous from the patterns of the world. We break things down and study them in pieces, and steadfastly deny that anything connects to anything else. But there are ways to restore that sense of wonder. One of these is divination, for divination demonstrates that patterns really do exist, the world really does fit together. "The first thing that happens," writes Stephen Karcher, "is that the world comes to life."

The courtship of Mars and Venus appears in the story of Rapunzel. The time when the prince wanders lost and blind is the long winter of the two planets' separation, symbolized in the Tower and the Moon. And the reunion, the return of love when the ice thaws and the waters of spring flow freely, appears as the healing of the prince's eyes and the card of the Star, when the Venus maiden pours out her endless flow.

Does the story of Rapunzel at last reveal the secret origin of the Tarot? Well, no and yes. No, because only a fool (Tarot pun intended) would argue that the anonymous creator of the fairy tale designed the Tarot. Yes, because both Rapunzel and the Tarot *tell the same story* and by their different disguises help to illuminate each other. The simple tale of Rapunzel brings together the sky and the Earth, the unchanging repetition of the planets with the ever-changing evolution of sexuality, of every mother, father, and child. These things appear in the Tarot as well, in a form as condensed and pleasant as the fairy tale.

Here is the great secret: Fairy tales and myths and Tarot cards do not code wisdom in simple forms in order to keep it from the uninitiated. In a sense, it's just the opposite. They do what they do because we can absorb wisdom best when it thrills and fascinates us. "Nothing is learned except through joy," said my teacher Ioanna Salajan many years ago. And if we truly love the images of Tarot, including those of pain and sorrow, we will know what she meant.

Is this cosmic/evolution story what makes the last seven cards so special, what brings us to the "frontier"? Not really. It is not the story itself but the way we read it. To learn the information will take us far, but we still need to take the most important step. We need to experience it. We can try to liberate the Devil with knowledge and more knowledge, but there will never be enough knowledge.

 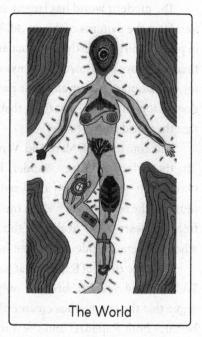

Awakening   The World

Awakening and the World from the Shining Tribe Tarot

The rich deep darkness of mystery will still call us to enter it, to go down. And we will only *know* when the lightning strikes. And we will only truly rise up (truly awaken, to use the title of card twenty in the *Shining Tribe*) when we have tracked through the moonlit night of the wild beasts, when we have poured out our sad and loving waters to reunite Rapunzel and her prince in the glorious light of the sun. And when we awaken, we will dance. We will know that we dance in the cosmos and the cosmos dances in us. We will *really* know, not as information but in our lives.

Short of such true gnosis, can we get the real message of the cards, or do we remain on the shore, stuck in the land of information, with only a glimpse of the light on the far side? There is a way, and that is the way of delight. When we truly play with the cards, when we gamble our lives with the Moon and read the stories hidden/revealed in the pictures, when we deeply love the images, we begin to become free.

The Fool from the Shining Tribe Tarot

The Fish

Eleven

The Woman with the Camel

An old television show used to begin with a shot of New York City and a voice that told us, "There are eight million stories in the Naked City. This is one of them." I'm not sure if the number of stories in the Tarot reaches eight million, but I would not be surprised. If we consider the possible stories that we can generate when we mix the cards and pluck out between one and seventy-eight of them, with all the possible combinations, both upright and reversed, we will leave eight million behind fairly quickly. But let us consider one of those stories, not chosen at random, but as in illustration of a special kind of journey we can travel in our spiritual lives, with Tarot as our vehicle.

A short while ago (in page count, that is; we have traveled several worlds since then) we looked at the High Priestess in the Rider Tarot as a representation of the idea of secrets on page 156. Let us move now to the other most famous modern Tarot deck, the Thoth deck, designed by Aleister Crowley and painted by Lady Frieda Harris. In Harris's picture we see a camel near the bottom of the card. Other decks have followed the Thoth, most notably in recent years the *Haindl Tarot* by the German painter Hermann Haindl.

The High Priestess from Thoth and Haindl decks

Why a camel? If we think of priestesses, we may imagine temples in ancient Egypt, but not even Court de Gébelin suggested that the pharaohs traveled around on camels. The most direct answer lies in the attribution of the twenty-two Hebrew letters to the twenty-two trump cards. In the Golden Dawn system, the card labeled Two actually got the third letter of the Hebrew alphabet, since the first letter went to card zero, the Fool, and the second to card one, the Magician. We'll look at this odd system in more detail in chapter thirteen. In Hebrew, the third letter is *gimel*, which literally means "camel."

So now that we know how it got there, what does it mean? Paul Foster Case, founder of the modern mystery school the Builders of the Adytum and creator of its thirteen-year Tarot correspondence course, gives various interpretations based on the camel's qualities. People used camels for transportation, so therefore it means "travel, communication, commerce, and like ideas." (Interestingly, these are all ideas associated with Hermes, a God usually associated with the Magician.) Because merchants and pilgrims used camels, and people in these professions work with others, Case sees the camel as a symbol of "association, combinations, co-existence, partnership and the like." (All Case quotations come from *The Tarot* by Paul Foster Case.)

Now, we can see these concepts with the number two, but not really with a veiled priestess. There is something schematic about these lists of qualities, like a chart written on a blackboard for a class to memorize before the next quiz.

The symbolism comes a little more alive when Case links the camel to the High Priestess's astrological association with the moon. The moon, he tells us, symbolizes personality and deep layers of memory. Like the camel that stores water in its hump (somewhat the shape of a lunar crescent), the subconscious stores and carries soul memories from one life incarnation to another.

We might say that like the camel, the subconscious is tough, irascible, and hard to approach. We also might think of Sherif Ali's line in the film *Lawrence of Arabia*, "If the camels die, we die." For a symbol truly to work it needs to do more than sum up a list of qualities. It actually needs to carry us, like a camel, across the desert of outer experiences to an oasis of meaning.

Angeles Arrien, a modern interpreter of the Thoth Tarot, points out that the camel stands in an oasis, rather than in the desert. The High Priestess archetype, she writes in *The Tarot Handbook*, "represents *the journey homeward* or the *return to oneself*." (Her italics.) The card for this archetype symbolizes the "return to the inner oasis, or the garden within." She sees the camel as "self-resourcefulness" for it can travel barren wastes "yet always find the oasis." (Actually, I would think that the camel rider directs it to the oasis. In other words, consciousness needs to direct instinct.)

Let us consider *gimel's* place on the Tree of Life (see page 192). The twenty-two letters/Tarot cards do not go on the sephiroth, but on the lines, or pathways, between them. These lines are mostly of equal length, except for one. A long line stretches from the top sephirah, Kether (Crown), to the middle of the Tree. In the Tarot Kabbalist tradition this is the line of *gimel*, the camel, the line of the High Priestess.

This line is the longest because there is a kind of empty space, an "Abyss," as the Kabbalists call it, between the upward-pointing triangle of the top three sephiroth and the downward triangle of the middle three. The first three sephiroth signify divine perfection, almost beyond human comprehension. The bottom seven bring us more to human consciousness. While still exalted, they are more accessible, more part of our lives. The journey between the parts of the Tree is difficult, even dangerous. Just as a camel can take us across a desert, so the qualities of *gimel*, the High Priestess, can carry us across the Abyss between the human and the divine.

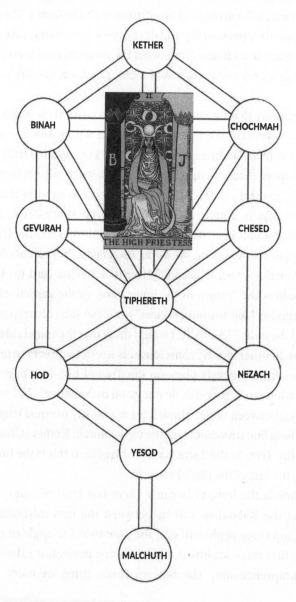

Crowley writes in his *Book of Thoth* that the High Priestess is the link between the archetypal and formative worlds. The camel is that which can carry consciousness on the great journey from pure ideal to physical reality. Intuition, silence, wholeness, inwardness, perfection, wordlessness, depth, all these come from the High Priestess. The formless *sea* of the unconscious becomes the *water* in the camel's hump that allows it to travel across the empty spaces.

I asked my friend Hercel V. Schultz, a Mormon elder and a true scholar of esoteric ideas (true because he relates them to the actual lives that people live) about camels and the High Priestess. Among his other comments, he wrote that if someone told him he had dreamed of camels, he would ask his friend to tell him three things that come into his mind about camels and the meaning would come out of his own words. Try this (you don't need to wait for a dream, you can do it with any image) and see what you discover.

Hercel went on to say that the High Priestess remains in one place while the camel travels all about, so that they appear opposites. In fact, they are deeply connected. The High Priestess dwells within "the Great Deep," Hercel's term for the formlessness of existence when we do not break the world down into mental categories. Just as the High Priestess card in the Rider deck reveals water inside the temple, so the qualities of water pervade Frieda Harris's Thoth painting, as well as Hermann Haindl's version. In the *Shining Tribe Tarot*, the masked priestess literally dwells in the sea.

The camel carries the Great Deep within his body. Sustained by this inner water, he travels across the emptiness. Without it, he dies. Hercel writes that we must have that deep inner water within ourselves or we will die spiritually. Certainly we move through a world that often seems barren and harsh. In fact, we do carry the Deep within ourselves, literally, for our tears are salty and our blood chemically resembles the waters of the oceans that first brought life into existence.

We begin to get a sense of it, but still an abstraction. Let us see if we can make it a little more concrete.

Since the camel is a Kabbalist symbol, and Kabbalah ultimately derives its symbols from the Bible, let's look at a place where the animal appears in the oldest and most mythic layer of the Bible: the Book of Genesis. You may

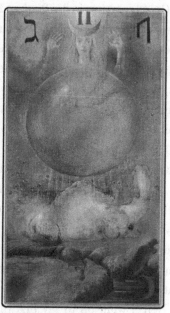

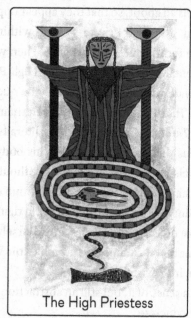

The High Priestess

The High Priestess from Thoth, Raziel, and Shining Tribe decks

recall that God tells Abraham to sacrifice Isaac on a mountaintop. Just as Abraham raises the knife, an angel stops his hand and tells him it was only a test of his willingness to submit to God. This episode seems very bizarre to us today, but at the time sacrifice of male children did sometimes occur. (In recent years, I've actually come to question this. It has struck me that accounts of children being sacrificed always seem to come from enemies or rivals of the people supposedly doing it—as in, "*Those people over there* sacrifice babies!")

The usual view is that people viewed blood sacrifice of precious lives as a kind of direct communication with the divine. When the angel stops Abraham, he moves humanity away from such literal—and monstrous—expression of religion to a subtler human-centered belief.

Two things signal this change—and they are not especially happy. One is that after this Abraham never speaks directly with God again. The second is that Sarah, Isaac's mother, dies. An old way ends to make room for a new.

As part of this change, the time comes for Isaac to marry, a ritual that always creates a new beginning, in myth as well as life. But where to find a bride? Even if they had had singles bars in Old Canaan, Isaac just wasn't the type. So Abraham sends his servant back to Abraham's homeland to search for a suitable young woman. In his instructions, Abraham says something odd. Even though he insists the bride must come from his homeland, he insists even more strongly that under no circumstances must Isaac go there himself.

The servant leaves with ten camels. When he arrives at a well, a woman (Rebecca) offers water, not only to him, but for his camels. Thrilled that God has led him to such a kind woman, he asks her father to arrange the match. The father asks Rebecca if she will go with the servant (very progressive for the times), and she says yes and they start out.

Meanwhile, Isaac has gone to a field to meditate. From a distance Rebecca spots him, and he appears so radiant that she *falls off her camel*. After the proper introductions, they marry. Isaac then leads her into Sarah's tent where at last he finds consolation for the loss of his mother.

What is going on here? What does it mean that Rebecca falls off the camel or that Isaac takes her into his mother's tent (presumably he owned his own tent)? And why does Abraham insist so vehemently on a girl from the old country but just as adamantly that Isaac mustn't go himself? What does all this have to do with the camel on the High Priestess?

Let's begin with the ten camels. Anytime we meet the number ten, we can think of the Tree of Life with its ten sephiroth. Some might argue that the concept of the sephiroth did not emerge until long after the Bible stories were set down. Historically we first encounter them in the *Sefer Yetzirah*, or *Book of Creation*, which scholar Gershom Scholem dated to around 400 CE.

Exactly when something was written down does not really matter here, for we have entered myth, and myth always shifts us out of history. Without that shift, we could never discuss Kabbalah and Tarot at all, for there is no evidence of any Kabbalist origin for Tarot cards. And yet, the connection works so well and fits so tightly that it brings the cards, and us, to deep levels when we allow ourselves to move outside historical fact.

So the Tree of Life, the ten sephiroth, the ten camels, move from Canaan to the homeland and back again, now bringing Isaac's bride. Let's make a suggestion. Let's suppose that Abraham's *homeland*, wherever it might appear on a map, is in fact the heavenly realm of pure spirit, the place of our origins, every one of us. In Welsh myth, a man named Gwion Bach goes through a terrifying transformation and emerges as a baby floating on the sea. Young as he appears, the child can sing and prophesy, so that when he comes to court, the amazed king asks him his name and where he comes from. "My name is Taliesin," the babe says, "and my home is the region of the summer stars." This is Abraham's home as well, the region of the summer stars, and our home, though most of us have forgotten. The Tarot helps us remember. The Tarot is our camel.

Years ago, during an extreme crisis in my life, I took out my cards and instead of asking questions or doing a set spread, I simply said, "Take me home." I do not remember the exact cards or even how many, but I do remember how contemplation of the images returned me to a knowledge of my deep self below all the surface storm of my immediate situation.

Crowley described the High Priestess as the link between the archetypal and the formative. The journey does not go only one way. We have come from the archetypal region of the summer stars, the kingdom of heaven as Jesus called it, and with our ten camels, the emanations of the Tree of Life, we can return there.

Rebecca can ride her camel from the archetypal through the formative, all the way to the *physical* world where she will fall from her camel to become Isaac's wife in his mother's tent. Abraham knows that Isaac's bride must come from that archetypal homeland, but he knows as well that Isaac cannot go there himself, for Isaac belongs firmly in this world. When the angel stopped the sacrifice and God ended his conversations with Abraham and Sarah died, then Isaac became rooted in the world of the human. And so the servant followed the path of ten back to the homeland. And so Rebecca comes riding on her camel back down the longest road on the Tree, only to fall off into the world of physicality at the sight of her destined beloved.

Rebecca's father asks if she is willing to go, something possibly unprecedented in that time and part of the world. No magic or power can draw spirit into physical reality against its will. The spirit light enters the world deliberately, of its own choice, and it does so as an act of love.

In a way, we are dealing here with the card of the Lovers. In the Thoth deck, we see the glory of alchemical marriage, the merger of male and female, that produces divine consciousness. In *Shining Tribe*, we see the embrace of the human and the divine. In the Marseille deck, a young man seems to move from an older woman—his mother?—to a younger. In the Rider, we see Adam and Eve by the Trees of Life and Knowledge; only the angel does not condemn or banish them, he blesses them, for they are Adam and Eve as they should have been, without sin. Isaac and Rebecca are Adam and Eve as they should have been.

Sarah was the priestess of the other world, of the old way of direct communication with the divine. Some people have suggested she was a Canaanite priestess. I do not mean to imply in any way that she presided over human sacrifice. In fact, a long midrash tradition claims that Sarah died from her horror at what Abraham was planning to do. (I recently wrote a story in which Sarah dies to become the angel who stops Abraham.) Nevertheless, as the priestess who dwells in the deeps she must give way to a new priestess, one who will become part of the new world. Rebecca is the priestess who travels on the camel to become the lover of this world.

The Lovers from the Thoth Tarot, Shining Tribe Tarot,
Tarot de Marseille, and Rider Tarot

And so Isaac makes love to Rebecca in his mother's tent and finds consolation for Sarah's loss. One way to interpret the Lovers card is to see it as the union between the seemingly opposite principles signified in the Magician and High Priestess.

Remember the story that God takes a rib from Adam to make Eve? If ever there was a story used for political purposes, it's that one, cited by countless generations of sexist men as proof of women's inferiority, even that men are closer to God because God made them first. Some Kabbalists have given it a less obnoxious interpretation. Adam and Eve, they say, were originally one being, a perfect hermaphrodite joined at the rib. But, as one creature, they could not make anything new, so the Creator separated them into two beings who seek each other to become whole. This, too, is the Lovers card, the wholeness of the two. We also might recall the Seven of Birds in the Creation reading, in the position of "source." There, too, oneness must form two aspects in order to know itself.

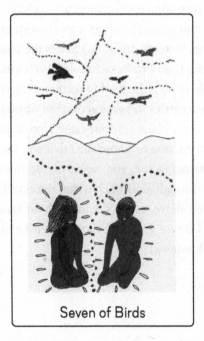

Seven of Birds

Seven of Birds from the Shining Tribe Tarot

Rebecca, the new priestess of human love, travels from the homeland, the highest sephirah on the Tree of Life, down into the heart of the Tree, sephirah six, the place of love (six is the number of the Lovers). To do so, she must cross the Abyss that separates the higher three sephiroth from the seven lower ones.

The camel, who holds the Great Deep within its body, carries her across. The camel is a fitting image for this longest journey on the Tree. Like the High Priestess, the camel keeps silently within itself the memory of our origins. The fall from the camel is like the Fool's fall from his mountain: not a sin or a disaster, but an act of love. Rebecca falls at the sight of her beloved. The Fool leaps into the splendor and variety of the material world.

The camel symbolizes something more than memory. Jewish tradition links the letter *gimel*, the camel, to the Hebrew phrase *gimalut chasidut*, "acts of lovingkindness." These include charity, and Jews sometimes describe a rich man running after a poor man to give him money (sadly, not something we see very often in contemporary society). Rebecca shows her true self to the servant when she offers water to a stranger *and* his camels. (In desert countries, water is precious.) She is the mistress of the waters, another aspect of the High Priestess, but she also is kind and generous.

Kindness and love hold the world together, they connect the material to the spiritual. Love carries Rebecca across the Abyss from the archetypal to the formative. Love will become our camel, too, to carry us home again. For it is not just meditation or knowledge that will transport us back. We need to make ourselves sacred, and we do not do this only through ritual or magic. We do it through gimalut chasidut, the camel of lovingkindness.

For much of the above, especially ideas about Isaac and Rebecca and gimalut chasidut, I owe a great debt to Avigayil Landsman, a woman of great wisdom and kindness.

Twelve

Opening the Heart: A Journey across an Abyss

I n our tale of the camel, we saw how acts of lovingkindness can take us across an Abyss that separates the higher spiritual levels from the lower, more accessible ones, for lovingkindness opens the heart. This concept—opening the heart—appears in many spiritual traditions. The Egyptians considered the heart, and not the head, the center of intelligence. Opening the heart is not simply a phrase for the nice glow we get when we do someone a favor or watch a movie where love triumphs. The phrase actually represents a complex idea with great importance for spiritual awareness and for how we understand Tarot.

In Indian teachings we learn that the body contains seven concentrations of energy that are also gates for the movement of consciousness. Each of these gates, associated with the body's endocrine system, shines with its own color. These are the colors of the rainbow, and because there are seven, they belong as well to the seven visible "planets," so that human beings become a mirror of the sky. The order of the gates, called *chakras*, and their colors matches the colors of the rainbow, *but only when the body is upside down.* In other words, red is at the top of the rainbow and violet at the bottom, while in the body we find red at the base of the spine and violet at the crown chakra on top of the head.

Hermann Haindl, creator of the *Haindl Tarot*, realized this when he looked at the precisely demarcated colors of a rainbow in Ireland. The Hanged Man, he understood, is the rainbow, and his position of surrender through reversal, his release of ego, shows a true state of spiritual openness. We align ourselves with the heavens, and indeed the Earth, when we reverse our normal condition. We might think about the fact that yogis famously stand on their heads, or that Saint Peter was crucified upside down, or that Kabbalists describe the *Aytz Chayim*, the Tree of Life, as a tree that grows upside down, with its roots in heaven and its branches reaching down to Earth.

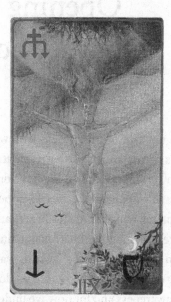

The Hanged Man from the Haindl deck

The energy that lives in the body, called *kundalini* in yoga, is both sexual and spiritual. These are really the same thing but expressed in different ways, depending on our level of consciousness. For most of us, the kundalini lies coiled at the base of the spine, like a sleeping snake, awakened only slightly through sexual arousal. Most of our chakras are only partially open, though they may open further in response to particular experiences. (For example, a psychic flash indicates a momentary opening of the third eye chakra in the forehead.)

For the kundalini to fully move through the body, we must open each gate. When that happens, the person experiences great heat that travels up the spine and out the top of the head, in a kind of lightning flash. The head seems to vanish, for the person loses the separation between self and God and the universe. This experience, this flash of revelation, is another way to look at the card of the Tower. The stone tower symbolizes the closed rigidity of ego consciousness, the illusion of separation from the rest of existence. The release of light shatters the illusion, and the divided dualistic ego finds itself thrown from the tower. In some versions we see the top of the Tower knocked off, as if to show the removal of head-consciousness.

As we saw with Rapunzel, a period of confusion and wandering in a wilderness may occur before the dualistic self truly heals. In the biblical story of Exodus, the Israelites wander in the desert for forty years, when in fact it is possible to cross the Sinai in a matter of weeks (Lawrence of Arabia did it by camel in just days). Forty is four times ten. Each of the four worlds of Kabbalah contains its own Tree of Life with ten sephiroth, so that in fact the Israelites were traveling through all the worlds during their time in the desert.

In Kabbalist symbolism, a lightning flash describes the way divine energy travels down the sephiroth on the Tree of Life. On some depictions of the Tower, we see lightning strike the building in exactly this form

Exercises and meditations exist to raise the kundalini. Not only are these difficult, however, they also can be dangerous. To raise up such energy, you first must prepare yourself. For this reason, Joseph Campbell writes in *The Inner Reaches of Outer Space* that most adepts raise the kundalini to the fourth chakra and then let it sink down again. Only those who have

XVI

THE TOWER

The Tower from the Tarot of the Spirit

203

done the necessary spiritual work can safely bring it past the fourth level and out the top of the head. The fourth chakra, then, acts as a kind of barrier. Chakra four is the heart.

Campbell goes on to describe Navajo sand paintings where worshippers paint a picture of a spirit and dance into it to transform their own spiritual consciousness. There are seven positions in the paintings. Only a very few of the dancers actually move all the way through the seven places and out the head of the spirit. The dance is far more than exercise or aesthetics. When they enter through the feet, they have left the ordinary world and moved into the cosmic body. To exit out the head means to open their own heads, their crown chakras. Those not ready to make such a full journey dance only as far as the fourth position, and then go back out the way they came, back to ordinary consciousness. In both Navajo and Hindu traditions, the heart becomes the stopping point, or the abyss, that separates above and below.

Many people will know the expression, "As above, so below," from the legendary founder of Western Hermeticism, Hermes Trismegistus. (Actually, that phrasing comes from a later time.) Usually, this means that the patterns of the heavens reflect our own lives or that we can know the Gods through a true knowledge of ourselves. It also can refer to the higher and lower chakras and their meeting place at the heart.

Now we switch our frame of reference and move back in time to ancient Egypt, where the Tarot legendarily began—Hermes Trismegistus being another name for Thoth. A papyrus painting from about 1300 BCE shows a mythological scene of a dead person's heart weighed against an ostrich feather. We will look more closely at this event in just a moment, but right now we give our attention to the center pole that holds the balanced scales. In the picture, the pole contains seven circles arranged vertically. The Goddess Isis, who re-membered, that is, reassembled, her torn apart husband Osiris, points with her finger at the sixth circle.

If the seven circles do indeed represent the chakras (centuries before the first known Indian references), then Isis points to the third eye, the place of psychic opening and knowledge of spiritual worlds beyond ordinary senses. In the Middle East and the Mediterranean, the Goddesses associated with love and sexuality were sometimes connected to the number six, the number of the Lovers card in the Tarot. The sixth chakra becomes a kind of stepping-off point to the ultimate oneness of the crown chakra, where the self dissolves, but also the individual Gods and Goddesses.

(Julie Gillentine, a Tarot teacher in the Paul Foster Case tradition, has pointed out to me that some say that the sixth chakra actually opens *after* the seventh. The energy travels up the spine and over the top of the head to come down the forehead and open up psychic awareness.)

There is another figure in the picture, one more directly relevant to our purposes here. A monster with the head of a crocodile, the hindquarters of a hippopotamus, and the body of a lion—in other words, all the dangerous beasts of the Egyptian countryside—points his crocodile snout between the third and fourth circles. This creature, who bore the name Ammut, occupied a special place in Egyptian beliefs about the afterlife, one directly related to the scales in the picture.

The Book of the Dead—the temple manuscripts, pictures, and hymns known collectively as *Pert Em Hru*, or *Coming Forth into Day*—tells us that the dead soul must go up for judgement before a court of the Gods. As part of this divine judgement, a Goddess named Ma'at, helped by our old friend Thoth, weighs the person's heart against an ostrich feather. If the heart does not weigh down the scale, the Gods dress the person in divine robes and lead them to a new life. But if the heart tips the scale even a small amount, then the person becomes a meal for Ammut.

When Ammut points below the fourth circle on the scale post, he suggests that for the Egyptians as much as the Hindus or the Navajo, the heart represents a border, and a place of danger.

The Woman with the Scales

The weighing of the heart actually appears in the Tarot, though in disguised form. In the card of Justice we see a robed woman who holds a sword in one hand and balanced scales in the other. The figure represents the Roman Goddess Justitia (Themis or Dike in Greek). Most people will recognize her from courthouses and movies about trials, where she appears blindfolded to signify equal treatment to rich and poor.

The Tarot Justice wears no blindfold, for spiritual Justice requires that we examine ourselves and our lives with absolute honesty and no looking away. It has long seemed to me that the eyes, piercing and direct in so many versions, represent the most important symbol here, for they signify the courage not to look away from anything.

In American courthouses, the scales tip, for in a trial a decision must come down to one side or the other. In most Tarot Justice images, the scales balance perfectly, for when we truly understand our lives, we realize that everything balances. The experiences that come to us from outside— our birth circumstances, the actions of other people, the effects of our culture—are balanced by our own response to life and its demands. We are not responsible for what others do, but we certainly are responsible for our own actions.

Both sides of the scales are important. That is, it seems to me that to think we are somehow responsible for what other people do—or the outer circumstances of our lives, our society or events—is just as unbalanced as to believe we are simply victims.

In older and traditional Tarots, Justice appears as trump eight, the start of the second group of seven cards. In this way she puts her mark on the whole sequence. The Golden Dawn moved Justice to eleven, and Strength, formerly card eleven, to eight. Strength at the beginning signifies the gentle inner strength we need to make the inward journey of transformation.

Justice fits position eleven very well. Eleven is the midpoint of the Major Arcana, for if we consider the Fool as the journeyer through the twenty-one numbered trumps, then ten cards precede Justice, and ten cards follow it. Like the heart chakra (number four out of seven), Justice becomes the place we need to go if we want to continue to a genuine death and rebirth (cards thirteen and fourteen, Death and Temperance) that can prepare us for the great revelations of the final seven cards.

We can look at Justice as a midpoint of our lives, no matter the time-line, for it is there that we really come to terms with who we are. We need to understand and finally accept the past in order to create a future, or as Stephen Karcher says about divination in general, Justice can free us from slavery to our conditioning. Another way to say all this is that Justice opens the heart.

For all these symbolic reasons, the image of Astraea works very well for the card, as well. But the woman with the scales also represents Ma'at, the weigher of hearts with her balanced scales. For this reason, many Egyptian-style Tarot decks show the actual moment when Ma'at and Thoth weigh the heart against the ostrich feather.

Justice from the Rider and Raziel decks

What does it mean, then, to open the heart? What closes it, and what weighs it down? How can we make our hearts as weightless as an ostrich feather and so open that divine energy can shine through them, as if they have become transparent? Why does a monster devour the heart that weighs itself down?

We speak of a kind person as openhearted, and a person without charity as someone who has closed the heart. In the story of Rebecca and the camel, we saw that gimalut chasidut, acts of lovingkindness, carry us across the Abyss, from the higher realms of the upper sephiroth into the heart of the Tree, Tiferet, with the implication that such acts can carry us back again. Kindness raises our spiritual awareness and makes us able to open ourselves.

In Kabbalist tradition, Tiferet is literally the heart of the Tree, for when we look at the sephiroth on the human body, we find Tiferet as the heart. Like the Egyptians, who saw the heart as the center of awareness, the Kabbalists considered the heart, not the head, as the seat of true knowledge.

The placement of knowledge in the heart matches yoga teachings. The description of the kundalini moving up the spine and out the top of the head simplifies a highly complicated technology of consciousness. As William Irwin Thompson writes in *The Time Falling Bodies Take to Light*, the communication between genitals and brain really focuses on male experience of deep meditation. The male yogi experiences both intense sexual arousal, without climax, and ecstasy focused in the brain.

For the female yogini, the vital connection runs between the womb and the heart, and the woman in deep meditative states finds a rapture that Thompson calls "an orgasm in the heart." He adds, "The sudden opening of the heart chakra causes an ecstatic experience of illumination; the heart of the woman becomes the center of the universe." The Sufis picture this experience as a winged heart. In Western culture, the most famous mythic representation comes in Gian Lorenzo Bernini's statue *The Ecstasy of Saint Teresa*. The saint lies in rapture, her head thrown back orgasmically, while an angel aims an arrow at her heart.

Thompson acknowledges that people can and do misuse the distinction between male and female bodily spirituality to "apologize," as he puts it, for patriarchal dominance of women. He points out, however, that when the yogi has opened "certain centers" in his brain, he learns to move his being to the heart, not the head. Ultimately, both women and men focus on the heart as the place where we open ourselves to the great love that fills the cosmos.

When I spoke with Julie Gillentine about the movement of the kundalini, she told me that it is a mistake to think of the energy as rising step by step from the base of the spine to the crown of the head. The adept learns to draw up the energy from below for the three lower chakras, but the higher energy comes down from above for the three higher centers. In this way the physical and the spiritual become united. As above, so below. The place where they meet—the border of above and below—is the heart.

The Ecstasy of Saint Teresa, by Gian Lorenzo Bernini

Kindness opens the heart because our natural state, our *sacred* state, is empathy or the sense of identification with others. We cannot expect to achieve oneness with the divine if we cannot find it with fellow creatures. This is why the Bible tells us to "Love your neighbor as yourself," and also "You shall love the Infinite your God with all your heart, and all your soul, and all your might." The two statements are the same, for they describe our natural condition when we do not close our hearts: to love the divine, love ourselves, and love each other.

We find the same idea in Wicca, in the statement "Do as you will and harm none." People sometimes find this contradictory, for they think of "do as you will" as arbitrary and selfish. But it really speaks of our condition of empathy. Wicca is a profoundly optimistic religion. Unlike more traditional organized religions it does not believe that we need to control people with rigid rules of morality and the fear of punishment. Instead, it trusts that the more we allow people to come to their true natures, the more they will harm none because that will indeed be their will.

Closing the Heart

At the same time, the world, and human culture with all its conditioning, does not always respond to kindness. From fear and confusion and the need to function in hard situations, we act against our basic nature. Sometimes it just seems to require too much from us to do what we know is right. We may feel that a certain job stifles us or requires us to act immorally (not illegally, but against our own sense of what is right), but to quit would mean to start all over. So we tell ourselves it's not that bad, it doesn't matter, we're just doing what's necessary.

The child, the infant, trusts the adult world to tell it what to do. Even when the instructions, or the life the adults give it, go against something deep inside, it listens to its parents and the messages of its culture. Inside, however, it knows that something is wrong. Inside it can feel the violation of the heart.

And yet, our instincts remain, always. We may feel a profound guilt, not just from social conditioning, but from feeling that we have betrayed who we are. Three things close the heart more strongly than any others: fear, guilt, and shame. These things come from within but also from without. We become ashamed when we do not follow our own truth, but also, very powerfully, when we discover that society and the people around us, especially our families, consider some aspect of our true selves unacceptable.

Many people must fight a constant battle against the shame of being the "wrong" color, the "wrong" religion, the "wrong" language, the "wrong" gender, the "wrong" sexuality. Contemporary terminology calls this self-hatred. In so many human cultures, virtually all girls learn shame just for being an "inferior," an unwanted, sex. Queer children, especially feminine boys and masculine girls, often face extreme physical danger just for behaving in ways that for them are natural. To avoid harm and ridicule and punishment, they try to conform. The price of this conformity, the denial of how they know they should live, is deep shame. The shame comes from outside, imposed by society's arbitrary values of good and bad, male and female, but also from inside, from the knowledge that they have betrayed their hearts.

Denial of our true selves is often deeper than the conscious compromises we make to get along in a hostile society. It can go back to infancy. The child instinctively loves the people and the world around it, and it expects love in return. It begins to deny itself when people, or simply existence, hurt it. It becomes confused and frightened. I believe that we all grow up with our instincts intact and an inner sense of how the world should be. We may not know this consciously. When our parents abuse us or simply withhold love, when we face cruelty and prejudice, when life is simply not the way we know deep down it should be, we become disoriented and fearful and begin to close down the heart.

At the deepest level, the process begins even earlier, in the first hours of life. We leave our mothers' bodies fully conscious, able to make eye contact and give and receive emotionally. But we have entered an entirely new universe, and within hours the mind of the infant shuts down.

We survive by learning the description of the world that our culture calls reality, including the variations that come from our parents or ethnic group or religion, all the external sources of information about life. We learn to see ourselves as separate from the universe and other people, contained and isolated in our bodies. This illusion protects us. To maintain it, however, we need to close down genuine—inner—awareness that the world is not really the way we have learned to think it is. We need to close off the information that comes from both above and below. To do this we close the heart, the center of instinct and knowledge, and seal it off.

Most of us close the heart so intensely we do not know, at least consciously, that we have done it. If we follow exercises meant to move energy through our bodies and out the top of the head—that is, open ourselves to existence as it really is—we may cause great disturbance. All that mix of fear and guilt and shame, all our unrecognized denials of our true nature, will resist exposure.

If the work is intense enough, the resistance can take on mythological form as a monster or demon. We can understand Ammut in this way, and also the Devil. The Hebrew word *Satan*, or *shaitan*, originally meant "adversary." He seems to have been a sort of prosecuting attorney accusing humans when they stray from the sacred way. How did this minor figure become the supernatural beast of Christian myth? Partly the idea of demons became a convenient way to attack the Pagan religions Christianity wanted to replace: they could not convince people that the Pagan Gods had never existed, so they denounced them as demons. But there also may have been a core of (distorted) psychic experience.

Imagine that a terrible figure appeared to early Christians who sought to "enter the kingdom of heaven" before they had truly opened the heart. They may have sought to absorb themselves into the divine "Father," as Jesus called God, without the cleansing necessary to free themselves of fear and shame. Such images are psychic projections, but they appear as real as they are terrifying.

When the Church began to solidify itself into a center of power, it formalized the Devil, constructed a mythology around the image, as a means to control people. (This is a simplified account of an important religious development, and I apologize for any distortions.)

We can put this problem in Tarot imagery and say that people who follow spiritual or meditative paths may try to go directly from the Chariot to the Devil and Tower. In other words, they believe that they can use a strong will to overcome all resistance and liberate spiritual light. But the Devil only feeds on such heroism. We will end up forging our own chains, for we cannot face this task before we have opened the heart and reached the level of Temperance. Possibly the desire to throw ourselves into intense magical experience is partly a desire to avoid self-knowledge.

The difference between exoteric and esoteric spirituality often comes down to an understanding of inner processes and states of awareness. As without, so within. What the outer religion describes as events—usually after death—the esotericist may understand as psychic states. So in Egypt the Book of the Dead seems to outline what happens in the Gods' judgement hall, with a monster that devours anyone whose heart cannot balance a feather. Modern people will read this account with amazement that anyone ever took it seriously. But the person used to symbolic texts reads an account of the need to free the heart in order to open consciousness.

In Christianity, too, the outer religion describes what happens after death. Those baptized in Christ survive the Last Judgement and enter the

Kingdom of Heaven; all others suffer eternal torment in Hell. But Jesus talked about cleansing and purification to enter the Kingdom in this life as much as in a world to come. Both the purification and the absolute commitment that Jesus demanded are approaches to open the heart. So is the famous statement to "become as a little child."

The Tarot adapts itself so well to so many esoteric traditions because it describes the process needed to move to spiritual transformation. The Tarot is not Egyptian or Kabbalist or Wiccan or Christian or Tantric. *It only can seem to be all of them by being none of them.* We can describe it instead as a map for the soul's journey from a narrow blinkered vision to the wide splendor of reality.

The Journey to Open the Heart

In the *Shining Tribe Tarot*, one particular card gives us a vision of the heart fully opened. The Seven of Trees (remember this card from the Easter reading?) shows the spinal column with the sun—the light of heaven—shining at the heart chakra. The column itself becomes a tree, the Tree of Life, now identified as the human body. The ganglia on either side become branches, for when we open our hearts to the sun, we discover our deep connections to all nature, not as a philosophical idea but as an experience deep within our bodies.

No head appears on top of the column. As we have seen, when the energy fully rises the head seems to vanish; we no longer believe in that strict border between ourselves and the world. Our senses no longer filter reality into a safe construction. We encounter the sacred winds of the cosmos in all its glory.

In the Tarot's middle line, cards eight to fourteen, we shift from the outer concerns of worldly success and willpower symbolized in the Chariot to the inner states symbolically shown in the angel of Temperance. As we have seen, however, the personal change does not represent the ultimate goal, though it may feel that way as we struggle with letting go of old ways and former values. In fact, the entire experience is a transition. We move from Strength to Temperance to allow ourselves to shift from personal outwardly directed consciousness in the Chariot to the path that will lead us to transcendent "super-consciousness" in the World.

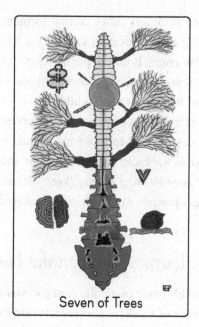

Seven of Trees

Seven of Trees from the Shining Tribe Tarot

Justice is the key, and the center of the line (at least in the Golden Dawn tradition), but it is not the only card to deal with these issues. The entire line, really, opens the heart so that we may ready ourselves to descend to the symbolic Devil and liberate the light of ecstatic love. We will follow the steps, briefly, and with the recognition that these descriptions form only one model for cards eight to fourteen. Many other interpretations exist, each with its own truth. The symbolic explication of the Tarot is not a competitive sport.

Strength shows us the basic commitment to open ourselves. It depicts the willingness to give up outer concerns and reach inward. It teaches us a passion for life, and for the world, that is deeply spiritual for it does not seek achievement or power but only love. The Hermit then begins to search inward. The traditional image of the Hermit often shows him on a mountain peak holding out his lantern, as if to light the way for others. We can imagine him on some rough climb away from the ordinary life to rare heights of wisdom. At the same time, we also can describe his lonely journey as a descent, for anytime we turn away from outer directedness and seek truth

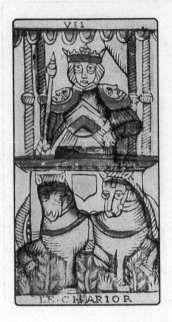

Chariot, Temperance, and the World from the Marseille deck

Chariot

Temperance

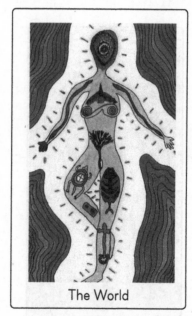

The World

Chariot, Temperance, and the World from the Shining Tribe Tarot

inside we make a descent through layers of culture, conditioning, and fear. As above, so below.

We can find a parallel to this ascent/descent in the meditative journeys of Jewish mystics (perhaps including Jesus) two thousand years ago. Before the formulations of Kabbalah, these early explorers would practice intense meditations based on the *Merkavah*, or chariot, vision of Ezekiel.

In the first edition of this book, I assumed that the Chariot was the vehicle of ascent. That is, Ezekiel gave such a detailed and precise description of the heavenly chariot that the mystics could visualize it as their own vehicle to move through seven heavenly "palaces" (for the seven planetary spheres). Since then, I have discovered that Ezekiel's Chariot was not the vehicle but the *goal*, for the rabbis considered that what the prophet saw was in fact the Throne of God.

When Robert M. Place and I created *The Raziel Tarot*, based on Jewish stories and teachings, I suggested we use Ezekiel's vision for the Chariot card. The image from traditional art is vastly complicated, but Robert had the inspiration to do a close-up that captured the essential details (see image on page 218).

Many of us have grown up with the image of God as a white-haired old man on a throne above the sky, and the image of a divine chariot conjures the vision of an ascent from the ground to the sky (paintings that show Elijah being taken to Heaven in a chariot indeed show it flying upward into the sky). And yet, the Merkavah mystics described their journeys as a *descent*: "The Descent to the Merkavah." They would indeed describe the movement through seven celestial "palaces" (which I take to be the seven planetary spheres of astrology), and yet the entire journey was seen as a going down.

Perhaps we might say that to travel such pathways we first must meditate into ourselves. Only then will we find the doorways to other worlds. The Hermit may stand on a mountaintop, but he shines his light into the depths.

We could describe the Wheel of Fortune as what the Hermit sees. The Wheel displays a vision, both of the person's individual life and of the mysteries of existence. Whether we call it the wheel of karma, or fate, or the seasons, or simply the cycles of life from birth to maturity to death, the image of a wheel draws people into a sense of destiny. In many decks, symbolic images surround the Wheel of Fortune. We may see a sphinx or other mythological

The Chariot from the Raziel deck

The Merkavah, the "chariot vision" of Ezekiel

figures. Winged creatures in the corners may represent the four "fixed" signs of the zodiac or the four evangelists of the New Testament. Animals, such as monkeys, may climb up and down the wheel.

After the vision comes the acceptance. Where the Wheel of Fortune impresses us with its symbols, Justice looks directly at us, its message clear: Weigh your life in the balance. Be honest. Accept who you are and what made you. Justice can be hard, powerful, frightening, deeply sorrowful. And yet, ultimately the experience is intensely joyous, for Justice liberates us. As in other situations we've encountered in these explorations, we need to remember that joy is not necessarily the same as happiness or pleasure.

In the same weekly class where Ioanna Salajan declared "Nothing is learned except through joy," we often entered into past pains and traumas. I remember one class especially where we went into old experiences of anger and saw the way even righteous anger would dance with fear, shame, and the ancient history of our childhoods and even infancy. The joy of Justice is the excitement and wonder of genuine freedom through truth. Through Justice we open our hearts, first to ourselves, then to those close to us, even those we think we've harmed and who have harmed us, and finally to both the sorrow and the beauty of the world.

Justice from the Rider and Raziel decks

When we open the heart to Justice, we discover something amazing. We do not have to face the hugeness of existence all by ourselves. The sense of a tiny isolated self alone in a cold universe becomes an illusion, and we discover ourselves connected to what people in Alcoholic Anonymous and other twelve-step programs call "a power greater than ourselves."

In the Egyptian after-death, the person who has passed the test, whose heart carries no burdens and so does not weigh down an ostrich feather, becomes dressed in the clothes of the God in preparation for passage to a greater existence. They do not *become* the God, whose costume they wear, but become *attached* to the God, in the deepest sense possible. This attachment carries the soul through death to new life.

In the Greater Mysteries of Eleusis, the celebrants—as many as several thousand—did not dress as Persephone, the Goddess who dies and returns (the Star card), even though the message was that death would not be permanent for them. Like the followers of Osiris, they too would pass through death to a greater existence. Instead, they all wore the mourning shroud of Demeter, Persephone's mother (the Empress card). When the nine-day ceremony had ended, the shrouds were cut up into swaddling clothes for newborn babies.

In the Tarot we find this profound attachment in the card of the Hanged Man. Most people who look at this card see the reversed position before anything else. Watch someone who doesn't know Tarot look through a deck; they will turn the Hanged Man card around, thinking it's the wrong way. Among the many possible meanings for this reversal, we find two important ideas. For the first, the initiate now follows a path so different from most of society that they will seem the wrong way around. The second reversal is really the same, but internal. The Hanged Man hangs upside down because he looks inward for truth, rather than out. Like the Hermit and the Merkavah journeyers, he has learned a great secret: the opening to vast worlds lies inside yourself, and to look up you must look down.

For many, inward vision comes with great difficulty, especially if the ego resists surrender to that sense of life beyond your own resources. This may be why so many people find the Hanged Man a disturbing image or assume it means suffering. The actual image on most cards is not disturbing. If we look at the very earliest version of it that we know, the Visconti-Sforza Tarot from around 1450, we see a beatific expression and no pain.

The Norse myth of Odin and the Runes illustrates the extreme steps necessary sometimes to turn attention inward and down. The Scandinavian God Odin sought the runes, a magical alphabet used for divination, spell casting, protection, and the greatest magic of all, writing. The runes lay in darkness, deep within the Well of Mimir, a God of knowledge. To compel Mimir to give up the treasure, Odin wounded himself in the side (a possible reference to meditative sexual disciplines) and tied himself to Yggdrasil, the World Tree, for nine days and nights. (The number nine has great mythic resonances, to the Great Year of 25,920 years—$2 + 5 + 9 + 2 + 0 = 18 = 1 + 8 = 9$—and to the nine lunar cycles of human pregnancy.)

Finally, Odin plucked out his right eye and threw it down into the well. While Mimir accepted his sacrifice, Odin reached down and snatched up the runes. The right side often signifies reason or outer consciousness, the left intuition or inward consciousness. (There are no universal symbols, but this distinction between right and left shows up around the world, supported by some modern brain research.) In other words, Odin had to go to extreme lengths to reverse his spiritual direction.

Artist Hermann Haindl views Odin's violent self-sacrifice as ego resistance, as well as the arrogance of separation from the Earth. For Haindl, the World Tree signifies nature, and Odin a culture—European primarily—that tries to force nature to give up its secrets. To illustrate the possibility of an alternative, Haindl actually painted Odin twice. The usual violent tale shows up as the King of Cups, while a joyous unmaimed Odin gives himself to the Earth in the Hanged Man.

While many people's first glance at the card of the Hanged Man focuses on the upside-down figure, the Tree is at least as important. Whether an upside-down *T* (a so-called *tau* cross, after the last letter in the Hebrew alphabet) or a branch or a fully flowering tree or a beam of wood, the Tree signifies finding a power greater than individual ego. Through this attachment we can go beyond our limitations. We can die.

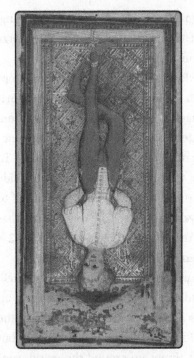
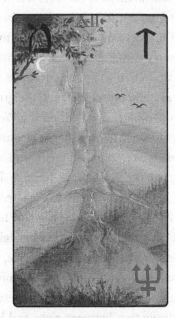

The Hanged Man from the Visconti-Sforza and Haindl decks

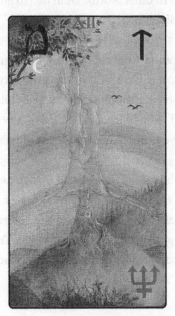

The Hanged Man and King of Cups from the Haindl deck

The Delicious Word "Death"

It may seem like a bad deal that Death follows the Hanged Man. Imagine a Tarot promotional campaign: "Surrender to higher consciousness and die!" Luckily, the Hanged Man does not look at things from the point of view of advertising (if he did, he would not be upside down). Death means release, freedom from past limitations. Rather than come before Justice, as in the Egyptian myth, death comes after surrender, and so it comes gently, without any Ammut to devour us.

But we need to be careful that we do not take it all too easily. Most modern Tarot readers will turn over the card of Death and rush to tell their questioners not to worry, no one is about to die, it just means the death of old ways, or as I've sometimes characterized the way we think of it, the-death-of-the-old-self.

The hyphens in that phrase indicate a glibness we sometimes assume about Death. We make it comfortable and safe when we assure ourselves that Death means a wonderful liberation of our best qualities, as if our superior sensitivity makes it easy for us to go through it. Death does come easily to the person who truly has opened the heart and attached themself to the Tree of Life, but most of us have not gone through those deep experiences of release and connection. So while Death liberates, it also frightens.

These are primarily psychological views of the Death card. We can take it to a more mythic or shamanic level, and indeed it often seems to me that such approaches are truer—and less comfortable—than the psychological. One hint of the kind of power found in Death is that in so many Tarot decks Death is the most evocative picture.

Partly this reflects Death as the Great Unknown, and therefore an opportunity for artists' imaginations to take flight. That very mystery can give Death its power. Once again we can cite all the esoteric traditions that clothe themselves in stories of the afterlife. Looked at structurally, the Egyptian story of the weighing of the heart and the Christian of entering the Kingdom of Heaven become remarkably similar, and both take place after death. In Pagan tradition as well, stories of psychic transformation often describe events that supposedly happen in "the Otherworld," also called the Land of the Dead.

Death

Death from the Rider, Marseille, and Shining Tribe decks

To fully open the heart, even beyond the honesty of Justice, to really experience the power of released energy, we must embrace death—once again, not as an idea but as an experience. We must invite it to us with arms open and minds clear. Jesus goes willingly to the cross when he so easily could have changed the course of events. The Greek Goddess Persephone, kidnapped by Hades and then liberated, eats several pomegranate seeds in the Underworld (the number varies in different tellings). Even though the Homeric Hymn describes this as a trick of Hades, the God of the dead, I and many other modern commentators believe that Persephone eats the seeds deliberately, to signal her willingness to return each year to give new life to the souls who move through her mysteries.

The lure and sensuality of psychic death emerges in Walt Whitman's magnificent account of his poetic awakening "Out of the Cradle, Endlessly Rocking." Whitman was America's most mystical poet, and also the most earthy. To those of us raised in traditions that see soul and body as enemies, Whitman's passion for the sacred and the sensual may seem strange. But Whitman, like the Persian poet Rumi or the composer of the *Song of Songs*, understood that to truly love God we must love the world, with all its joys and challenges. This is one reason why the card of the Lovers comes early in the Major Arcana, for without passion our spiritual devotions remain lifeless. Doreen Valiente evoked this idea beautifully in her ritual poem "Charge of the Goddess," in which the Goddess declares "All acts of love and pleasure are my rituals."

In "Out of the Cradle," Whitman describes how as a boy he watched two birds by the sea sing their love for each other. Every day he would go watch and listen. Then, one day the "she-bird" vanished, "may-be kill'd," and never returned. For the rest of the summer, the "he-bird" sings out across the ocean waves, as if the water somehow has taken his beloved. Those readers who know Greek myth will recognize the story of the poet-seer Orpheus, yet another variant on the widespread myth of the search for the lover taken into the Underworld.

Orpheus lost his Eurydice to death and failed to bring her back when his nerve failed. When he himself died, torn apart by wild women, his head survived, floating on the waves forever to sing of his lost love.

As the child listens to the bird, he discovers, "Now in a moment I knew what I came for. I awoke" as "a thousand songs . . . started to life within me, never to die." But if the bird has aroused poetry and longing in the child, he knows that a greater truth, "a word . . . supreme to all" lies within the sound of the sea, our original mother. And so he begs the waves, "If I am to have so much let me have more!"

The sea answers him, "Whisper'd to me through the night ... the low and delicious word death/And again, death, death, death, death." From that hour, Whitman wrote, his own songs truly awakened.

We cannot embrace Death with the careful thought that we only do so to get the good stuff afterward. Such knowledge helps with our fear, but in fact it will not work if we look right past Death, if we see it only as death-of-the-old-self. We must love Death and join with it.

If we align the seven middle cards of the Major Arcana with the seven chakras of the body, then Death, chakra six, becomes the third eye. In the row above, the Lovers opens the sixth chakra, while below Death, in the final row of seven, the third eye opens for Judgement, or in the *Shining Tribe Tarot*, Awakening. It is no accident that the vertical sequence runs love, death, resurrection. We might describe true liberation as the moment when these three experiences fuse together into one. Maybe this is why Isis points to the sixth chakra, because she knows that we cannot discover our true selves until we have embraced this great trio: to love with all our hearts, to give ourselves to death, and to awaken to light.

And after Death comes the final release, the angel of Temperance. Aleister Crowley called this card "Art," and some modern decks, such as the *Haindl Tarot*, label it "Alchemy." As described above, some people find this card dull. After all we've been through, after Death itself, our reward is to stay calm and balanced? I confess that when I first looked through the Rider cards years ago, I did not respond immediately to Temperance as I did to, say, the Magician or the Star.

The change in my visual response (as compared to symbolic analysis) came when I realized that the wings unfurled so powerfully the picture could not contain them. Intense energy flows through a serene state. Many of us think that serenity means we have to close ourselves down, not let life get to us. We assume we must avoid passion in order to stay serene—untouched. But imagine a state in which you could allow the strongest emotions to move through you, take firm action whenever necessary (after all, this is the angel who threw Satan down into Hell), love, cry, and dance and never lose your ground, your knowledge of who you are and what really matters. Imagine that you *know*, not as an idea but as knowledge in every part of your body, and every action and every emotion, that the divine moves through you like a river. Or like a stream of bright water that passes from one cup to another.

Our culture has stripped angels of their original power and turned them into fluffy little guardians or wise upholders of moral virtue. The ancients who created this tradition recognized angels as beings of immense power, filled with the glory of God. As the Gnostic literary critic Harold Bloom described in his book *Omens of Millennium*, angels originally were not sexless. They included male and female angels, and they not only made love, they reproduced.

Nor did people simply make them up as a clever symbolic device. Ancient mystics and artists *saw* angels and talked with them in shamanic journeys and in mystical meditations, like the "descent" to the Merkavah. Many modern psychics continue this tradition when they speak of getting messages from "angels and guides." Interestingly, if we remember the Hebrew way of looking at only consonants as official letters, *God*, *Good*, and *Guide* are all the same word—*GD* (which of course, is the way some often refer to the Hermetic Order of the *G*olden *D*awn).

Temperance from Rider and Shining Tribe decks

Trump fourteen is not a vision of something out beyond ourselves. We have gone past that. Temperance is the angelic part of you, that part that thrills to eternity without ever losing track of time or responsibility. Temperance is what you can become if you open your heart and embrace Death.

A Reading to Open the Heart

We need to remember when we work with the Tarot that it does two things for us. First, the story of the cards, the symbolic sequence from the Fool to the World, plus each suit in its order, teaches us traditions of wisdom. If we want to learn what it can mean to open the heart, we can identify this concept with the card of Justice and then extend it on either side to the seven cards that form the middle of the Major Arcana. That's the first thing. The second, however, is the possibility for us to apply the concept directly to our own lives. We do that with readings.

When we read the cards based on ideals of sacred transformation, we tend to "step down" the energy, or at least the grand ideas, to our actual lives. This does not make readings shallow, for when we deal with the reality of who we are and what we have faced in our experience, we can come to profound discoveries. Divination brings us to the possibility of true liberation, for in divination we go beyond theories to an honest look at the actual gifts and forces that have shaped us.

Here then on page 229 is a reading spread to open your heart in your daily life. The positions come from discussions between myself and my friend Zoe Matoff.

Here are the positions:

```
        4

6   3   1   5   7

        2
```

1. What is the heart of my heart? We chose this expression to emphasize that we want to look at a person's essence. What makes a person unique? What are their challenges and opportunities?

2. What closes the heart? What past experience or fear or repression keeps these special gifts hidden? What narrows the person's life and leaves them in that blind tunnel where awareness of life's wonders becomes darkened?

3. What surrounds or obscures the heart? What layers have built up around that initial closure? What must the person clear away to get back that unique connection between the self and the world?

4. What is my heart's aspiration? Zoe and I discussed this one for some time. We wanted position four to act as a pivot for the whole reading, the place where we shift from what closes the heart to what opens it. As card four of seven, it represents the heart itself, and thus the core of the issue. Zoe suggested the idea of aspiration. What does the essential heartself desire? To put it another way, what does Spirit call a person to do? Here it is important to see the card as something positive. With the Rider Five of Pentacles (the beggars outside the church), for example, we might be called on to help those who suffer.

5. What will help open it? To begin the process of self-discovery, we need help to get past our fears or guilt or shame. This card may represent a quality that will help the heart seeker or some spiritual energy that they might envision as a Goddess or God, or even an actual person, such as a teacher, counselor, or friend the seeker can trust with deep confidence. As with card four, if the card here is challenging, we should not reject it. Often the qualities that we shy away from can act most powerfully.

6. What will carry me through? In most cases, the process of self-discovery takes time. Just as the initial steps are difficult or fearful, so the journey as a whole can require special qualities to help the person not retreat behind layers of protection and avoidance.

7. What will I experience? The cards cannot, and should not, tell us everything that will happen, for the open heart experiences life as constant wonder. At the same time, a sense of what we might find can inspire us to continue.

Thirteen

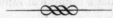

A Short Leap to the Place
of the Fool

An interesting problem comes up over and over in Tarot history. Where do we put the Fool? We would think that as zero it precedes one and would go at the beginning. The Golden Dawn did indeed place it there, and most modern decks have followed their example, but the problem is not as simple as it seems. Zero means nothing and implies no fixed place. In many versions of the card game tarocchi, the Fool seems to occupy no precise place in the hierarchy; you can play it to avoid being forced to give up a high-value card, but it has no value of its own. By comparison, the Fool's "cousin," the Joker, can become anything, but only when placed alongside other cards. By itself it doesn't exist (if we were to interpret playing cards in the same psychological way we interpret Tarot, we might call the Joker the ultimate codependent).

Most modern interpretations of the Fool describe the card as a journeyer who travels through all the other cards. They all stay in their places, but the Fool dances from one to the next. It's fascinating to see how many people who explore the Major Arcana describe it as "The Fool's Journey." Often they arrive at this expression independently, with no realization that others have come up with the same expression. Disclosure: I have used this expression in *Seventy-Eight Degrees of Wisdom*, but I will not pretend that everyone who has used it since has gotten it from me.

The problem becomes acute, however, when we look at the Kabbalist interpretation of the Tarot. This approach depends on fitting the twenty-two cards to the twenty-two Hebrew letters, and through the letters the twenty-two pathways on the Tree of Life. In the Hebrew alphabet, every letter and word has a numerical value. No letter in the Hebrew alphabet signifies zero. They begin with one and continue on to the end. Similarly, no pathway on the Tree of Life carries the symbolic idea of nothingness. The pathways go in order: one to twenty-two. Nothingness is sometimes seen as an aspect of the unknowable divine energy beyond the Tree, called *Ain Soph*, Without Limit. But this idea does not help us place the card of the Fool, for if we remove it from the Tree proper, there are no longer twenty-two cards for the twenty-two pathways.

What effect does it have that the Fool is zero and the first Hebrew letter/pathway is one? Well, if you make card zero the first letter, then card *one* becomes letter *two*, and card two becomes letter three, and so on all the way to the end, with the card that bears the number twenty-one—the World—as the representation for the twenty-second letter and pathway on the Tree. This clearly sets up a problem. Many times in classes or workshops I have seen how confused people can become when I try to explain that card two, the High Priestess, with all the symbolism of twoness (duality, female openings, etc.), in fact represents the third letter, *gimel*, that camel that carries us down the longest pathway on the Tree of Life, which is, of course, pathway three. See? It's confusing even to read, isn't it?

For the Tarot Kabbalist, this becomes much more than a curiosity or even a philosophical problem. If you accept that the Tree diagrams existence itself and that the cards give you the key to understand that diagram, and still more, to make use of it for magic or mystical enlightenment, then it becomes vitally important to figure out just where the cards go on the pathways. In that enterprise, the place of the Fool becomes a significant question.

There are other questions. The Golden Dawn switched the numbers, and therefore the pathways, for Strength and Justice. Crowley switched the Hebrew letter designations, and pathways, for the Emperor and the Star. (Crowley kept the traditional numbers on the cards, which created its own confusion, since the Hebrew letters for those two cards no longer corresponded to their numbers.) But the Fool has the capacity to shift everything around.

Éliphas Lévi solved the problem by making the Fool next to last. That way, only the last card, the World, moves one number out of place; that is, card twenty-one becomes letter and pathway twenty-two. All the other cards, from the Magician to Judgement, follow the same sequence as the letters. The Magician, card one, becomes letter one. Judgement, card twenty, becomes letter twenty. Lévi could have made the Fool the very last card, which would have given the World, card twenty-one, the twenty-first letter. The World, however, seems so clearly the final card, the culmination, that it becomes difficult to think of it as anything but the last card.

Another reason to make the Fool card twenty is that letter twenty, called *shin*, means "tooth" in traditional Hebrew symbolism. Many of the older Tarot decks depict the Fool as someone bitten by an animal.

The Hebrew letter shin *and the Fool from the Marseille deck*

At the same time, the symbolism of a letter, and its use in Tarot, does not always depend on its original Hebrew meaning. The first letter, *aleph*, literally means "ox," but most Kabbalists do not focus much attention on that image. Other qualities matter more, such as the fact that the *aleph* is silent (more about this in a moment). When A. E. Waite designed the Rider deck, he instructed Pamela Smith to paint the Fool in a posture that resembled the letter itself. The animal remained, but changed from a hostile cat to a friendly dog. The body's movement, and its position at the edge of what looks like a cliff, suggested the idea of a fall from a high place.

The Hebrew letter aleph *and the Fool from the Rider deck*

The Fool was the first card I drew for my *Shining Tribe Tarot.* Impressed by a painting I'd seen of a child with its arms out, I drew the Fool as a young child who has leapt off a cliff to follow a bird. In its unconscious purity, the child flies across a wide landscape toward a range of mountains.

It always seemed unsatisfactory to me to insert the Fool between the last two cards. Possibly I felt this way because I began my Tarot explorations with the Rider deck and

The Fool from the Shining Tribe Tarot

so absorbed the idea of the Fool as the beginning. I went on to develop the idea of the Fool as actually apart from all the other cards, the character that moves through them. The Fool to me represents the energy that resists complacency. When we come to some valuable place, such as the Chariot, where we might want to stop or tell ourselves we've reached the ultimate success, the Fool pushes us onward. Only a Fool would give up the power and control of the Chariot and go on to open the heart in cards eight through fourteen. And having reached the angelic state of Temperance, only a Fool would then descend into the realm of the Devil.

Aside from the symbolic attractions of the Fool as the first card, it always seemed awkward to me to insert the Fool next to last, as if we could not figure out what else to do with it, like the eccentric relative at a family party. Some time ago, however, I began to think about what it might mean for the Fool to appear between Judgement and the World. The more I thought about it, the more interesting it became—not as a replacement for the Fool at the beginning, but in addition. In other words, we can think of the Fool as the start of the journey, and then again as a necessary step before the final liberation, a leap from the Awakening of card twenty to the cosmic consciousness of card twenty-one.

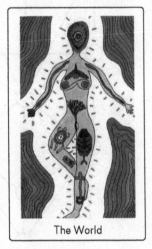

Awakening

The Fool

The World

Awakening, the Fool, and the World from the Shining Tribe Tarot

I realize that this approach does not solve the Kabbalist number-letter problem. We might say that it makes it worse with the addition of what amounts to an extra card. Readers of this book probably will have guessed, however, that symbolic *meaning* concerns me much more than symbolic *structure*. Since I consider the Tree of Life an image and not a scientific description, I would rather play with many possible meanings than insist on one absolute truth.

The fact is, there are several different versions of the Tree itself (the sephiroth remain in the same place, but the twenty-two pathways differ a good deal), and the Tree that most Tarotists consider universal truth actually varies significantly from the one found in traditional Jewish Kabbalism.

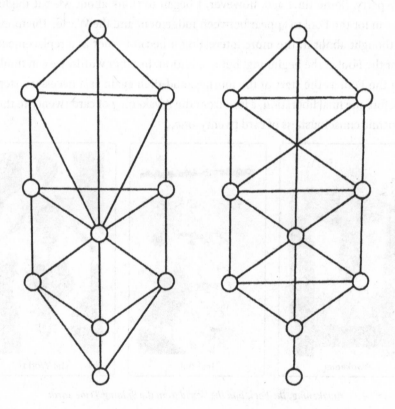

The Tarot Tree (left) and Luria Tree (right)

So let us look at some meanings for the Fool, both as the start of the whole process and in that odd place between the last two cards.

Maybe we should change the first part of that description—not the start, but the card *before* the start. The Fool is zero, after all, and zero means "nothing." If you are nothing, then you are no-thing, that is, not any fixed definition or category. When people try to pigeonhole us or attach us to their own ideas or their group identities, the Fool reminds us that none of these things can really pin us down. So it is with the Major Arcana as well. Zero sets the Fool apart from all the specific numbers that come after it. One, two, three, and all the rest all have very special qualities. The Fool journeys through all of them but remains . . . nothing.

Through quantum physics, we have learned to acknowledge that reality is not as solid and unchangeable as it appears to our everyday senses. I happen to be writing these words in a hardbound notebook on a wooden table in the second floor of a house in Minneapolis. All these things appear solid and fixed. But in fact, if I could perceive reality at its deepest level, I would recognize the book and the table and the house (and the city of Minneapolis) as a field of particles that are themselves part matter and part waves of energy. These wavicles are not really *things* but probabilities that "collapse" into reality when a consciousness observes them.

This makes the Fool truer than all the other cards. The Magician, the High Priestess, and all the others, in a sense signify those various moments when energy collapses into specific realities. Years ago, I read a wonderful quantum description of an electron: "nothing spinning." We might describe the Fool—and ultimately ourselves—as nothing dancing or flying. The Fool as the beginning card dances and flies, as well as jumps.

Let us play a moment with the idea that the Fool can exist in old mythologies. So we might say that when Thoth creates the Tarot to gamble with the Moon and create five new days outside the calendar, he can do so because the spirit of the Fool has entered him. Like a gambler, the Fool takes chances. It leaps. It refuses the demand to become safely *Something*, and remains, dangerously, *Nothing*.

As the first card, the Fool takes on the Hebrew letter *aleph*. Aside from its appearance as a leaping or flying child, the *aleph's* most interesting characteristic is that it actually makes no sound. It exists in words only as a carrier for vowels. By itself, the *aleph* creates a mouth that opens and makes no noise, like a blank canvas whose emptiness contains the potential for all possible paintings. The silence of the *aleph* makes it the perfect expression of the Fool's zero. Zero, no-thing, carries all possible things. This is one reason why modern Arabic numerals draw zero in the shape of an egg. (The oldest representation was as a point.)

We have looked a number of times at the Tree of Life and its importance in Tarot. The Kabbalists teach that the sephiroth emanate from God and contain God's essence in different aspects, but God's totality remains beyond the Tree, without limitation or definition. As mentioned above, they call this divine totality Ain Soph, "Without Limit." Now, the first letter of *Ain* is *aleph,* and so mathematicians use the *aleph* as the symbol for infinity. Infinity and zero, everything and nothing, are really the same, for both exist outside normal consciousness, indeed, outside normal reality.

As described earlier, Jewish and Kabbalist tradition consider the four-letter name of God unpronounceable. This does not mean that we've lost the secret of how it sounds, but that the human mind, with its limitations of language and culture, cannot encompass God's name. (The four letters actually form a variant of the verb *to be, to exist,* but in a form outside any grammatical tense or person.) Modern Kabbalists sometimes describe the Name as a breath rather than a sound. The mouth opens to breathe life into the universe. This nonsound, this open mouth breath, also describes the silent *aleph.*

Here is a myth that expresses the power of *aleph.* I do not present it as a literal account but as a story that can help us grasp what silence can mean to us.

The Bible tells us that all the Israelites assembled at the foot of Mt. Sinai to hear the voice of God give the ten commandments. All the other commandments on how to live and be holy, some 613 of them, God gave to Moses and Moses passed them on to the people, but the people themselves heard the basic ten.

But how much did they hear? Did they hear every word or just a portion? The full experience might have so overwhelmed them that maybe the divine voice only spoke the most essential part to the mass of people. That way, they would know the reality of God and still survive.

Like the Tree of Life, with its three higher and seven lower sephiroth, the ten commandments (the Hebrew phrase actually means ten statements) separate into three declarations of holiness (e.g., Honor the Sabbath and keep it holy) and seven moral directives (e.g., You shall not commit adultery). For this reason, some people who looked at this question said that the Israelites only heard God speak the first three, and then Moses conveyed the other seven. But were all three necessary? The first statement runs "I am the Infinite, your God, who brought you out of slavery in the land of Egypt." (This is the Jewish version—some Christian Bibles have the first one slightly different.) Surely this announcement of God's reality was enough to let everyone experience the divine power that fills all our lives.

Or maybe more than enough. Why not simply the word "I am" (*anokhi* in Hebrew)? Imagine yourself part of the people in the desert. Your leader Moses claims to speak to God and then let you know what God wants. Like everyone else, you wonder about this claim, but you have to admit that Moses has performed some amazing stunts. The plagues, the splitting of the sea— well, they were certainly impressive, however he did them. Now he's climbed a mountain and disappeared into rock and clouds, with some promise that God will speak, not just to Moses but to everyone. And that includes you.

Nervously, you look up. Thick clouds gather all around the peak. Great bolts of lightning tear open the dark sky. Your weaknesses, your vulnerability, all your narrow outlooks on life, they dart through your mind and then vanish as you look at that great sky in astonishment. And then—a voice booms through the lightning. Louder than an earthquake, softer than a mother's whisper to her sleeping child, it fills the sky, penetrates the Earth, sounds through every particle of your body. **I AM**. Would you really need to hear any more? Would you *want* to hear any more?

Ah, but wait. The mystics took it a step further, as they so often do. Why the whole word? they asked. Why not just the first letter? Wouldn't that alone fill people with the knowledge of divine existence? Only—the first letter of *anokhi*, "I am," is *aleph*. The silent letter. Without the addition of a vowel, it doesn't even make the sound "ah." Like the Fool's zero, the silence of the *aleph* contains everything, and that *silence* becomes the ultimate truth.

With so much symbolism and story to support the Fool as the start of the Major Arcana, why would we even consider a move to next to last? But remember, we do not have to *move* it, we can *add* it. If we look for meaning, then the Fool only gains if we consider it in both its traditional places. And we may discover a connection or relationship between the two ideas.

We begin as nothing and move into something. Alan Moore, in his wondrous comic book series *Promethea*, which is partly Tarot based, describes the creation of the universe—something out of nothing—as the ultimate act of magic. Significantly, the second Hebrew letter, *beth,* which means "house," begins the Bible, and therefore the story of creation. The famous phrase "In the beginning" translates the Hebrew word *B'raishith.* In other words, *beth* begins the physical something out of the nothingness of original existence. Remember, too, that *gimel* follows, the woman with the camel who travels the long road from the "supernal" world of divine principles down to the more accessible world of human understanding. So after Nothing we begin our journey through various stages of Something, more and more complex until—

We come to card twenty, Judgement, or Awakening, or Aeon, as Crowley called it.

Aeon from the Thoth deck

Judgement from the Marseille deck, and Awakening from the Shining Tribe Tarot

After the card of rebirth, or "regeneration," to use Paul Foster Case's term for Judgement, do we just move smoothly into the state of divine consciousness depicted in the World? It seems to me that a radical break occurs between Judgement and the World. Judgement continues the long sequence of somethings. It culminates them, but it also belongs to them. The World is not just a better or more complete Something. In the same way that the Fool is Nothing, the World is Everything.

We do not get to Everything by accumulating more Somethings. In fact, we need to let go of all those specific states of awareness that began with the Magician and the High Priestess and moved to Judgement. To really free ourselves, to really know Everything, we first must return to Nothing. For as we saw with the number zero and God's silent thunder at Mt. Sinai, *Nothing* contains *Everything*. In Tarot, the letter *aleph* signifies zero; in mathematics it means infinity. Divide any number by zero and you get infinity. On a National Public Radio program, I heard someone describe the singularity that existed before the universe as "God divided by zero."

Lévi's placement of the Fool contains great wisdom, for we need the Fool's freedom to gain the World. That wisdom becomes truest, however,

The Fool

Magician

High Priestess

The Fool, Magician, and High Priestess from the Shining Tribe Tarot

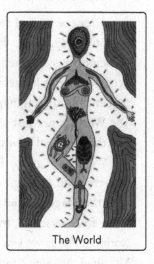

Awakening

The Fool

The World

Awakening, the Fool, and the World from the Shining Tribe Tarot

when we also place the Fool at the beginning. And since the Fool is zero, why not allow it to go wherever it can do the most good?

Along with the idea of Nothing, we find the symbolism of the fall, or leap, from a high place. In the Rider version, we see a white sun, to indicate spiritual light. So what does this fall mean? Does it refer to the "big mistake" Adam and Eve made when they ate from the wrong tree? And what is the difference between a fall and a jump?

We are going to spend a little time here looking at the most famous story of a fall in Western culture, the loss of Paradise in the Garden of Eden story. Some readers may reject this tale, almost on principle, as something they learned in Sunday school, used by religious leaders to control people. Others may wonder what it has to do with Tarot. I will ask readers to bear with me, for the story, especially in its more subtle meanings, has greatly influenced Western esoteric thought, and therefore the Tarot.

Stories of what happened long ago are a lot like stories of what happens after death. They arise partly from the need to explain facts about the world and partly as outer expressions of inner discoveries. The story of a fall from paradise gives an explanation for the fact that life is so unsatisfying. We live a short time; we get sick or debilitated; our relationships turn to bitterness; good people get cancer . . . and the yearning that many of us feel to know divinity directly meets only silence and a universe so vast we become less than insignificant. In the face of all this pain does it seem strange that people would develop a story of a perfect time ruined by some stupid mistake?

And yet, there is more going on in this story than a justification for life's miseries. For one thing, the basic intuition of myth often gets clothed in what we might call politics. This would seem to be the case with embellishments in the story of Adam and Eve. The issue of disobedience, and Eve's weakness and God's curse, often gets used to support such ideologies as the command to women to submit to men or the treatment of nature as an enemy or the authority of a priesthood that can threaten people with eternal torture. And since the Goddess-centered religions of Canaan used groves of trees as ritual spaces to the Goddess Asherah, the story of fruit from a forbidden tree may have helped the Hebrew priesthood turn the people against their rivals, the priesthood of Asherah.

Still there is more. If origin myths reflected nothing more than explanations or politics, they never would last for thousands of years. A deeper perception lies in such tales. That perception comes to us articulated by mystics and hinted at by psychologists and, increasingly, by scientists. The perception is this: what we think of as reality is an illusion. Our true state lies in a kind of flow and oneness with all existence. In our genuine existence, light fills the world and us. In fact, we cannot really say that light *fills* the world, for we ourselves become pure light, a "light" that can be expressed physically in dark night as well as sunshine, and the distinction between our own sense of self and the divine presence simply vanishes.

If all this sounds idealistic, or just fantastic, please put aside your doubts for a moment (we will come back to these questions shortly) and pretend that the mystics have got it right. How, then, did we lose our sense of our true state? This is where the distinction between a fall and a jump comes in. If we have fallen into a world of separation and isolation, then either we did something very bad or very stupid. The Bible story, at least on the surface, lies on the very bad side. Adam and Eve had the chance to live in Paradise with God, and ruined it all by disobedience. But what sort of God demands obedience as a price for perfection? And if they needed the fruit to understand right from wrong, *and* the fruit (the Bible never says "apple") came from the Tree of Knowledge of Good and Evil, then how would they have known they were making a mistake? To put it another way, they could only have disobeyed if they already had separated their consciousness from the Creator.

What about the rest of us? Saint Augustine, hyperaware of his own human weakness, developed the idea of original sin inherited from one generation to the next, all the way back to Adam. If Augustine had known about genetics, he might have said our DNA carried the sin. Instead, he claimed the inherited sin lies in the father's semen. For Augustine, our conception in sex fills us with Adam's sin, and only Christ's sacrifice can erase it.

By contrast, the early rabbis rejected the idea of inherited sin. They could hardly see sex as a transmission of evil, for the first commandment in the Bible tells humans to "go forth and multiply." So they suggested that our *own* sins deny us paradise and eternal life. Adam sinned once, they say, and had to die; we disobey all the time, so what else should we expect? (Interestingly, they do not blame Eve at all; God gave Adam the instructions, the rabbis argue, and Adam did not convey them correctly to Eve, so he gets the blame.)

Some later Kabbalists looked more in the direction of stupidity. The original being, the hermaphroditic *Adam Kadmon*, looked upon the Tree of Life and became entranced by the final sephirah, Malkuth (Hebrew for "kingdom," as in "the kingdom of this world"). Because Adam made the mistake of taking Malkuth for the entire Tree, s/he became separated from the divine consciousness, and also divided in two, as (fallen) Adam and Eve. (Kabbalist myth tells us that the two halves had been joined at the rib, and so were separated there, giving rise to the biblical account that Eve came from Adam's rib.)

In the Kabbalist view, we repeat that same illusion, generation after generation. We do not see reality but only its most obvious aspect, and think that we see everything. This idea resembles the Buddhist doctrine that we separate ourselves from divine bliss when we allow desire to create ego.

All these concepts and stories make up the belief in a fall from a divine state to a state of illusion and isolation. The most extreme versions of this belief speak of physical existence, matter, as a prison for the pure light of our genuine nature. The Gnostics, a sect of early Christians, developed a myth that the God of Genesis was a false deity who created the world as a trap for free souls. In their view, the serpent becomes the hero of the story, for its attempt to liberate Adam and Eve with knowledge. (The word *gnosis* is Greek for "knowledge.") While many people will identify with the concept of a rebellion against a God who demands obedience, the Gnostics went on to describe the world, and bodies, in the most negative terms. Occult doctrine has inherited this bias against the physical.

Some mythologists and feminists, notably Joseph Campbell and Merlin Stone, author of *When God Was a Woman*, have developed a different way to reinterpret the Genesis myth. They point out that before patriarchal religion, people worshipped Earth Goddesses in groves and gardens. Snakes often figured as the companions of the female deities. In some places, particularly Greece, the Goddesses held an apple, with its five-pointed star in the center, as a sign of the unity between heaven (that five-petaled flower in the sky formed by the planet Venus over eight years), the natural world of

The Empress

Lovers

The Star

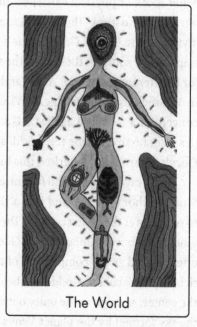

The World

The Empress, the Lovers, the Star, and the World from the Shining Tribe Tarot

The Empress, the Lovers, the Star, and the World from the Rider deck

plants, and the human body, which forms a pentagram when we stand with our arms out to the sides and our legs apart.

In this reimagined version of the Paradise myth, the Goddess welcomes us into her garden, where she and her snake, who may signify the kundalini life energy in the human body, *give* us the fruit of knowledge. Instead of the enemies of spirit, nature and the human body become the means to rediscover our divine selves. We can trace this myth in such Tarot cards as the Empress, the Lovers, the Star, and the World.

If the idea of a fall leads us to a negative view of the world as a prison, what of the Fool as a leap? In this version, the Fool does not sin or make a mistake, but chooses joyously to enter the world of experience and sensuality. In this way, that great act of magic, the creation of Something out of Nothing, becomes a choice not an accident; a celebration not a disaster. The movement from the Fool to the Magician—from silent *aleph* to *beth*— becomes a deliberate act. The Rider deck shows a beautiful youth, joyous and unconcerned. The *Shining Tribe* shows a child who leapt off a cliff after a bird and now flies across a wide landscape dotted with energy lines.

The Fool from the Rider and Shining Tribe decks

Does any of this make sense, other than a kind of poetic intuition? Can it actually be true we are really creatures of light and divine energy who somehow have come to believe in our isolation and mortality? After all, we do have bodies, and our bodies do get sick and die.

Let's turn away from esoteric doctrine for a moment and consider a seemingly very different source of knowledge (gnosis) about light: Albert Einstein's special theory of relativity.

We saw earlier how an experiment to discover the presence and effect of ether—the fifth element, or quintessence—led to two startling results. First, as far as anyone could tell, the ether simply did not exist. This meant that light waves somehow traveled through space without any substance to move through. A sound wave moves through air; the air vibrates and carries the sound. Without any air, no sound is possible. Remember the slogan from the classic movie *Alien*, "In space no one can hear you scream"? The wave a surfer rides moves through water. Without water, no wave. Light waves seemed to travel under their own power. This alone gave light a special status. Later, physicists would acknowledge this special quality with the controversial idea that light could act as a particle *or* a wave, depending on how you approached it. They called this principle "complementarity."

The second result of the experiment to find the ether was even more startling, for it seems to shake our very sense of reality. The experiment, done by two scientists named Michaelson and Morley, demonstrated that the speed of light is absolute. Indeed, it seems to be the only absolute thing in the universe, against which everything else becomes relative, which is why Einstein called his work a theory of *relativity*.

To get an idea how radical this is, how counterintuitive, to use a popular expression, consider the following example. Under ideal conditions, that is, in a vacuum with nothing to block it or slow it down, light travels at 186,282 miles a second. Let's say I somehow build a spaceship that can zoom along at 100,000 miles a second, and let's say you're on the ground, ready to wave at me as I flash by. Just before I pass you, I send out a beam of light. Maybe the spaceship has headlights and I've just remembered to turn them on. (I was busy reading Tarot for my copilot.)

Now, if both of us measured the beam of light, how fast would it travel? From my viewpoint in the spaceship, I turn on the light and it shoots out at 186,282 miles a second. However, as you watch me, my ship is already moving at 100,000 miles a second, so you would expect the light to travel at 286,282 miles a second, its own speed plus the ship's 100,000. Wrong. As you measure the light, it goes at only 186,282 miles a second, exactly the speed at which I measure it. Even worse is if the spaceship has taillights and I turn them on at the same time as the headlights, and someone on the ground is measuring how fast the light moves *backward*. You would expect to measure the speed as slowed down by the forward movement of the ship, but the taillights also beam out at 186,282 miles a second, for whoever measures them, in whatever direction.

How can this be? The answer is that *time changes* according to how fast you are moving. The speed of light is absolute for all observers, the *only* thing in all existence, and that means that time, the very pace of time, changes constantly, speeding up or slowing down according to how fast an object is traveling. We do not notice this effect because we all move so slowly, but scientific observations have confirmed it over and over again. The relativity of time is why we sometimes read that if you could take a trip in a spaceship at, say, 90 percent of the speed of light, time would slow down so much for you that you could spend a short time away and hundreds of years would have passed back on Earth.

Does that sound at all familiar? In so many of the stories of people who enter the Land of Faerie, the Celtic world of spirits, the hero goes for a night and comes back to discover that a hundred years have passed and everyone he knows has died. If we think of this in relativity terms, the spirit world moves much closer to the speed of light than ordinary reality.

Actually, three things change as something accelerates. While time slows down, mass increases, but length actually decreases. What this means is that something gets both heavier and shorter at the same time. Mass isn't really weight; we might describe it as an object's physical presence. So, paradoxically, an object becomes smaller and smaller (contraction of length) while denser and denser, with greater and greater presence. And time gets slower and slower.

Now—imagine you could not just get closer and closer to the speed of light, but actually reach light speed itself. Your mass—your presence—and maybe, just maybe, your consciousness would be everywhere at once. However, you also would have no length. You would become a point, without dimension, that is, without physical form, *everywhere* but not pinned down to *anywhere*. And time would no longer exist. Put in spiritual terms, you would become joined to divine consciousness. You would *be* divine consciousness.

Most physicists will say that matter cannot become light, and light cannot become matter. Put another way, scientific descriptions exist for what will happen to an object that reaches 99.999 . . . 9 percent light speed, but not what would result if it actually crossed the barrier. So there is not a progression from light to matter and matter to light. Instead, we find a radical break.

But if there is no scientific description, there is, in fact, a spiritual one. It occurs in the Tarot. The movement from the Fool to the Magician—from Nothing to Something—is the transformation of light into matter. And the movement from Judgement to the World—with the Fool between them as the moment of liberation—is the transformation of matter into light. We call it the World because consciousness becomes everywhere, without physical limit and outside of time.

Consider again the esoteric creation story, with its fall, or leap, from a state of pure light to a state of matter, and now think of another aspect of special relativity, the very famous equation $E = mc^2$. This says two very remarkable things: first, that matter and energy actually are the same, only in different forms, and second, that a tremendous amount of energy exists in a very small amount of matter. If you think of how much destruction comes from a bomb made from a single pound of plutonium, imagine how much energy lies bound up in your own body.

The Fool "descends" from a place, or state, of pure light beyond our knowledge. If we think of this as a leap rather than a sin or a mistake, then the spirit light *chooses* to become matter in order to experience that different condition. It must do so as a leap because light cannot gradually become matter.

But when it has experienced all the different states and knowledge of matter, all the stages of existence symbolized in cards one to twenty of the Major Arcana, when the only step that remains is to return to its full knowledge of itself as pure light, everywhere and nowhere and beyond time—well, then it must leap once more, for matter cannot gradually become light. And so we come to Éliphas Lévi's wise understanding that the place of the Fool comes between cards twenty and twenty-one.

Awakening

The Fool

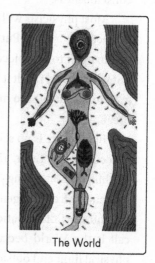
The World

Fourteen

A Final Gamble, Alternate
Major Arcanas

We will end with a return to a theme that has become an old friend by now: the idea that Thoth gambled with the Moon (or as the Moon himself, gambled with the other Gods), and in fact invented the Tarot for just this purpose. While we do not know what game they might have played, or the rules, we can give it a title. Let's call it the Game of Destiny, or maybe the Game of Life. How would we play such a game? What might it mean to use the Tarot to gamble with fate?

Any reading is a form of gambling. This may shock some people, for after all, the Tarot tradition assumes that the cards tell the truth, and therefore the way they fall in a reading is not at all a matter of chance. People who wish to discredit the whole enterprise will point out that if you shuffle the cards again, some other message will emerge. In reply, Tarot readers, myself included, will dutifully insist that the message will stay very similar, even if slightly different cards appear. Now, this does happen, and often many of the same cards actually show up in the second reading, but maybe that is not the point. Maybe we should acknowledge that we take a risk every time we mix the cards. Maybe instead of looking for some secret agency that controls the outcome—higher self, synchronicity, the unconscious, the spirit world—we should play with the idea that *nothing* controls the cards, and it is entirely this lack of control, this gamble, that makes possible the discovery of new wisdom.

So, to end this walk through the forest of souls, we will gamble with that most hallowed of all Tarot traditions: the Major Arcana itself.

• • •

The Major Arcana comes to us in a numbered sequence, and over time that sequence has become a vital part of the cards' interpretation. Most Tarot commentators do not look to the Magician only for its individual qualities but as card one, the beginning of the journey. We have seen that for Kabbalists, the order of the cards determines what pathway each one occupies on the Tree of Life. And yet, part of the glory of the Tarot lies in the fact that these are *cards* and not a bound book. Instead of a fixed sequence, they actually form an entirely new order every time we shuffle them.

In fact, the sequence has always been a matter of some question. Some very early decks do not follow the order that became fixed in the Tarot de Marseille. The very earliest cards known to us display no numbers at all on them. There is even some question as to whether there were always twenty-two cards. As the occult tradition flourished, people began to argue over the correct sequence. Éliphas Lévi, as we saw in the last chapter, placed the Fool next to last, while the Golden Dawn set it at the beginning. Remember, the Golden Dawn magicians also switched the numbers for Justice and Strength.

One thing that unites all of these switches, however, is the insistence on a good reason, even if, occasionally, the reason given is divine revelation or information channeled from disembodied spirits. People argue, often vociferously, for these changes. Their new order, they will say, *explains everything*. All the laws of the universe will fall into place once people accept their arrangement of the cards. Few people have considered that we might scrap the entire sequence, *just for the sake of doing so*, just to see what happens if we gamble. If we call the Tarot the *instrument* of our wisdom, why should we expect it to play just one song, no matter how exquisite? Why not let the cards themselves improvise new compositions?

Let us imagine, for the moment, that the Tarot indeed comes from the God of Everything Worth Knowing. If Thoth had wanted to give his original disciples a fixed sequence of symbols, he would have handed them a single table or a sewn book. Instead, he gave them cards, and cards, unlike most sacred texts and/or divine messages, do not have to remain in their original order. What new, or alternate, major arcanas might you get if you take the twenty-two Major Arcana cards, shuffle them, and lay them out in a new sequence?

People call the standard sequence "The Fool's Journey" because the prime card, the Fool, shows a carefree traveler. I have no desire to dismiss the significance of this journey or diminish the deep perceptions that have come from its contemplation. The previous chapter gave us some glimpses of the wonders we can find in the traditional sequence. And yet, it still remains only one possible sequence, one Major Arcana out of a huge range of possibilities. (To get the actual number of possible sequences using all twenty-two trump cards, multiply $22 \times 21 \times 20 \times 19$ and so on. I have not done it, but I promise you it would be a *very* large number.)

If we mixed the cards and the first card, the theme card, became the High Priestess, we might call the Major Arcana as a whole "The High Priestess's Meditation" and see it as a vast meditative vision. There are, in fact, many possible Fool's journeys, for all the different number sequences that might begin with card zero.

As jazz musicians have long known, even the freest improvisations work better with a structure. To aid our interpretations we can follow any of the patterns first discovered in the traditional order. There are many such patterns, probably as many as there are interpreters, and any of them will give us a way to understand the cards. We might look at the Tree of Life, for instance, in all (or any) of its historical or occult variations.

Or we might use different myths and stories as guidelines. As described in previous chapters, my own favorite structure for the Major Arcana sets the Fool aside, as the focus card, and then lays out the rest in three rows of seven. Over the years I have worked with this pattern the different positions have taken on clear meanings. Here, once more, is the pattern:

From the Rider deck:

Row 1: Fool

Row 2: Magician High Priestess Empress Emperor Hierophant Lovers Chariot

Row 3: Strength Hermit Wheel of Fortune Justice Hanged Man Death Temperance

Row 4: Devil Tower Star Moon Sun Judgement World

The initial card, the Fool in the standard version, becomes the theme card. Each of the three lines below it contains the same structure. The first two cards lay out the basic issues for that line. For example, in the standard sequence the Magician and the High Priestess symbolize the basic opposites of life—active and still, light and dark, speech and silence, conscious and unconscious. The middle three cards show the "work" of that line: the issues we must face if we want to grasp the message of the cards, and especially if we want to experience them and make sense of them in our lives. The Empress, the Emperor, and the Hierophant symbolize such triads as nature, society, and tradition; or mother, father, and education; or Goddess, God, and Priesthood.

In each line, the card right in the center forms a test or crisis. The Emperor is a difficult card for many people. It confronts us with society, with rules and restrictions. They might see the father as distant and remote, or harsh and judgmental. If we wish to acknowledge the Emperor in ourselves, we have to set boundaries and organize our lives. We need to learn to claim and defend our territory. Since Tarot enthusiasts are typically empathetic and caring people, we shy away from the Emperor's seeming coldness. But if we want to journey through the various stages, we must come to terms with the Emperor and his structures.

The final two cards represent the achievements of the line. Card six shows a direct experience we get after we accomplish the work, while seven indicates something we can become. In other words, by going through the life work of Empress, Emperor, and Hierophant, the Fool gets to experience the passion of the Lovers and take on the successful persona of the Chariot.

The other two lines repeat the same pattern, going to deeper levels of knowledge and wisdom. As we saw in the standard sequence, the second line may reverse many of the values of the first, as the person looks inward to open the heart. The first line deals with outer challenges, the second with inner exploration. The third, then, goes beyond the personal to discover greater principles, and even a liberation of the soul.

Not every new version of the Major Arcana will produce the deep insights of the traditional structure. Esoteric students have studied and pondered this pattern for over two hundred years and linked it to spiritual concepts that go back for thousands. And yet, there is value in newness as well, as shown in the vast number of new Tarot decks currently appearing almost every day.

With the three lines (or any other structural system) in mind, we can mix the Major Arcana and gamble with what we will find. There are two ways to do this. You can shuffle all twenty-two and set out your initial card as your theme. If the first card you turn over is Justice, you will have a Justice Major Arcana, in which you will learn about the issues, challenges, and life experiences that arise from this subject. If the card is Strength, you will learn what tests and rewards come as we learn how to be spiritually strong. And what if the first card we turn over happens to be the Fool? Well, then we will have a *new* Fool's Journey.

The second method allows us to examine a chosen theme. Suppose you feel challenged by questions of love and relationship. You could set out the Lovers card, mix the remaining twenty-one Major Arcana cards, and lay them out in rows of seven below the Lovers. The pattern would illustrate the question of love in your life.

Here is an example of the first method, shuffling all twenty-two. The deck used was *Shining Tribe*, my default deck for spiritual wisdom.

The theme card is the Chariot. Like the Fool, it suggests a journey, but where the Fool acts instinctively, the Charioteer drives the wagon with consciousness and purpose. We might describe the basic issue as how we become forceful in the world, or how we express our will. What follows is a brief interpretation.

The first line begins with the Emperor and Justice. The Emperor tells us that to ride our Chariot in life, we need to be strong and set boundaries. But we also need to act with Justice, for if we do not act justly and honorably, the Emperor can become a tyrant. The three work cards are the Spiral (Wheel in traditional decks) of Fortune, the High Priestess, and Strength. A forceful Charioteer needs to know to adjust for turns of fortune. They need inner Strength to give real depth to the outward-directed will. The crucial test, however, is the High Priestess, symbol of inner mysteries, for the Chariot tends to direct all its attention outward.

From the Shining Tribe Tarot
Row 1: Chariot
Row 2: Emperor Justice Spiral High Priestess Strength Magician World
Row 3: Temperance Death Lovers Hermit Fool Star Tradition
Row 4: Tower Sun Devil Moon Hanged Woman Empress Awakening

Having done this work, we experience the Magician, that is, the magical creativity of a directed will. Interestingly, in the standard sequence, the Magician begins the line, and the Chariot ends it. Both cards involve the development of will and its use. If will is to become the theme of this new Major Arcana, then it makes sense for the Magician to fill the place of what we can experience. After the Magician, the card of what we can become gives us the World. The card has moved from the end of the *third* line to take a place at the end of the first. It balances the Chariot's outward power with spiritual meaning.

The second line goes to a more internal level. Temperance and Death are both challenges for the Chariot. The first demands calm and balance, while the second confronts us with loss. Both involve surrender of control. Curiously, the two have reversed their usual positions. That is, in the standard sequence Death is in the sixth position of line two, followed by Temperance. Here Temperance is first, and Death second. In the work sequence of this line, both the Lovers and the Fool call on the Charioteer to further give up control. The Hermit, as the central test, requires the Charioteer to enter that state first described in the card directly above it, the High Priestess. The Charioteer must learn to direct attention inward. Having followed this theme of surrender, the Charioteer finds a return to consciousness in the Star. Through this return, the spiritual truths of Tradition (Hierophant in traditional decks) are discovered. The Charioteer *becomes* Tradition, a master of spiritual wisdom.

The final line goes still further in exploring these themes. The Tower and the Sun are opposites. The first symbolizes moments when everything seems to fall apart, the second times of simplicity and pleasure. Both are very intense, filled with energy. They create a kind of duality of power. If the Chariot wants to go beyond personal will, it must deal with such universal energy.

The work cards continue the intensity. At this deepest level, the Charioteer must confront an internal dark Devil and find the greater values of the World Tree in the Hanged Woman (or Man). In between, the Chariot must be driven through the half-light of the Moon, the card of deep instinct. Notice the connection between the cards of each row. The High Priestess, the Hermit, and the Moon all look inward. They test the Chariot by taking it to deep places where an outer-directed will is simply not enough. Notice as well that the Moon has shown up here in its usual place. For any journeyer, whether a Fool or a Charioteer, the Moon signifies a strange and difficult passage.

Remember as well—this was a random shuffle, and yet the three center cards of the High Priestess, the Hermit, and the Moon are all similar and certainly all a test for the outer directed will of the Chariot.

The final two cards allow the Charioteer, originally focused on success, to enjoy the wonders of the Empress's pure passion followed by a spiritual Awakening. In the previous chapter we examined the idea that we need the Fool once again between Awakening and the World so that we can leap free to the state of pure being. Something similar happens here. In the Empress, the Charioteer reaches a state of bliss. Put mythologically, the Charioteer dwells inside the very body of the Great Mother. But this is not the end. The Charioteer needs to return once more to the outer world, symbolized in the card of Awakening by the city, with its twenty-two lights and twenty-two windows. To do that requires *will*, but a will now beyond personal concerns. From the experience of the Empress, the Charioteer has discovered divine joy. To fully Awaken, the Chariot itself needs to be recognized as a vehicle of divine love. In other words, the Chariot needs to reappear between the last two cards.

This layout of three levels follows one particular pattern. You could set alternative Major Arcanas in any system. If you wished, you could lay the cards on the Tree of Life and discover what it might mean, for example, that the Chariot now appears on the path between Kether and Chokmah, the Emperor between Kether and Binah, and so on. What matters is the freedom the alternatives give us to play and explore the cards in new ways.

We will end this book with an image of Thoth—ibis-headed, dedicated, brilliant. Imagine the God, our Tarot ancestor, our teacher and friend, standing quietly, smiling softly, slowly, slowly shuffling the cards.

Tarot Deck Acknowledgments

The Brady Tarot, by Emi Brady. © Emi Brady. Used by permission. All rights reserved.

Haindl Tarot, by Hermann Haindl, used with permission of U.S. Games Systems, Inc., Stamford, CT 06902. © U.S. Games Systems, Inc. All rights reserved.

Motherpeace Tarot, by Vicki Noble, used with permission of U.S. Games Systems, Inc., Stamford, CT 06902. © U.S. Games Systems, Inc. All rights reserved.

The Raziel Tarot, by Robert M. Place with Rachel Pollack. Reproduced by permission of Robert M. Place. © Robert M. Place. All rights reserved. *www.robertmplacetarot.com*.

The Rider Tarot, by A. E. Waite and Pamela Coleman Smith, published 1909, London. Reproductions of the original courtesy of Holly Voley, scanned for the public domain.

Sacred Circle Tarot, by Anna Franklin and Paul Mason, is used with the permission of Llewellyn Worldwide Ltd.

The Shining Tribe Tarot by Rachel Pollack. Used by permission of Rachel Pollack. All rights reserved.

Tarot of Ceremonial Magick, by Lon Milo DuQuette. Used by permission of Lon Milo DuQuette. All rights reserved.

Tarot de Marseilles, this version circa 1700. Photographic credit: Isaiah Fainberg/Shutterstock. Used by permission for editorial use only.

Tarot of the Spirit, by Joyce Eakins and Pamela Eakins, used with permission of U.S. Games Systems, Inc., Stamford, CT 06902. © U.S. Games Systems, Inc. All rights reserved.

Thoth Tarot, Aleister Crowley and Lady Frieda Harris. Used by permission. © Ordo Templi Orientis and AGM-Urania. All rights reserved. Thoth Tarot is a trademark of Ordo Templi Orientis.

Visconti-Sforza Tarot. "Fortitude, recto." Milan, Italy, ca. 1480–1500 Pierpont Morgan Library. Manuscript. M.630.8. Photographic credit: The Morgan Library & Museum, New York.

Wheel of Change Tarot, by Alexandra Genetti. Used by permission of Destiny Books, an imprint of Inner Traditions International, Rochester, VT. © 1997 Alexandra Genetti.

Wirth Tarot, Oswald Wirth, this version 1889. Rights: public domain, via Wikimedia Commons.

Recommended Reading

Note that the many Tarot decks featured in *A Walk through the Forest of Souls* are listed in the Tarot Deck Acknowledgments on page 263.

Amaral, Geraldine. *Tarot Celebrations.* Red Wheel/Weiser, 1997.

Anonymous. *Meditations on the Tarot.* Element, 1985.

Besserman, Perle. *The Shambhala Guide to Kabbalah and Jewish Mysticism.* Shambhala, 1997.

Black Elk (Joseph Epes Brown, ed.). *The Sacred Pipe.* University of Oklahoma Press, 1953.

Boer, Charles. *The Homeric Hymns.* Swallow Press, 1970.

Calasso, Roberto (Tim Parks, trans.). *The Marriage of Cadmus and Harmony.* Alfred A. Knopf, 1993.

Calvino, Italo. *The Castle of Crossed Destinies.* Harcourt, Brace, Jovanovich, 1976.

Campbell, Joseph. *The Hero with a Tiiousand Faces.* Bollingen, 1949.

———. *The Inner Reaches of Outer Space.* Harper and Row, 1986.

Case, Paul Foster. *The Tarot.* Builders of the Adytum, 1974.

Chatwin, Bruce. *The Songlines.* Penguin, 1987.

Chilton, Bruce. *Rabbi Jesus.* Doubleday, 2000.

Critchlow, Keith. *Time Stands Still.* St. Martin's Press, 1980.

Crowley, Aleister. *The Book of Thoth.* U.S. Games Systems, 1977.

Decker, Ronald, Thierry DePaulis, and Michael Dunmiett. *A Wicked Pack of Cards.* St. Martin's Press, 1996.

Diller, Annie. *For the Time Being.* Knopf, 1999.

Dummett, Michael. *The Game of Tarot.* U.S. Games Systems, 1980.

DuQuette, Lon Milo. *Tarot of Ceremonial Magic.* Weiser Books, 1995.

Eliade, Mircea (Willard R. Trask, trans.). *Shamanism.* Bollingen, 1964.

Ellis, Normandi. *Awakening Osiris.* Phanes Press, 1988.

Fairfield, Gail. *Choice-Centered Tarot.* Newcastle, 1985.

Giles, Cynthia. *The Tarot: History, Mystery, and Lore.* Paragon House, 1992.

———. *The Tarot: Methods, Mastery, and More.* Simon & Schuster, 1996.

Gleason, Judith. *Oya: In Praise of the Goddess.* Shambala, 1987.

Gray, Eden. *The Tarot Revealed.* Inspiration House, 1960.

Greer, Mary K. *The Complete Book of Tarot Reversals*. Llewellyn, 2002.

———. *Tarot for Your Self*. Newcastle, 1984.

———. *Women of the Golden Dawn*. Park Street Press, 1995.

Grimm, Jakob and Wilhelm. *The Complete Grimm's Fairy Tales*. Pantheon, 1944.

Huson, Paul. *The Devil's Picturebook*. G. P. Putnams Sons, 1971.

Kaplan, Rabbi Aryeh. *The Living Torah*. Maznaim, 1981.

Kaplan, Stuart. *The Encylopedia of Tarot*, vols. 1–3. U.S. Games Systems, 1978, 1986, 1990.

Karcher, Stephen. *Ta Chuan: The Great Treatise*. St. Martin's Press, 2000.

———. *The Illustrated Encyclopedia of Divination*. Element, 1997.

Karcher, Stephen, and Rudolf Ritsema. *I Ching*. Element, 1994.

Kerenyi, Carl. *Eleusis: Archetypal Image of Mother and Daughter*. Princeton, 1967.

Kliegman, Isabel. *Tarot and the Tree of Life*. Quest, 1997.

Kusher, Lawrence. *Honey from the Rock*. Harper and Row, 1977.

Lao Tzu (Gia-Fu Feng and Jane English, trans.). *The Tao Te Ching*. Vintage, 1989.

Moakley, Gertrude. *The Tarot Cards Painted by Bonifacio Bembo*. New York Public Library, 1966.

Nichols, Sallie. *Jung and Tarot*. Samuel Weiser, 1981.

O'Neill, Robert V. *Tarot Symbolism*. Fairways Press, 1986.

Opsopaus, John. *Guide to the Pythagorean Tarot*. Llewellyn, 2001.

Patai, Raphael. *The Hebrew Goddess*. Avon, 1967.

Pollack, Rachel. "Aphrodite: Transsexual Goddess of Passion." *Spring Journal* 57, 1995.

———. *The Body of the Goddess*. Element, 1997.

———. "Breaking the Will of Heaven." *Spring Journal* 60, 1996.

———. *Complete Illustrated Guide to the Tarot*. Element, 1999.

———. "The Four Rabbis Who Entered Paradise." *Spring Journal* 66, 1999.

———. *The New Tarot*. Aquarian, 1989.

———. *Seventy-Eight Degrees of Wisdom*. Weiser Books, 1980, 1983, 1997.

———. *Shining Tribe Tarot*. Llewellyn, 2001.

———. *Shining Woman Tarot*. Thorsons, 1994.

————. *Tarot Readings and Meditations.* Aquarian, 1986. (Previously titled *The Open Labyrinth.*)

Pollack, Rachel, and Caitlin Matthews. *Tarot Tales.* Random Century, 1989.

Rosenberg, David. *Dreams of Being Eaten Alive: The Literary Core of Kabbalah.* Harmony House, 2000.

Scholem, Gershom. *Major Trends in Jewish Mysticism.* Schocken, 1941.

————. *On the Kabbalah and Its Symbolism.* Schocken, 1965.

Schwartz, Howard. *Gabriel's Palace: Jewish Mystical Tales.* Oxford University Press, 1993.

Teutsch, Rabbi David A., ed. *Kol Haneshamah, The Reconstructionist Prayerbook*, third edition. The Reconstructionist Press, 1994.

Thompson, William Invin. *Imaginary Landscapes.* St. Martin's Press, 1989.

————. *The Time Falling Bodies Take to Light.* St. Martin's Press, 1981.

Waite, Arthur Edward. *The Pictorial Key to the Tarot.* William Rider and Son, 1911.

Whitman, Walt (James E. Miller, ed.). *Complete Poetry and Selected Prose.* Houghton Mifflin, 1959.

Williams, Charles. *The Greater Trumps.* Gollancz, 1932.

About the Author

RACHEL POLLACK is a prolific author of fiction, nonfiction, and comics. Among the world's foremost authorities on Tarot, her bestselling *Seventy-Eight Degrees of Wisdom,* published in 1980 and never out of print, is widely considered to be the most authoritative book on the topic. Rachel is the winner of the 1989 Arthur C. Clarke Award, given for best science fiction, for her novel, *Unquenchable Fire;* the 1994 Nebula Award for Best Novel for *Temporary Agency;* and the 1997 World Fantasy Award for *Godmother Night.* A master of many genres, Pollack is renowned for her run of issues 64–87 of *Doom Patrol* (Vertigo Comics), and for the books for *The Vertigo Tarot* and *Salvador Dali's Tarot,* among others. She is the creator of her own *Shining Tribe Tarot.* With famed Tarot artist Robert M. Place, she created *The Burning Serpent Oracle,* and *The Raziel Tarot.* A member of the American Tarot Association, the International Tarot Society, and the Tarot Guild of Australia, Rachel has taught at the famed Omega Institute for over thirty years. Find her at *www.rachelpollack.com.*

To Our Readers

Weiser Books, an imprint of Red Wheel/Weiser, publishes books across the entire spectrum of occult, esoteric, speculative, and New Age subjects. Our mission is to publish quality books that will make a difference in people's lives without advocating any one particular path or field of study. We value the integrity, originality, and depth of knowledge of our authors.

Our readers are our most important resource, and we appreciate your input, suggestions, and ideas about what you would like to see published.

Visit our website at *www.redwheelweiser.com*, where you can learn about our upcoming books and free downloads, and also find links to sign up for our newsletter and exclusive offers.

You can also contact us at *info@rwwbooks.com* or at

Red Wheel/Weiser, LLC
65 Parker Street, Suite 7
Newburyport, MA 01950